Alienation and Authenticity

BRIAN BAXTER

Alienation and Authenticity

SOME CONSEQUENCES FOR ORGANIZED WORK

TAVISTOCK PUBLICATIONS
LONDON AND NEW YORK

First published in 1982 by
Tavistock Publications Ltd
11 New Fetter Lane, London EC4P 4EE
in association with Methuen, Inc.
733 Third Avenue, New York, NY 10017

Photoset in Great Britain by
Rowland Phototypesetting Ltd
Printed in Great Britain at the
University Press, Cambridge

British Library Cataloguing in Publication Data

Baxter, Brian
Alienation and authenticity.
1. Alienation (Social psychology)
2. Alienation (Philosophy)
I. Title
302.5'44 (expanded   HM291   ·

ISBN 0-422-78280-7

Library of Congress Cataloging in Publication Data

Baxter, Brian.
Alienation and authenticity.

Bibliography: p.
Includes indexes.
1. Alienation (Social psychology) 2. Work environment
– Psychological aspects. 3. Organizational behavior.
I. Title
HM291.B373   302.5'44   82-5695
ISBN 0-422-78280-7   AACR2

To my parents

Contents

Introduction   1

1   The Self and the Other: an exploration of the forms of
interaction between them as a preliminary to
understanding the psychological qualities of
authenticity and alienation   5
2   Forms of authentic awareness   38
3   The aetiology of estrangement in a closed form of
authentic existence   70
4   Alienation and estrangement in the open form of
authentic awareness   113
5   The transcendence of alienation and estrangement in
organizations: the quest for self-actualization   164

References   189
Name index   203
Subject index   207

Acknowledgements

The photograph on page 6 is by William Vandivert and was first published in *Scientific American*, April 1960.

The illustration on page 7 is from Held and Hein, *Journal of Comparative and Physiological Psychology* 56:873. Copyright 1963 by the American Psychological Association.

Introduction

This book grew out of my desire to explore the phenomenon of 'work alienation'. I thought initially that the first stage in developing this interest would be to obtain a suitable measure of alienation and then to conduct field studies to discover its association with other factors of relevance to man's behaviour in organizations. Through analysis of this mix of data I hoped it would prove possible to understand the effect of alienation on workers, both in their jobs and in their private lives. An appreciation of these effects would then allow me to specify the circumstances where alienation at work could be minimized, if not removed altogether.

However, a search of the literature intended to obtain a suitable measure of alienation turned up an extraordinary wealth of measures and 'operational definitions', each claiming to be the most suitable way to approach the quantification of the concept.[1] The

---

[1] Compare, e.g. Goffman 1957 (alienation as personal non-involvement); Seeman 1959 (alienation as a psycho-social phenomenon); Feuer 1963 (alienation as a lack of understanding of one's environment); Scott 1965 (alienation as a series of deficiencies); Aiken and Hage 1966 (alienation as dissatisfaction in social relationships); McDermott 1969 (alienation as the price one pays for a growing culture); Touraine 1974 (definition of both socio-psychological alienation and socio-economic alienation); Seybolt and Gruenfeld 1976 (alienation as the opposite of job satisfaction); Kaplan 1976 (alienation as an inherent component of the human condition); Gouldner 1980 (the term alienation as a part of the lexicon of philosophy). This welter of conflicting views on alienation led Lee (1972) to write an 'obituary' for the concept.

only common element in these studies appeared to be their uncertainty about the exact nature of alienation.

At this point, I realized that either to develop a new definition of alienation or to use an existing one and to proceed with the planned research would be fruitless, only adding yet another study to a tangled literature. What was required, it seemed, was a fresh analysis of the concept of alienation from its roots in general social theory to its specific expression in the work context, so that a new synthesis of the concept's disparate elements could be obtained. This, of course, entailed a complete reappraisal of the approach to be adopted in researching into alienation as a concept, and required a broadening of the range of issues to be considered. This form of reappraisal of the research approach and topic range in the field of the behaviour of individuals in organizations has gained increased support in recent years. For instance, F.A. Heller (1976: 45), in his Chairman's address to the Occupational Psychology section of the British Psychological Society, called for new research work which would by-pass the four key obsessions at present occupying the time of researchers. The issues to be avoided were, he said: (1) 'academic boundary disputes' (the insistence on keeping strictly within the parameters of one's 'subject area'); (2) 'holier-than-thou scientism' (an insistence on applying the methods of physical science to social research);[2] (3) 'compulsive causality' (the consequence of scientism that leads to the assumption that changes in a research project's independent variables are the cause of variations in its dependent variable), and (4) the 'subjectivity phobia' (the distrust of non-objective measures).

My own studies, by using other areas of literature perhaps unfamiliar to organization scientists (notably the wealth of philosophical[3] and theological studies available) to develop a coherent picture of the phenomenon of alienation has, I hope, largely avoided the problems to which Heller has drawn attention. When exploring these areas of thought new to organization scientists one is struck most forcibly by the relevance of their approach to problems central to a study of man's relationship to his work context. On reflection, it is not surprising that this is the case, because much of philosophy has been concerned with understanding the individual's relationship with his environment, and theology with his rela-

---

[2] Goldmann (1969), Wilden (1972), Bateson (1972), Maslow (1976), Heidegger (1977), and Waddington (1977), among other noted researchers, have all offered criticism of this approach.
[3] The philosophy that contains the richest source of information on alienation and its related phenomena is generally of European origin. The British school of philosophy is as yet mainly oriented to the empiricist tradition.

tionship with God as the Supreme Being whose presence permeates all man's actions. More specifically, each of these areas has established a comprehensive literature that examines the individual's alienation both from his environment and from God. I have sought to abstract from and rework areas of this literature to draw insights from these fields into the comparatively arid confines of organizational science. This fertilization has produced a number of simple but key factors, the understanding of which is essential to an appreciation of the phenomenon of alienation.

The first factor is found in the realization that to be alienated from something presupposes the existence of an opposite state of non-alienation. MacIntyre (1965) has said that 'alienation is essentially a contrast concept', that is, before one can understand alienation one must be able to determine the nature of un-alienated life. This I have endeavoured to do through an exploration of the nature of what may be called man's authentic existence – the possible state he may attain if he is unalienated.[4]

The second factor evident in the non-organizational literature that assists in the understanding of the phenomenon of alienation is that it implies the presence of a potential dialogue between the individual and the context from which he is alienated. I have explored the nature of this dialogue through an analysis of the degrees of autonomy or independence possible between the individual, whom I term the Self, and his environment (which includes other people) and which I describe as the Other because it is something *other* than the Self. By understanding that under the different circumstances of Self-Other interaction there can be different forms of dialogue I can add t.. is to a range of parameters that specify the possible presence of alienation.

A third factor that influences alienation is the nature and level of the individual's awareness of his particular context. Without a knowledge of the stage attained by the individual in the development of his awareness, both of himself and of others, one cannot be sure that he comprehends the nature (alienating or otherwise) of the influence of the forces he encounters. This leads to two other related factors that non-organization behaviour literature can assist us to formulate: first, if the individual is aware of alienation, does he see it as a personal, psychological issue or as part of a general social problem that has befallen him through his contact with a particular framework of socio-economic and political circumstances? Second,

---

[4] It is to be realized that the terms 'alienation' and 'authenticity' are intentionally used rather loosely in this Introduction: the wealth of associations surrounding them dictate this for the moment.

if one can establish sufficient parameters to specify the presence of alienation, does its influence actually affect man's behaviour and if so, how? An aspect of this is to see if there are circumstances where the individual may actively seek to be alienated from the environment in which he finds himself.

The common theme uniting these factors is that man is not treated as a 'black box' – a mysterious transformer of the input of environmental influences into an output of responses and actions – but is perceived as passing through different stages of psychological development and having different forms of psychological awareness that respond to different aspects of the context of ecosystem of which he is a part. In fact, man is to be seen as a *psychosystem*, a dynamic, ever-changing network of relationships in constant two-way interaction with his environment, both changing and being changed by other systems with which he comes in contact.

I shall make few specific references to the unconscious as a force influencing man's behaviour. The reason for this is that because man is perceived as a psychosystem, I take it that his 'psyche is in fact a conscious–unconscious whole, an all embracing One' (Jung's view, reported in Franz 1975: 124). Thus, the unconscious is not to be seen as a (Freudian) receptacle for repressed desires that influence man's behaviour, but as that which contains 'many matters which are so familiar that we do not need to inspect them' (Bateson 1972: 114). However, part of the researcher's task is to re-inspect these familiar matters so that he can perceive afresh and with a critical eye the assumptions that underlie the individual's daily thoughts and actions. This book places considerable emphasis upon this task, because it can yield insights into the particular expression of the phenomenon of alienation as manifest through the nature of the individual's awareness.

Indeed, the questioning of assumptions has a crucial application to the general research process itself, and because my concern has been to allow the emergence of new perspectives on the concepts of alienation and its counterpart, authenticity, I have sought to develop layers of arguments that allow me to build up a picture of the wealth of issues involved in understanding the concepts of alienation and authenticity, then to abstract themes from these arguments to allow an appreciation of the particular significance of these concepts to man in both his private and his working life. In this way, I hope that the scene may be set for further research into these areas, because although some issues may prove to lead up cul-de-sacs, others may allow those concerned with man's behaviour in organizations to gain fresh insights into their own work.

1

The Self and the Other

The significance of work as an active force in man's development: two illustrations of the danger of passivity

'The secret of the human condition is that there is no equilibrium between man and the surrounding forces of nature, which infinitely exceed him when in inaction, there is only equilibrium in action by which man recreates his own life through work.'

(Weil 1972: 157)

The appreciation that one's activity is a *self-creating* force can impart a special significance to research that explores what is meant by the phrase 'alienation from work'.[1] If man is 'alienated' it implies that his existence is in some way incomplete, because he has lost the opportunity for self-creation. Although Weil presupposes that working to restore the 'equilibrium between man and the surrounding forces' is inherently sufficient, she gives no indication of the different possible *natures* of man's working relationship to those forces.

This chapter explores this issue and uncovers three distinct forms of interaction between man and his environment. Associated with each form is a particular kind of work activity necessary to sustain man's connexion with the surrounding forces, thus suggesting that 'alienation' can take three forms too. In fact, it will become clear as

---

[1] This phrase, often found in organization behaviour literature (see Finifter 1972: 103ff for a brief summary of its appearance), is placed in quotes until I reach the stage where it can be defined with some precision.

this discussion unfolds that an understanding of 'alienation' is complicated by a further series of qualifiers.

As a starting point, I will take up Weil's comment that through inactivity, man allows the surrounding forces to 'infinitely exceed him', to his detriment. Her concern throughout her short book is that man must retain *control* of his environment through his activity: loss of control leads to an incomplete or false understanding of that environment, a falseness that is compounded because further actions are based upon it.

This point can be illustrated by using one of a series of experiments by the psycho-physiologists, Held and Hein (1963). They studied kittens reared under different conditions of sensory deprivation, to ascertain the importance of self-directed activity in visually guided behaviour. It was found that a freely-moving kitten develops an awareness of its environment that is considerably more sophisticated than that of a passive kitten whose actions are not self-controlled by the relation of its actions to the perception of its environment. The difference in awareness levels between the active and passive kitten was tested on an apparatus called a 'visual cliff' (Walk and Gibson 1961), consisting of on one side, a ledge and a large drop (covered by a pane of glass) and a small drop on the other side, thus:

Figure 1(1)

◄——— Upper ———►◄——————Ledge——————►◄ Cliff ►◄ Lower ►
　　　Surface　　　　　　　　　　　　　　　　　　　Surface

　　　　　　SAFE SIDE　　　　　　　　　DANGEROUS SIDE

Normally reared kittens, with normal perception, notice the large drop and avoid it: the experiments wanted to see if passive kittens, having no control over their actions, could exercise similar judgement. To ensure that both active and passive kittens had the same visual evironment Held and Hein used a carousel 'gondola' device, as illustrated in Figure 1(2), which restricted one kitten's movements while allowing its partner relative freedom.

The passive kitten (P) was restricted by putting it in a closed gondola then giving it a neck-yoke and body-clasp to ensure it did not escape. The active kitten (A) also had a body-clasp and yoke, but this was to allow its actions to be transmitted by the system of levers through to the passive kitten. Thus the latter's perception of the striped walls and its approaches to them had no relation to its movement, which were all contained within the gondola.

Results showed that the passive kitten (P) failed the 'visual cliff' discrimination test, by stepping off the dividing edge and walking on the glass that covered the dangerous cliff as often as it stepped onto the other, safe, side. Once having had the chance to practice in a normal environment, away from the restrictions of the gondola, these kittens, formerly deprived of control over their own actions, were then able to make the distinction and avoid the cliff-edge.

This experiment illustrates that the restricted kitten lacked an

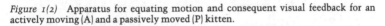

Figure 1(2) Apparatus for equating motion and consequent visual feedback for an actively moving (A) and a passively moved (P) kitten.

appreciation of the significance of the cues present in its visual field because its actions had been dictated by the other (unrestricted) kitten's movements, and although it encountered the same visual information as did the active kitten, it could not comprehend its significance for its own actions. That is, the kitten in the gondola was deprived because its actions were not of its own will, but *other-directed*.

The deprivations of the kitten in this example are readily observable, but there are other instances when an outside influence takes a more insidious form, yet is no less restrictive of a person's actions. For example, a letter written in 1833 by a teacher (formerly a hand-loom weaver) describes a life of ceaseless toil endured by a particular family of hand-loom weavers, a man, his wife, and two small boys (seven-and-a-half and nine years old). The four of them earned a total of nine shillings per week, from which was made the following necessary weekly deductions:

	£	s	d
'For wear of material and rent of shop for 3 looms		3	0
Fire for house and shop		1	0
House rent for one apartment		1	0
Oil for house and shop		1	0
Starching, twisting and carriage		1	0
Amount of deductions		7	0'

(Quoted in Gaskell 1836: 379f)

Thus, two shillings were left to feed and clothe the whole family for a week. When asked how he managed, the father retorted that he did not know; on being further questioned on what the family ate, he replied that they could manage only 'parritch in the morning, and potatoes and salt to dinner, and the same to supper, or sometimes a wee drap brose' (a dish of oatmeal with boiling water).

The family's activity was so curtailed by the necessity to work that their existence was merely one of survival. In the manner of the deprived kitten, the weaver and his family were moved by forces apparently beyond their influence: work occupied and moulded their daily thoughts and activities to the extent that its dominance went unquestioned. Could the weaver possibly have comprehended the significance of James Joyce's enthusiastic outburst 'Welcome, O life! I go to encounter for the millionth time the reality of experience and to forge in the smithy of my soul the uncreated conscience of my race'?[2] One may imagine that the weaver's response would have been one of amazement, if he did not dismiss

[2] In *A Portrait of the Artist as a Young Man*.

these sentiments outright as artistic fancy. Caught up by the inevitability of the forces about him, the weaver cannot conceive of the possibility of using his activity and his experience to enhance the quality of his life, and perhaps that of others with whom he comes into contact, let alone of using them as a creative, artistic force.

The concept of work as a creative, *self-productive* force, not simply in the materialist sense, but as the key to man's psychological growth, is central to the writings of Karl Marx, who, we shall see in Chapter 4, has offered one of the most profound interpretations of alienation to date. In his examination of alienation, Marx's use of the term 'production', which covered all forms of work activity, is not simply to be seen in the way the weaver understood it – the production of cloth – but involves, as Lefebvre has pointed out:

> 'On the one hand *spiritual* production, that is to say creation (including social time and space) and on the other, *material* production or the making of things, it also signifies the *self-production* of a 'human being' in the process of historical self-development which involves the production of *social relations*.'
> (Lefebvre 1971: 30f, emphases added)

Contrast the breadth of this definition with the conventional view of the organization scientists Parker and Smith (1976) who see the terms of work, production, effort, labour, and employment as the antonyms of rest, leisure, recreation, and play. For them, employment presupposes a social relationship bound by contract between employer and employee, while effort and labour include both the rendering of services and the production of goods. There is no mention of the developmental or self-productive qualities of work. This lacuna, not unique in the organization behaviour literature,[3] ensures that the full significance of 'alienated work' is not realized and consequently efforts to overcome it are inadequate. Because Marx saw that productive work had spiritual and social values, together with the more apparent material significance, his study of 'alienated work' included an examination of man's awareness of himself in the world, and of his relationship with other people. My own approach towards an understanding of the nature of 'alienated work' likewise treats work as the key medium through which man creates himself. More than this I seek also to understand the psychological issues confronting man in his efforts to use his work self-productively.

---

[3] E.g. See also Gross (1961) or Dumazedier (1967): both assume that work is contractual employment and that self-development only occurs through non-work activities or play.

The timeless nature of the Other's presence

We have seen that together with the passive kitten, the weaver faces life as a blinkered being; but although his constraints are as physical as the experimental harness, their force has a particular psychological aspect in the stoic acceptance of his life-style. This gives the constraints he encounters a double strength because they are sustained both *internally*, by his own attitude and behaviour, and *externally* by his social and economic position.

The theologian, Martin Buber, has elaborated this difference between the internal and external into a distinction between the I-world and the It-world (Buber 1970: 87ff); the former contains feelings, the 'in-here', and the latter is the 'out-there' and is composed of institutions where one 'works, negotiates, influences, undertakes, competes, organizes . . .' (p. 93). In terms closer to social science usage the I-world corresponds to the Self,[4] and the It-world, the non-Self or Other.[5] Man's awareness of this fundamental dichotomy far antecedes Western theological and philosophical thought. For example, in the Frankforts' (1949) noted analysis of the ancient civilizations Egypt and Mesopotamia, they argue that in search for the cause of things, man asked 'Who made this happen?' not 'How did it happen?' The 'who' was their Other, manifested in the form of the gods that abounded in the earth and heavens.

To perceive the qualities of the world around us and abstract them into a whole that confronts us as a living presence, that is not of the Self, locates the nature of the Other, whether it is as venerable as Horus the Egyptian god of heaven or as modern as capitalism. The realms of Self and Other are coextensive, their influence is dialectical; that is, each can only exist in the presence of the Other. The Greek, Heraclitus, described their interconnexion as being like that of the 'bow and the lyre' (Fragment 212). Other ancient philosophies sought to illustrate the psychological significance of the Self-Other union: for example, followers of the southern Hindu school of occultism held that 'samadhi' or ecstasy, the fourth and highest state of man's consciousness, was the outcome of the merging of the Self and Other and, as such, epitomizes the attainment of cosmic consciousness. The Alexandrian philosopher, Plotinus, likewise contended that man's relationship to the non-Self passed through several stages: *opinion* – founded upon the senses – *science* – founded upon dialectic – and ultimately *illumination* – founded upon the identity of the Self with its opposite.

[4] With a capital 'S' unless is conjunction with another word, e.g. 'self-assert'.
[5] With a capital 'O'.

However, it has been twentieth-century work on psycho-analysis that has given the Other its most complex role. Freud argued that the infant directs his attention towards the Other in an effort to become attached to it. The infantile sexuality, Freud proposed, adopts two methods to achieve this attachment: 'identification' and 'object-choice'; the former is an expression of the childish effort to be like the Other, while the latter indicates his desire to possess it. The child's love of his father is a manifestation of identification, while love of his mother is one of possession, hence the significance of the Oedipus myth to Freud's work. Lacan (1977), the French psychoanalyst whose thinking owes a greater debt to Hegel's writings than to Freud's, argues that initially the Other is perceived by the Self as a mirror-image of its own ego. Without this perception the Self cannot sustain inter-subject (or Self-Other) communication. Laing (1969) generalizes the Self-Other connexion even further by describing the Other as 'either an internal or external object or a fusion of both' (Laing 1969: 19).

At a different level, where the Other's qualities are less personable and more abstract, the Self-Other interaction can be illustrated by noting that semiologists (who study systems of discourse between man, his fellows, and his environment in terms of sign systems) have made the distinction between the linguistic system and its quotidian expression: between *langue* and *parole*.[6] Culler has cogently summarized the differences between these terms: '*La langue* is the system of a language, the language as a system of forms, whereas *parole* is actual speech, the speech acts which are made possible by the language' (Culler 1976: 29). The individual speaks from the reservoir of language and in turn 'the existential-ontological foundation of language is discourse (*Rede*)' (Heidegger 1978: 203). That is, although the Self operates within the presence of language it cannot exist and is meaningless without the Self's life-giving breath.

The creative power of this interaction is not to be underestimated: Artaud, the surrealist playwright, has argued extensively that twentieth-century man has lost the ability to use the poetry of language and the richness of mythology to project himself beyond the passive forces that surround him into the arena of (dangerous) possibility, and instead has succumbed to a one-dimensional picture of tame

---

6 The French terms are generally used in the literature, where '*la langue*' approximates to 'language', and '*parole*' to 'speech' (after Barthes 1967: 14). But note that Ogden and Richards (1923) and Derrida (1976), both from different perspectives, argue that Saussure, the founder of semiology, based his use of '*langue*' upon a metaphysical conception of language. Thus, we can broaden the concept of '*langue*' to include the Other-based aspects of culture and myth.

representation. As a consequence, theatre, which Artaud sees as the true offspring of language and myth has now become:

> 'A kind of frozen world, with players frozen in gestures that were no longer of any use to them. . . . with music reduced to kinds of ciphers whose signs were beginning to fade, and kinds of luminous explosions, themselves solidified and corresponding to the traces of moves – and all about an incredible fluttering of men in black suits busy arguing over receipts by the entrance to a white-hot box office.'   (Artaud 1974: 31)

This state of affairs would appear to be a particular expression of the modern phenomenon explored in the writings of Marcuse. He has contended that the power of the Other has lost its benign appearance and taken on an overwhelming, totalizing, or all-embracing quality, because the Self's actions rest upon uncritical nimesis of the Other's shallower qualities. This leads to a 'flattening out of the contrast (or conflict) between the given and the possible' (Marcuse 1964: 21), a flattening which, he states, is an expression of man's 'alienated' existence, because man has passively succumbed to a world of work which imposes upon him 'alien needs and alien possibilities' (1964: 17).

The impersonal power of the Other can acquire such an authority that it appears to be a 'law of nature'. This assumption was made by the traditional Marxists who argued that an understanding of the Other's force could emerge only when man realized the objective law that gave force its potency. This interpretation of the Other's significance led Lenin to remark that:

> 'For until we know a law of nature, it, existing and acting independently and outside our mind, makes us slaves of "blind necessity". But once we come to know this law, which acts (as Marx pointed out a thousand times) *independently* of our will and our mind, we become masters of nature. The mastery of nature manifested in human practice is a result of an objectively correct reflection within the human head of the phenomena and processes of nature, and is proof of the fact that this reflection (within the limits of what is revealed by practice) is objective, absolute and eternal truth.'   (Lenin 1972: 222)

To argue that the acts of the Other can be translated into objective, eternally true laws, while providing the theory behind a Marxist view of revolutionary practice, is to omit consideration of the psychological forces that can mould man's behaviour and, through him, that of the Other in an evolutionary manner. Man's actions are thus relegated to those of an inquirer in search of laws as a prelude to revolutionary change, and the dynamic dialectic between the Self and the Other, which *itself* is the source of change, is arrested and transformed into passivity.

There is another change immanent in a call to man to turn his efforts towards uncovering 'objective laws': it assumes that man is an amorphous presence whose collective *persona* is subjugated to the Other without distinction. Each individual is seen as a shard of the hologram 'man' or, at best, one who belongs to a sociologically specific sub-group of the genus 'man': that is, average or 'modal man'. In line with my desire to avoid treating man collectively or modally – this would be a reversion to the 'black-box' approach – I examine the different possible psychological connexions between the Self and the Other to allow an understanding of the circumstances in which the Self is active or passive in the face of the Other.

To do this effectively I shall be using an Other with qualities that extend from the intimately personal to the powerfully impersonal: God.

God chosen as the most complex Other: three forms of relationship between man and God as Other

The choice of God as Other has a number of points in its favour: first, the connexion between man's work activity and God is well known through the biblical account of Adam's Fall from God's Grace; second, the philosophical and theological literature may be drawn upon for examinations of the relationship between man and God; third, the potency of God as Other is appreciated in many different cultures and conveyed through many myths, and fourth, the variety of God's connexions with man on the personal, cultural, and mythical levels together with the breadth of attitudes held by man towards God allow for the Self–Other relationships of matchless psychological complexity.

The particular quality underlying God's power as an Other is that He can be both adored and reviled by man. On one hand His actions are seen as originating in a force of omnipotent benevolence under which man may bow down to worship and receive His protection, thereby fulfilling himself through obedience to God's Will. On the other hand, man may perceive God's domination as an unwelcome yoke which he refuses to accept because he sees Him as a threat to his fulfilment. This conflict between protection and threat inherent in the Self's perception of God has a parallel in the mythologies of the Ancients. They categorized all abstract Other-based forms into two camps: on one side were ranged the gods of day, light, life, fertility, wisdom, and good; and on the other the demons of night, darkness, death, barrenness, and evil. The majority of myths indicated that men spent their time wooing the gods of light and good and appeasing or warding off those of darkness and death, because their will and influence were awesome powers to be obeyed.[7]

Between the Self's polar perceptions of God as Other there lies a compromise not commonly found in ancient religions, where God appears neither as an omnipotent master nor as a human manifestation of mastery over one's own fate, but rather as a supportive friend with whom one can enter into a dialogue. This view is exemplified by the writings of the twentieth-century theologians Dewart, Barth, and Buber. If their perspective of God is included, we now have three broad forms of the Self–God (as Other) relationship each having in common a statement about man's autonomy or lack of it in his dealings with the Other. By accepting and welcoming God's omnipotence, my first form, man's actions are *not autonomous* or Self directed: man derives his fulfilment only by acting in the context of God as the Other who decrees that all actions are for His ends alone. The theology of the Reformists, notably Calvin, is based on this view of the Self–Other interaction. In the middle form, God, as Other, provides a strong supportive role but man's actions are not inextricably linked to His Will, instead his behaviour may be described as *semi-autonomous* because he uses the assistance of the Other to support his present condition and to extend the possibilities of his Self. The third form, where the Self seeks completely to transcend the Other's presence is the result of a determination to make actions *fully autonomous* of the Other's influence in the belief that only through surpassing all domination can the Self be truly of his own making: this is the creed of the existentialists.

---

[7] However, in Celtic mythology, the influence of these gods was treated by man with contempt because he believed that he had as his ancestor the god of death – that is, Celtic man saw that his fate ultimately lay in his own godlike hands. This unusual mythology first came to light when Caesar reported that the Gauls believed themselves to be descended from Dis Pater, the god of the underworld (the Gallic Wars, Book VI, Ch. XVIII). In gaelic mythology Dis Pater was called Bilé, a name containing the root 'bel' meaning 'to die'. 'The God Beli in British mythology was no doubt the same person, while the same idea was expressed by the same root in the name of Balor, the terrible Fomor whose glance was death' (Squire 1900: 120).

The contrast between the psychological qualities of authenticity and sincerity

I wish to emphasize that each of these three forms of Self–Other interaction can be perceived by different people as the one offering the key to their authentic existence in the world. Imprecisely used thus, the term 'authentic' is intended to convey an awareness, either intuitively felt or consciously realized, that a certain relationship with the Other is the most rewarding or stimulating for the particular individual in question. By implication, if a person felt that he could not establish a satisfactory relationship (and even the act of surpassing the Other's influence presupposes an initial relationship) then perhaps this provides an early formulation of the nature of 'alienation'. Certain organization scientists thought so (e.g. Seeman 1959; Blauner 1964), by discussing 'alienation' in terms of an individual's feelings of powerlessness and meaninglessness in the face of an all-powerful Other – in this case capitalist society and its work environment. However, these insights, although limited by being drawn from the Self's interaction with a pervasive but shallow Other, were then generalized by other writers in the organization behaviour field (e.g. Hajda 1961; Fromm 1963) to formulate a universal notion of 'alienation', thus losing the personal quality of its significance. Understanding the different modes of Self-Other interaction can provide a key to understanding the individual's psycho-system because it offers a methodological tool to examine 'alienation' as a psychological phenomenon, but, one may ask, what precisely is meant by describing a Self–Other interaction as *authentic*?

The literary critic Trilling (1972) has pointed out that authenticity is a concept with polemical qualities, which by its nature deals aggressively with 'received and habitual opinion, aesthetic opinion in the first instance, social and political opinion in the next'. The questioning aggression associated with authenticity is channelled through the Self into a committed awareness of his circumstance that ensures that he is never lost in passive complacency or uncritical acceptance of his relationship towards the Other. To allow one to appreciate the active, inquiring quality of authenticity, Trilling contrasts it with *sincerity* and argues that the search for authenticity suggests a

> 'more strenuous moral experience . . . a more exigent conception of the self and of what being true to it consists in, a wider reference to the universe and man's place in it.'
>
> (Trilling 1972: 11)

On the other hand, to be sincere implies a strong moral or heroic quality, because sincerity depends on a certain self-conscious awareness of one's goodness. Furthermore, society demands of man that he *appears* sincere, and the best way to satisfy this demand is to ensure that each man sees to it that he really *is* sincere. Thus man plays the role of being sincerely himself so the 'judgement may be passed upon our sincerity that it is not authentic' (Trilling 1972: 11).

Sincerity becomes a cocoon in which to wrap oneself as a protection from issues that could otherwise force themselves upon one's consciousness. Mannheim (1936), among others, has called this state of awareness 'false consciousness'; the term adds a political significance to the moral factors that Trilling associated with authenticity. Its political importance arises because it makes the point that man is inauthentic if he acts and understands or interprets his actions solely within the given of his socio-economic context: he does this because he has succumbed to the potent will of the Other, the institutional environment in which he is located. Marx, like Trilling, saw inauthenticity as man's estrangement from himself and the result of an alienation of his will to the Other's. The connexion between these two writers lies in their mutual debt to Hegel's writings. Hegel had exposed the inherent hypocrisy of man's sincerity through an analysis of the progression of the 'honest soul' – a stage of the Self's psycho-historical development – by contending that for the Self to develop fully it[8] must pass through a phase of intense self-doubt where received values are inverted and the significance of every action questioned. The act of questioning signifies the emergence of authentic behaviour because the outcome is a heightened awareness of the Self's relationship to the Other. With this heightened awareness the Self may choose to reaffirm its original sincerely held position, for example, to accept that the divine Will is the originator of his activity (what I have called the non-autonomous form of Self-Other existence), or the Self may wish to transcend its submission to the Other in an effort to ensure that its destiny lies solely in its own actions (full autonomy of the Self from the Other).

The distinction between sincerity and authenticity that is highlighted by Trilling is paralleled by a much older contrast between the Apollonian and Dionysian principles of existence: that is, the constructive and destructive forces inherent in each Self.[9] Etymologically, the Latin word *sincerus* means pure or

[8] Hegel treats the Self as an impersonal entity.
[9] A distinction that was revived in Freud's writings through his use of the terms 'superego' and 'id'.

whole; a sincere body was one untainted by corrupting influences. The Apollonian principle likewise sought order, unity, and completeness and is manifest in the Self's desire to attain certain specific criteria, moral rectitude for instance. The Dionysian principle was associated with bacchanalian licentiousness and revelry, the priests of that cult pretended to eat raw flesh, wore serpents in their hair, carried phalli on the ends of long poles, and 'by the wildness of their looks and eccentricity of their actions feigned insanity' (Lempriere 1865: 234). These actions were done to encourage followers to cast off and forget the accepted morals and conventions that surrounded them so that they could regain their own *original authority* or *'αυθεντια'*.[10] The presence of Dionysus ensures that the Self 'experiences himself and his world as an Open Field' (Cooper 1976: 1001); a field where the emergence of expressive systems are possible through one's activity. An expressive system is one where the Self, through his own self-development, can establish a particular relationship with the Other in the awareness of alternative Self-Other inter-relationships. To describe a Self-Other relationship as authentic is to indicate that the Self has passed through the Apollonian and Dionysian phases of existence to acquire a new awareness of his position *vis à vis* the Other.

Trilling, however, takes his remarks on authenticity one stage further, arguing that man's authentic life is to be found in the 'here and now and not susceptible to explanation by some shadowy there and then' (Trilling 1972: 139). This ignores the psychologically beneficent qualities provided by being able to strive towards the goal of 'there and then', factors that are at the foundation of metaphysical and theological systems and in themselves possible routes to an authentic existence. My intention is not to lapse into prescribing *one* form of authentic life,[11] but to discuss its manifestation in the three forms of Self–Other interaction as a prelude to understanding that as man's life within any of these forms of existence can be a realization of his authentic state, so may they each be a manifestation of his 'alienated' life. That is, the nature of the Self's activity *per se* is secondary to the nature of his activity in the face of the Other. Failure to see self-development, through active involvement with the Other, as the gestation of its particular manifestation of authen-

[10] i.e. Authentia, the Greek root of 'authenticity'.
[11] Trilling does this because his arguments rest on the assumption that the Self *must* have autonomy of the Other before he can attain authentic life – a position held also by Sartre who contends that the Other's influence upon the Self *always* thwarts authenticity through the crushing of his possibilities and his freedom. Man 'is alienated in the presence of the Other's pure subjectivity', i.e. the Other's will for itself (Sartre 1966: 489).

ticity, may cause one to assume that the sincere Self has transcended 'alienation' when in fact the question of his 'alienation' has not even occurred to him. The significance of work as self-directed activity is thus central to a theory of 'alienation' because it incorporates an appreciation of the importance of man's self-development with a statement about how he expresses himself towards the Other. Without an appreciation of the permutations of these factors, the psychosystem of the weaver who labours under the shadow of the Other (manifest as socio-economic conditions) is indistinguishable from that of a Christian mystic whose union with the Other (as God) gives him deep insight into his condition and that of his fellow men.

The Fall of Adam as a metaphor for the loss of man's harmony with the Other: the significance of the Fall for the nature of man's activity in the face of the Other

For the elucidation of the psychology behind the different forms of the Self–Other dialogue I shall start by noting the special psychological importance of the mythologies and theologies that blossom from interpretations of man's fall from grace, or his loss of unity with a supreme deity, or Other. The Judeo-Christian tradition holds that the Fall of Adam and his subsequent expulsion from the Garden of Eden represented man's loss of primal unity with God, that is, a breakdown of the special harmony between man and the Other, which man could only regain either through the Will of God (e.g. Calvinism) or through activities directed to the 'greater glory of God' (e.g. Victorian 'self-help' theology[12]). Other cultures have formed their own particular traditions and myths describing man's associations with the gods. In Greek mythology the fall from harmony with deities is described in some of the early Greek texts (e.g. Empedocles' *Purifications*) as being due to man eating the flesh of human sacrifice, while in the later (Homeric) writings there are accounts of man's efforts to reunite himself with the gods, thereby ending his subjection to them. Like the Christians, they saw that this act of union is one that allows man to regain an insight into all the non-Self forces surrounding him, which in his isolated state, confront him as alien and mysterious entities whose dominion over the Self can never be overcome. This is the significance of the tale of the mortal Bellerophon who sought to fly to heaven to see the gods

---

[12] Samuel Smiles was one of the most noted exponents of this view through his book *Self Help* (1908).

and so cross the borderline between them, but his winged horse was stung by an insect sent from heaven by Jupiter, causing the horse to start and throw Bellerophon to earth where, according to Homer's *Iliad* (Book 6: 201), he died in misery 'hated by all the gods'. The essence of all metaphysical systems, of which mythological thought is the prototype, is that it offers man, through glimpses of the unseen (that realm of the Other lying beyond natural vision) both a goal towards which he can direct himself and the method of activity required of him to achieve that goal. Bellerophon's downfall, and Adam's too, occurred because their efforts to attain the goal were not approved by the Other.

Jane Harrison, discussing the nature of religion in ancient Greece, conveys the psychological importance of the link between the unseen force of the Other and the nature of man's actions in the face of that Other:

> 'Every religion contains two elements. There is first what a man *thinks* about the unseen, his theology, or if we prefer so to call it, his mythology, second, what he *does* in relation to this unseen – his ritual. In primitive religions, though these two elements are to be distinguished, they are never, or very rarely separable. In all living religions these two elements are informed and transfused by a third impulse – that of each man's personal emotion towards the unseen, his sense of dependence on it, his fear, his hope, his love.' (Harrison 1905: 7–8)

Man seeks through activity to attain a union with the omnipotent Other to allay his fear, fulfil his hope, and share his love, but this activity in metaphysical systems is not self-directed, it is *ritualized*. Its qualities and significance derive from the special meanings that the ritual contains, its power lies in that one's actions are directed to the Other and can never be idiosyncratic. In Judeo-Christian theology the book of Genesis states that Adam's ritualized activity to regain his former unity with God takes the generalized form of labouring. God's command to Adam is: 'In the sweat of thy face shalt thou eat bread until thou return unto the ground' (Genesis III, vs.19).

MAN'S DILEMMA AFTER THE FALL: AUTONOMY OR HOMONOMY AS THE WAY TOWARDS SELF-FULFILMENT

The relationship between God and Adam, treated as a timeless expression of man's psychological involvement with the Other, reveals the dilemma at the root of the formation of man's psycho-sytem: the break from the Other's benign but total control compels man to decide either that he should seek a reunion to give his life meaning through a new active association with the Other (the only way to salvation, or fulfilment, in Christian terms), or that he should try to continue striving for a way to free his actions from all Other-based influences (the way towards authenticity for existentialists).

Attention to this dilemma has been drawn in the social science literature by Angyal (1965) and Maslow (1968, 1976) who argued that within man two contrasting directions, or needs, seek control over the Self, one towards autonomy and the other towards homonomy. Homonomy is a tendency towards giving up self-will, self control, or autonomy and to submerge oneself in the Other, while autonomy is manifest by a self-directed will to strive towards self-sufficiency, towards fuller development of man's unique Self out of its own laws, 'its own inner dynamics, autochthonous laws of the psyche rather than of the environment' (Maslow 1976: 157). Maslow's obvious enthusiasm for autonomy is a reflection of his commitment to ensure that man *actualizes* himself: that is, actualization is to be understood as making actual or manifest, through self-directed activity, one's inner potential to be self-creating. Nevertheless, Maslow's view of autonomy is not as broad as that implied by my own use of the expression 'full autonomy' which, I argue, is a form of existence that seeks constantly to shrug off the Other's influence. True self-actualization, as Maslow made clear throughout his writings, could only take place through the medium of the Other as a base from which the Self could work, thus his actualization occurs in what I have called the semi-autonomous Self–Other existence, or as he would see it, in a position of dialetic balance between the poles of autonomy and homonomy. Maslow saw that advocacy of one form against the other could lead to undesirable extremes; for instance, he thought of masochism as a 'sick' form of homonomy where blind obedience and self-denial is maintained to the extent that one may suffer psychological and physical harm. It is interesting to note that the very behaviour Maslow rejects as psychologically undesirable, because he sees it to be non-actualizing, is no different in many respects from what was believed to be saintly behaviour in the sixteenth century. Martin Luther, before he began to question the principles of Roman Catholicism, believed that self-abasement was necessary to achieve approval from the Other, God, and hence the way to actualize himself in His sight, despite the toll on his physical wellbeing.

'I was a good monk, and I kept the rule of my order so strictly that I may say that if ever a monk got to heaven by his monkery it was I. All my brothers in the monastery who knew me will bear me out. If I had kept on any longer, I should have killed myself with vigils, prayers, readings and other work.'

(Luther, *Weimar Ausgabe* XXXVIII: 143, quoted in Bainton 1950: 34)

For the young Luther these, to our eyes, extreme actions were expressions of his desire to be true to God's Will, no compromise or semi-autonomous connexion with God was adequate. By appreciating that actualization is ultimately a personal affair I cannot, like Maslow, treat one specific form of Self–Other interaction as the approved mode of self-fulfilment, although one may agree that in the context of twentieth-century life his route to self-actualization is the most practicable – a point raised again in the closing Chapter.

THE FALL AS THE EMERGENCE OF INDIVIDUAL SELF–AWARENESS

Turning once more to the theme of the Fall of Adam to understand why the abnegation of the Self to God's Will can be self-fulfilling, I shall refer to the work of Jean Calvin, who was one of the clearest exponents of the principles behind the Reformation. He saw the events in the Garden of Eden as a trial of obedience which failed through Adam's insult to God in assenting to the force of evil, Satan (Calvin 1960, II: i, s.4).[13] St Augustine, from whom Calvin drew much of his inspiration, was more specific about the nature of the evil that Adam was accused of. He saw that Adam's actions originated in self-love, rather than love of God, a self-love indicative of a confidence in his own abilities, and a forgetting that they were God-given. The consequence of losing the trial by pandering to self-love was man's estrangement from God and hence the loss of his soul, the core of his authenticity before God. Adam's trial failed because he ate of the fruit of knowledge having succumbed to the snake's[14] suggestion that by doing so he could be as a god, knowing good and evil. Although the snake is seen in Judeo-Christian theology as a creature of evil who tempted man to sin by offering him

---

[13] This refers to his main work *Institutes of Christian Religion* first published in Latin in 1536 and then finally in 1559–60. It is largely upon this latter edition that the English text is based. The book chapter and section numbers are as in the original.

[14] The snake may be seen as a symbol of the phallus, the primary source of new life. The connection appears both in classical mythology (through Hermes in Greece and Osiris in Egypt) and, more recently, in the writings of Jung. His first dream was of a giant enthroned phallus which, as a primitive life-force, had supplanted the king who had formerly held that throne (God) (Jung 1963: 11).

knowledge, in Indian mythology its actions are venerated because it used its hood to protect the Buddha from devilish influences at the moment of Enlightenment: that is, in his breakthrough into self-knowledge.

The knowledge that the snake offered Adam and Eve was not confined to an awareness of objects in their world, it was primarily a self-knowledge, which shattered their sincere blindness and forced them to look at themselves. Their first act (clothing themselves) was done in shame of their nakedness, of their self-exposure, the second (hiding from God) done because they understood that He was no longer as themselves but now appearing as an *Other*: Adam's self-conscious action in concealing himself is his first act as an *individual*.

The arguments surrounding the issue of individual self-knowledge together with the emphasis upon self-directed activity keenly divided the existentialists (who argue for self-autonomy) and the Calvinists (arguing for non-autonomy), because although both see its key importance to man's psychological development, no reconciliation can be found in their views on how self-knowledge is to be attained. Calvin has expressed sentiments with which, at face value, both camps would agree:

'It is not without reason that the ancient proverb so strongly recommended to man the knowledge of himself. For if it is deemed disgraceful to be ignorant of things pertaining to the business of life, much more disgraceful is self-ignorance, in consequence of which we miserably deceive ourselves and so walk blindfold.'   (Calvin 1960: II, i. s.1)

However on the ways that self-ignorance is to be overcome these two polarized camps cannot reach accord because of the fundamental difference in how each understands the nature of *work*: is it primarily for the Self, or must it be for the Other? This polarity is not confined to academic or theological settings; I am arguing that it lies at the core of each individual's efforts to exist in the world and in their quest to derive meaning and significance from the ecosystem. Through a dialogue with the forces he encounters, man's involvement with the Other penetrates and enriches his psychosystem. Whether the Other is perceived as the force guiding one's life or as a force to be transcended is a *personal* issue, the essence of one's authenticity. Thus, it should be clear to those within the specific context of studying behaviour in work organizations that any assessment of 'alienation' based on large-scale surveys or *ex cathed-*

ra generalizations from analysis of groups' behaviour cannot hope to appreciate what each individual has as his or her own image of 'alienated' work, because these surveyors of behaviour have no way of discovering the personal, psychological significance that a particular mode of work may have.

The nature of man's activity in a non-autonomous existence between himself and the Other: Calvinism

Although Calvin's writings directly concern themselves with the individual's relationship to God, his understanding of the individual's psychological make-up was rather one-sided. He believed that although each individual had particular God-given abilities, all men had a common failing: they had the psychology of Adam. Calvin, unlike the Scholastics before him, was quite certain that Adam's actions in Eden foredoomed all mankind and not just himself and Eve. Through the generations of man 'the implicity of parents is transmitted to their children so that all, without exception, are originally depraved' (Calvin 1960: II, ii, s.6). The source of this depravity, like the Fall, lies in the individual succumbing to wilfulness, that is, self-directed activity that questions and supplants God's Will. To ensure that acts of wilfulness are properly contained, Calvin argued, requires the renunciation of oneself to God, knowing that 'no one has duly renounced himself until he is so resigned to God that he willingly suffers his whole life to be governed at God's good pleasure' (Calvin 1960: III, vii, s.10). Many Protestant theologians since Calvin have amplified his remarks on this issue. Shewen, for instance, writing in the eighteenth century, preached that *all* self-directed actions had to cease before one could achieve union with God.

> 'True rest and peace is obtained, or comes through a true self-denial: a dying to the self-sinning, and self-righteousness, self-thinking and working, contriving and inventing, self-wisdom and understanding also: all these things must be denied, annihilated or brought to nothing, and confounded.'
>
> (Shewen 1826: 185–86)

The sentiments expressed by Shewen convey the rigorous attitudes underlying Protestant thinking and action, attitudes with which the Roman Catholics could find little sympathy. For although they, like the Protestants, believed that man could not redeem himself through his own actions, the Roman Catholics argued that salvation may be attained by gaining the approval of the Church, because God's Grace 'is communicated by and through the ministrations of the Church' (Warfield 1935: 18). This logic justified the practices of confession of sins and the purchase of 'indulgences', both of which were widely promoted by the Roman Church: through these means, the priesthood assured men that their sinning actions were forgivable. Clearly, to Calvin, and to Luther before him, to forgive through these or any other means was tantamount to supplanting God's Will and hence forbidden.

In fact, as is well known, the purchase of indulgences to accumulate money for the building of St Peter's church at Rome was the catalyst for Luther's rejection of the established (Roman) church and its practices of sacerdotal authority. The people of Luther's day widely believed that the Pope held jurisdiction over purgatory, 'the post-house on the road to heavenly life', and that if one subscribed to indulgences one would enjoy complete remission of sins. If sufficient payment was made, it was possible to release from purgatory one's deceased relatives too. In the words of an old jingle:

'As soon as the coin in the coffer rings
The soul from purgatory springs.'
(Bainton 1950: 60)

The coin represents man's labour turned into an objectified form: thus, because money and not pure activity itself became a form of spiritual credit it was possible, Reformists argued, that wealth accumulated in the course of one's activities – regardless of whether or not these activities had been accomplished with the intention of fulfilling God's Will – could then be directed to obtain absolution of sins committed during the acquisition of that money, a self-deception unappreciated by the sacerdotalists.

Countering the Roman Catholic position, Calvin saw that man's spiritual deformity, arising through his sinning, could only be redeemed through God's benign Grace manifested through the coming of Christ (Calvin 1960: II, i, s.6). That is, in more familiar language, man could only regain his true nature through the direct benevolence of the Other. All *personal* striving after such truth through one's own self-directed activity was folly, because in Calvin's interpretation of man's psychology, man's life activity was not to be seen as a method to transcend either the knowledge or the condition of his depravity and ignorance, it is to fulfil God's design and to unquestioningly effect His Will.

'For it is not right for man unrestrainedly to search out things that the Lord has willed to be hid in himself, and to unfold from eternity itself the sublimest wisdom, which he would have us revere but not understand, that through this also he should fill us with wonder. He has set forth by his Word the secrets of his will that he has decided to reveal to us. These he decided to reveal in so far as he foresaw that they would concern us and benefit us.'

(Calvin 1960: III, xxi, s.1)

A parallel may be drawn between Calvin's comments on man's relation to God, as Other, and the profane world of a paternally run business organization: both exert power over the individual through the selective dissemination of information and both ensure that fulfilment and security of the individual depends only on the Other's requirements. In the case of a paternally run organization a fulfilled and secure existence is seen largely in social and economic terms, while in Calvin's system these factors are realized spiritually, that is, psychologically[15] through the salvation of man's soul, possible only through reunion with God. Moreover, and this is the linch-pin of Calvin's beliefs, because it lay completely within the power of God as the Other to decree whether or not an individual could find salvation, it meant that not everyone could achieve this measure of fulfilment, regardless of whether or not their sins were remitted by priestly intervention. Furthermore, no amount of self-directed activity could counter God's inexorable Will, which is why man's existence within this system can be described as truly non-autonomous. Man's individual destiny was God's choice, and one that he could only discover through the revelation that the message of salvation taught by Christ through the Gospels was for him. Nonetheless, despite this revelation man could not change his destiny in any way in the face of the absolute independence of the Divine Will, because he was, to use Calvin's term, *predestined* to fulfil the internal necessity of the condition, salvation or damnation, imposed upon him by God. St Augustine captured the 'heads I win, tails you lose' quality of Calvin's view on predestination when he said in his *Sermons* (II: 768) that if we are damned it proves God's justice, but if we are saved it shows his mercy. Only those 'elected' or chosen by God could be saved, Calvin stressed, but man had to live his predestined life in as useful a way as he could, not because he

---

15 If the connexion between these two terms appears unfamiliar, both have a common link in the notion of 'the life breath': spirit is derived from the Latin 'spiritus' which is used to translate biblical passages containing either the Greek 'πνευμα' or the Hebrew 'ruah', both associated with breath as a life-force. 'Psychology' is derived from the Greek formative root ' ψυχη ' meaning all of 'breath', 'life', or 'soul'.

was doing it for himself, but because he was simply fulfilling God's Will.

Without the utter conviction that the power of the Other was quite absolute and must be carried out, the individual could well be forgiven for thinking that because his actions were wholly irrelevant to the attainment of salvation or fulfilment he could then indulge himself in a life of debauched pleasure knowing his fate was pre-ordained anyway. To Calvin such a positive decision by a person to 'indulge himself' was quite impossible, because this would pre-suppose the re-establishment of a causal connexion between pre-destination and personal foreknowledge of one's condition. This would subject and hence limit the Will of God to external, selfish factors and so weaken the supremacy of the Other's potency. Cal-vin's assessment of man's psychology allowed him to believe that if a man did evil it was in God's design that he should do so and for reasons understandable only by Him. Similarly, if a man were to do unpleasant work he would not seek to question it because he knew it was decreed by God, the Other, through His divine Will, yet it was also expected that this man should find reward and fulfilment in his work knowing that his actions were ordained and beheld by the Other. The reward was thus primarily spiritual, elevating the most mundane task through faith in the Will of the Other, into an act of willing homage to affirm the Self's complete and desired depend-ence on the Other.

It is essential to appreciate how notably this submission of personal will to the divine Other's differs from the submission of one's will to equally arduous tasks when the commitment to work is sustained not through *spiritual* enrichment, but by *material* rewards, for example, the money and role status offered by most modern work-organizations. In these cases the imposition of the dominant will of the Other (the work-organization's *mores*) is less obvious, but at the same time psychologically harmful for the Self. Cooper has pointed out that the poet, William Blake, writing at the dawn of organizational society, foresaw that we would 'endure a profound psychic hurt in serving systems and not being allowed to find our own deep centres. The result is an inner rage which often disrupts' (Cooper 1976: 1015). The Other's presence still limits the actions of the Self, by requiring it to accept the organization's will, yet this is not balanced by any significant attempt to offer the strong, enriching spiritual or psychological support that Calvin understood to be a crucial aspect of work done for God. Without such psychological support the Self's intimate (non-autonomous) relationship with the Other subtly alters to become oppressive of the Self, or as Marx would say, exploitative. As we shall see in Chapter 4 it is in this form of Self-Other interaction that Marx was able to locate the act of alienation and discern the presence of estrangement.

However, Calvin's perception of exploitation was not centred on the imposition of the Other's will on the Self as it was for Marx, but on the Self's usurping of the Other's divine Will. Man abused God's Grace by succumbing in ignorance to the belief that he could find salvation or fulfilment through his own endeavours. Calvin saw these efforts of self-assertion which, in effect, question the predestined nature of existence, as 'not less insane than if one should propose to walk in a pathless waste or to see in darkness' (Calvin 1960: III, xxi, s.2). Calvin understood that man cannot exist without structures, not necessarily physical ones, but spiritual supports which ensured that he did not have to face life alone or in psychological darkness. Calvin consequently exhorted his followers to ensure, through prayer, that the *political* stability of their country was maintained: 'We hold that all Christians are bound to pray to God for the prosperity of the superiors and lords of the country where they live, to obey the statutes and ordinances which do not contravene the commandments of God, to promote welfare, peace and public good' (Calvin 1954: 32). In this respect his sentiments are echoed in the work of the sociologist Durkheim, who argued that a sound moral fabric was essential to man's survival within society because it provided man with a spiritual base or frame of reference in times of uncertainty and change.

It was completely alien to the Reformers' way of thinking to see that a constant interaction with the unknown, the pathless waste, could be an alternative way to establish spiritual fulfilment. This existentialist view is grounded in a perspective of man's psychology that is completely different to Calvin's: the influence of the Other is, without exception, coercive and deleterious to the Self's drive towards fulfilment in his own terms. For the existentialists, the Self's endeavours to assert himself against the Other is itself an affirmation of psychological fulfilment: to accept one's given lot and to trust in the benevolence of the Other, as advocated by Calvin, is to succumb to an existence akin to the passive harnessed kitten in Held's and Hein's (1963) experiment.

In summary, this difference in views between the advocates of non-autonomy and those supporting autonomy rests on the contrast in perceptions of the influence of the Other upon the Self: Calvin's interpretation of the Other is as a presence in which the Self can find psychological support through faith and trust in its power, while the existentialists perceive the Other as a potent threat to their psychological growth, so they are sceptical and mistrustful of its presence and actively seek to transcend it. Thus love, the closest connexion between the Self and the Other, is understood quite differently by each group. The French writer, Malraux, has said in his *Antimemoirs*:

> 'The genius of Christianity is to have proclaimed that the path to the deepest mystery is the path of love. A love which is not confined to men's feelings, but transcends them like the soul of the world.'
> (Malraux 1968: 179)

Yet Sartre sees love purely as a selfish act, 'an organic ensemble of projects towards *my own* possibilities' (Sartre 1966: 477, emphases added).

The nature of man's activity in a semi-autonomous existence between himself and the Other: the emergence of capitalism

The unrelenting emphasis that Calvin and Luther placed on man's non-autonomous unity with God raised a question particularly difficult to resolve: if God's Will over the Self is supreme to the extent that all man's doings are decreed by that Other, does it not follow that man's behaviour is *de facto* blameless? Pelagius, the fifth-century British monk, was the first to raise this issue by questioning the doctrine of the transmission of original sin through succeeding generations, and proposed instead that it was possible for man to lead a virtuous life through his own self-directed effort and receive due reward in heaven. Man's actions are thus not completely pre-ordained through the Will of God, the Other, but can, through an assertion of his own willed action, gain the Other's approval; that is, his actions are *semi-autonomous* of the Other. For Pelagius and his followers, man is sustained by God's guiding presence and his work is carried out as an act of creative furtherance of God's Will, and not done simply because He decreed it. This view, familiar to modern church-goers, was considered by St Augustine as quite sacreligious because it questioned the absolute Will of God:

> 'The recent Pelagian heretics . . . hold a theory of free choice of will which leaves no place for the grace of God, since they hold it is given in accordance with our merits.'
> (St Augustine 1955: I, ix, s.3)

Nonetheless, the support for the Self's semi-autonomous existence from God gathered momentum in the fifteenth and sixteenth centuries: Erasmus, in a celebrated pamphlet to Luther (*On The Freedom of Will*), rejected St Augustine's view and elaborated on the arguments of Pelagius in a passage worth quoting at length:

'How is it that we hear so much about reward if there is no such thing as merit? With what impudence is the obedience of those who obey the divine commands praised, and the disobedience of those who do not obey condemned? Why is there so frequent a mention of judgement in Holy Scriptures if there is no weighing of merits? Or, why are we compelled to be present at the Judgement seat if nothing has happened through our own will, but all things have been done in us by sheer necessity? . . . Why does he [God] wish anything to be unceasingly prayed for which he has already decreed either to give or not to give, and cannot change his decrees, since he is immutable? Why does he command us to seek with so many labours what he has decided freely to bestow?'

(Erasmus 1969: 87f)

Luther responded with quite unecclesiastical venom to Erasmus's ideas,[16] and instead of answering the specific questions put to him, he warned Erasmus that if the supremacy of God's Will was doubted then man's soul would be at the mercy of forces beyond the realm of certainty and would be ruled by 'the false idol chance, at whose nod everything happens at random' (Luther 1969: 228). Luther's rhetoric against Erasmus was not directed solely against sentiments questioning the supremacy of God's Will, but arose in part from a deeper psychological fear of the loss of God's complete control over man's actions.[17] By questioning the inevitability of God's Will, the Self no longer could have utter confidence in the protective power of that Other, but instead would have to find in himself a measure of strength to create his own salvation. Luther argued that man cannot have the depth of faith in his own willed actions to find his own salvation, even if this was theologically acceptable. For him there could be no alternative way to lead one's life because existence itself was an act of faith fulfilled in God's Grace and not by random chance. Both Luther and Calvin argued that the act of faith was founded on the *revelation*, to each person, of the potency of God's

---

[16] 'Your book struck me as so cheap and paltry that I felt profoundly sorry for you, defiling as you were your very elegant and ingenious style with such trash, and quite disgusted at the utterly unworthy matter that was being conveyed in such rich ornaments of eloquence, like refuse or ordure being carried in gold and silver vases.'

(Luther 1969: 102)

[17] Luther suffered throughout his life from bouts of intense depression brought on by a fear that God had deserted him – he often refers to this in his writings.

Will as expressed through Christ's presence on earth: the inner spiritual sustenance derived from this revelation should, they pointed out, manifest itself externally through a life of hard work, frugality, and moral uprightness. Ironically, their assessment of man's psychology failed to appreciate that these qualities, shorn of the spiritual value of revelation, and applied to the world of business, could provide man with the tools to help him face the rational immediacy of the market place. 'Religion', as the methodist Wesley pointed out, 'must necessarily produce both industry and frugality and these cannot but produce Riches' (quoted in Samuelsson 1961: 2). This money could be used to accumulate possessions and to acquire power over others through the purchase and control of labour. Increased productivity was seen as the way to enhance the use of God's resources. Thus, the spiritual value of work as the direct means of acting out God's Will, had altered to work for an economic purpose and accomplished with His benign approval. Moreover, the changing nature of work allowed man to establish even more firmly his self-confidence as a being who could determine his immediate fate through his own actions and acumen.

Max Weber attributed the alteration of attitudes and the growth of materialism to the 'secularization of all ideals through Protestantism' (Weber 1958: 40). Samuelsson (1961), on the other hand, argued that this change of attitude was part of a larger movement, a new spirit which he said revealed itself in the fifteenth and sixteenth centuries as creativeness, as protest against the establishment, as economic progress and the break with Catholicism. It is not my intention to become involved in the imbroglio that surrounds the difference of views held by these two writers on how the attitude change to work arose, (see Anthony (1977) for a recent extensive reassessment) but to note one key feature that they both agree upon. That is, whether one wishes to follow Weber who wanted to explore the religious conditions 'which made possible the development of the capitalist civilization' (Tawney in Weber 1958: 16), or others like Samuelsson (e.g. Robertson 1933, or Wallace 1959) who argued that the capitalist civilization and its associated work ethic was the consequence of man's desire to manage and control his *own* destiny, either way what was emerging was a new psychology based on self-assurance[18] and with it a new *purpose* for work.

Man in his daily business had forgotten or discounted Calvin's

---

[18] This 'new' psychology, it should be noted, was already well established in India: the Buddhist quality of '*saddha*' although often translated loosely as 'faith' is more accurately rendered as 'self confidence based on knowledge' or 'the confidence that there is a goal to be reached' (Saddhatissa 1971: 24).

warning that the righteousness of his activity must be justified through his faith in God and must be 'included in it and referred back to it, as the fruit to the tree' (Calvin 1960: III, xvii, s.10). The function of God had become subtly transformed to that of a supporter of man's self-directed deeds. Whereas before, under strict Calvinism, worldly success was not a matter of personal rejoicing, because God had Willed it for His own purpose, the sixteenth-century business man could now offer thanks to God for his own good *fortune*. Indeed, the successful business man compounded his evilness, in Calvin's eyes, by allowing feelings of self-satisfaction and moral superiority to emerge when his works were contrasted with his less successful counterparts, whose lack of prosperity was assumed to be rooted in personal idleness. As Anthony has pointed out,

'once work is dignified it is a short and almost inevitable step to dignifying the worker and when work is set up for enthusiastic comparison with idleness it is difficult to avoid admiration for the worker and contempt for the idle.'   (Anthony 1977: 44)

To be fair, this attitude was not intended by the early Reformists: Luther had denounced the ceaseless activity of prayers, fasting, and self-mortification in monasteries as simply 'busy leisure' (Luther 1958 (I): 213), because it was done purely functionally, without the revelation of faith in God that gave both work and rest their true meaning.[19] R.C. Cooper (in correspondence) has drawn a modern parallel with the world of business. He describes the bustling activity of the office environment as mere 'busyness' – a function for its own sake, devoid of any deeper personal meaning.

We shall see that Anthony has pinpointed the thinking still underlying certain conceptions of work when I come to consider (in the concluding Chapter) the enthusiasm for the introduction of work purported to be personally fulfilling or 'self-actualizing'. Briefly picking up one facet of this topic to illustrate it from the specific viewpoint of the Self's relation to the Other: although 'actualizing' jobs may appear to have a large *discretionary* content, rather than prescribed routine, to use Jaques's (1951) terms, the employees' powers of discretion (or as I have called it, his self-willed

---

[19] The bible, too, contains passages criticizing a preoccupation with work for merely material ends: 'Consider the lilies of the field, how they grow: they toil not neither do they spin. And yet I say unto you that even Solomon in all his glory was not arrayed like one of these. But seek ye first the Kingdom of God and his righteousness; and all these things shall be added unto you' (Matthew, 6, vs.28).

actions) are limited to the organizational context in which he works. Through its more potent will, the organization as a powerful Other ultimately decrees the parameters of any self-willed activity, thus making certain that the Self's actions are at best semi-autonomous of the Other's. Although this relationship can provide psychological support, because the Other is a medium through which the Self can act, it is not necessarily self-fulfilling, because it does not allow an authentic expression of that Self's disposition to emerge. That 'self-actualizing' work may not be authentic holds true for another reason: because of the work-organization's functional nature it does not usually provide the spiritual or psychological qualities that allow the semi-autonomous relationship inherent in man's relationship to that Other to attain its fullest expression, that is, love.

In a non-autonomous relationship between the Other and the Self the latter must admire and worship the former, but in a semi-autonomous relationship a supportive reciprocity emerges between the Self and the Other akin to the relationship between a loving father and his child. De Chardin believes that man should perceive God in this way. Through His presence man's behaviour is guided without being commanded, and His power over man is a creative presence which does not fashion man 'as though out of soft clay; it is a fire that kindles life in what ever it touches, a quickening spirit' (De Chardin 1970: 107). Or, as he says in another instance, God's presence can be perceived as a 'palpable *influence*, on our world, of an other and supreme Someone' (De Chardin 1959: 298, emphasis added). His influence lies in the power to connect and unify men with each other and with Him. By comparison, the shallowness of the work-organization as Other is notable; its interaction with the Self is grounded in mundane contact, not love: 'Contact is still superficial, involving the danger of yet another servitude' (De Chardin 1959: 265). The Self, aware of the servitude inherent in organized work, can attempt to minimize it by playing the *role* of a person committed to his given tasks. His conduct is thus functionally driven, and although appearing to his colleagues to be a spirited performance, actually lacks the animating spiritual qualities that allow interaction between the Self and the Other to go beyond simple contact and emerge into the realm of a mutually supportive, semi-autonomous existence. Although the external expressions of the functional and spiritual forms of commitment to one's work are indistinguishable, the psychological difference is deep and ever-present because a sizeable proportion of man's daily activity is being channelled into enhancing the role he plays, not the person himself.

Thus, minimizing the commitment of the Self to the organization as Other by role-playing is accomplished by reducing the Self's intrusion upon the Other's presence; the Other's requirements, not the Self's needs, stay supreme because although work organizations often wish to establish a semi-autonomous relationship with the working individual, their functionally based nature is coercive and fails to respond to the myriad needs of the live, non role-playing Self.

An alternative to the self-sacrifice entailed in role playing is to reduce the Other's intrusion upon the Self, not by hiding the Self behind a role but by treating the Other's requirements with a fair measure of indifference: the instrumental attitude towards work – i.e. work done largely for money without regard to the nature of the task – takes this approach (see Goldthorpe 1966). This attitude is a logical conclusion of the role-playing technique because it arises through the same calculating dissociation of the individual from his work context. Whereas role-playing is an instance of a loveless semi-autonomous existence between the Self and the Other which can result in distortion of the Self, the attitude of instrumentalism, which makes no pretence of showing love or commitment to the work-organization as Other, can be a manifestation of the Self's desire for a break from the attitudes, values, and customs that perpetuate the organizational Other's authority over the Self. This rejection of the covertness of role-playing in favour of overt indifference towards traditional values of work signifies the emergence of the Self's aspiration towards a *fully autonomous* existence.

The nature of man's activity in a full autonomous existence between himself and the Other: existentialism

This, my third and final form of Self-Other interaction, is of relatively recent origin, having gained prominence through the writings of the existentialists. The form's most noticeable quality and that which gives the diverse writings of the existentialists their unity is that for them, 'individuality is not retouched, idealized or holy; it is wretched and revolting, and yet for all its misery, *the highest good*' (Kaufmann 1975: 12, emphases added).

Because individuality is the 'highest good', man's self-expressive existence is its own reward: no gods, no supports, either material or immaterial, and no wilful Others are permitted to impede the process of sustaining his quest for Self. Kierkegaard, one of the first Western writers to discuss the issues central to this perspective of man, begins his book, *The Sickness unto Death* (originally pub-

lished in 1843), with a compact outline of the existentialists' view of
the nature of the autonomous Self:

> 'But what is the self? The self is a relation which relates itself to
> its own self, or it is that in the relation that the relation relates
> itself to its own self; the self is not the relation but that the
> relation relates itself to its own self. Man is a synthesis of the
> infinite and the finite, of the temporal and the eternal, of freedom
> and necessity, in short it is a synthesis. A synthesis is a relation
> betwcen two factors. So regarded man is not yet a self.'[20]
>
> (Kierkcgaard 1954: 146)

What Kierkegaard wishes to point out is that the Self, as a self-
relating presence rather than an Other-relating one, is in a constant
dialectical interaction with itself, both within the limitations of its
existing relations and its possibilities or relations-to-be, and it is this
constant dynamic reappraisal that goes on throughout man's life
that makes him realize that his Self is not a complete synthesis in
itself but must constantly yearn towards the unknown or non-Self
infinity that lies before it. Man's *actions* must be used to transcend
the necessity of the finitude of his existing relations, to precipitate
himself towards the possibilities inherent in his autonomy in an
effort to complete the synthesis of his Self. Yet, by being fully
autonomous, man can never complete this synthesis because his
freedom to act as a self-transforming being is itself infinite.

Western culture, enmeshed in a functional, Other-based life, still
finds it difficult to respond to a perception of man as an autonomous
self-transforming person, but other cultures have it as central to
their way of life. For example, Whorf (1956: 80ff) has reported that
North American Indians, the Hopi, use words and expressions that
are without equivalent in European tongues to represent man's
self-transformation in the course of his active engagement with the
world. As a consequence, their awareness of an individual's personality is less definite than ours in terms of its needs and limitations.
The immutability of the personality favoured by European man is a
legacy of the Calvinist view that man's whole life was pre-ordained
through God's Will, and is reflected in the modern emphasis upon
one Self playing various roles. Both attitudes hinder acceptance of
new relations and new transcending syntheses, the primary factors
in autonomous man's psychological growth.

Although the Self's task of precipitating itself towards the un-

---

[20] This convoluted style of writing seems to be a hallmark of existentialists. See, e.g.,
Sartre (1966: 123f) for his assessment of the Self. In existentialist writings the Self is
generally treated as an impersonal entity.

known through open-ended activity is one of immense seriousness to existentialists, the qualities of the task accord closely with Schiller's understanding of *play*, which involves: 'free movement of the poetic faculty, or of grasping the concrete individuality of things with a sense innocent of pre-conceptions and [yet] faithful to the object' (Schiller 1965: Letter 6, s.13). The Self, at play, forgets itself and suspends its assumptions in an attempt to perceive afresh. The act allows a re-orientation of one's perceptions and a formulation of untried relations. The existentialist Heidegger saw that man's primordial act of orientation was the establishment of a *Spielraum*, literally a playing-space into which man projected himself to create a new correspondence with the played-upon (Heidegger 1962: 75). Thus, we can see that Adam's eating of the apple in Eden was a playful act; not a frivolous gesture, but an active attempt, through self-assertion against God's Will, to create for himself his own possibilities and meanings in his own context. One may imagine that if Adam and Eve saw themselves as the first existentialists they would have said to themselves whilst they ate the apple: Eden may be paradise, but:

> 'There is literally nothing to do or to accomplish. We are petrified and impotent beneath a divine gaze, reduced to the condition of visible things. All our inner resources are alienated by an infinite wisdom which has already disposed all things well.'
>
> (Masterson 1973: 144)

To be cast out of Eden is not the *penalty* for their self-assertion, it is the necessary first step to take to find out whether they can live up to the challenge of eating the fruit. God's command to Adam that he must work in order to live is not man's burden but his release, if we understand work to be a self-creating activity. We shall see in Chapter 4 that this formulation of work, in fact no different from play, is what Marx understood to be unalienated work; not because it is pleasant to do, or carried out in comfortable surroundings, or with agreeable colleagues, but specifically because it is done for the Self and not for the Other.

Although it may be possible to conceive of work done by the Self for its own ends, rather than for those of the Other, the psychological hold by the Other's presence upon the Self remains powerful. Sartre, for instance, has argued that even the Other's *look* causes the 'solidification and alienation of [one's] own possibilities' (Sartre 1966: 352), that is, the look restricts his powers of self-expression, because it reduces the Self to a perceived object. This treatment is likewise meted out by the Self through his efforts to reduce the non-Self to an object. The dialectic of this joint deadening of possibilities competing with their mutual efforts to transcend each other's powers of solidification is, for Sartre, the process that creates one's self-awareness: 'I need the mediation of the Other in order to be what I am' (1966: 384).

In brief, to describe a relationship between the Self and Other as autonomous is to indicate that the Self is continually seeking actively to transcend the Other's will, to establish his own meanings and thereby create himself.

> 'It comes down in the end to how we use ourselves. If there is nothing "in here" there is nothing (of ours) "out there". Process begins with oneself and moves out from here. One is ever open. The alternative is the rule of structure outside you, in fact, that which measures you – and to which, having no measure to call your own, you refer everything. You are thus always closed, you do not own the key.'   (Cooper 1976: 1015)

Summary

This chapter has developed and looked at three main forms of relationship the Self can have with the Other. I have sought to establish the understanding that these relationships are alive in the psychological, or spiritual, realm of man's existence: that is, their focus is not upon man's epistemology (or how he comes to know and understand the world about him) but rather upon his *ontology* (or his being in the world as a self-consciousness).

Thus the forms of non-, semi-, and full autonomous existences are *forms of ontological life*, and as I have stressed before, each form is entirely psychologically valid because each can offer a different way through which the Self perceives the Other.

The Self's awareness of the difference between the forms provides the ground for the Self's *authentic* existence within any one of the forms, an authenticity which is then expressed through his full commitment to one particular form. Grasping that there exists an ontological choice that faces each individual is a necessary first step in understanding what happens when that person is 'alienated' from either making his or her choice or fulfilling it.

Figure 1(3) summarizes the main aspects of each form.

I have indicated that an *aware* choice is an essential element for authentic life in each of the three ontological forms, but have not yet explored the *nature* of awareness that gives authenticity its particular ontological significance. I now turn to this task.

Figure 1(3) Forms of ontological life

	Category	Nature of Activity	Relationship to the Other
(1)	The Self in *non-autonomous* existence with the Other	Actions are Other-directed	Adoration
(2)	The Self in *semi-autonomous* existence with the Other	Actions are jointly attempted or Other-supported	Respect or love
(3)	The Self in *full autonomous* existence of the Other	Actions are for the Self's own ends and/or 'playful'	Indifference or hostility

2

Forms of authentic awareness

Introduction: the importance of the individual's perspective of the world as a preliminary to understanding the nature of 'alienation'

The previous chapter sought to set the scene for discussions on the contrasting natures of authentic and alienated life by considering the two core aspects of man's existence: first, the importance to man of his active involvement with other people and objects in his ecosystem, and the different forms through which that involvement may be manifest, and second, how these different forms influence the development of self-awareness and the Self-Other interface – man's psychosystem. Thus, using man's relationship to the archetypal Other, God, as a medium for the discussion, it became possible to establish three theoretical forms of Self-Other interaction, each characterized by a different kind of ontological autonomy for the individual. It was argued that each of these three forms had a desired mode of existence, or Being, which, to the person within each form, appeared under certain conditions as an authentic and sincere way of life. This endeavour made it clear that the general approach to the quest for authentic life was to emphasize the individual's point of view not exclusively, but enough to draw away from the organizational science treatment of man as a 'black box' interacting with other 'black boxes'.

Four archetypal forms of awareness used by the Self to comprehend the world both epistemologically and ontologically

This chapter is an extension of that approach, and I now turn to an examination of four modes of awareness derived from the classical philosophical distinction between epistemological and ontological awareness. The former focuses on how we come to know entities in the world and asks the question 'What is such and such?'. The latter is concerned with man's awareness of himself in relation to the world and asks the question 'What ought to be?'. Although certain subtleties exist within each category[1] we can highlight two subdivisions within each of them. Epistemological awareness may be said to have two focuses, *long* and *short*, while ontological awareness may be divided into *open* and *closed* awareness.

Without the realization that these distinctions exist any further discussion on 'alienation' or authenticity will be seriously hindered because it will have not been made clear (as so often happens in discussions on 'alienation') upon what premises and conditions the analysis is being based.

From these four modes a four-box matrix is constructed to highlight their interconnexion with the three authentic forms of non-, semi-, and fully autonomous states of existence. Once this is accomplished I then turn, in Chapters 3 and 4, to a close study of the concept of 'alienation' as manifest in each of the four quadrants of the matrix, each of which represents a specific form of psychological archetype. I shall now examine in turn the four proposed modes of awareness; as the arguments unfold, some of the other areas within man's psychosystem that influence his appreciation of authentic and 'alienated' existences are mapped out.

If one puts into temporary abeyance the many possible ideological overtones and moral judgements that may be made about man's preferred mode of interaction with the world, either political or psycho-social, one sees that its essence is that of being able to rise to the challenge, which man himself creates in his self-directed activity, of choosing, out of a series of alternatives, an existence that ensures his self-preservation throughout his dealings with the Other. Man's response to that challenge, in the form of his style of ontological life, can offer a basis for describing what form an authentic existence may take. Thus, as a first step it was possible to distinguish between sincere and authentic awareness: in sincerity

---

[1] I shall discuss the more relevant of these intricacies over succeeding chapters, but Ayer (1956) and Heidegger (1978) offer useful contrasting assessments of each of the term's particulars.

man could live within any *one* of the categories of autonomy by holding one form of Self-Other relationship or one ideological stance: authenticity in one's ontological life emerged only when the individual gained an awareness and appreciation of the nature of the alternative possible relationships with the Other. That is, man's authenticity is the ontological proof of his awareness, while the adherence or deviation from the norms *within* each Self-Other relationship, is a measure of the individual's sincerity.

SHORT AND LONG FOCUS: THE EPISTEMOLOGICAL BASIS FOR MAN'S AWARENESS OF HIS PSYCHOSYSTEM

However, a consideration of man's awareness of others simply in terms of acts of self-preservation immediately reveals two further (contrasting) forms of awareness. First, the *short focus* where the sincere immersion by the Self into the prevalent culture is evidence of a good adaptation to the present circumstances. In this instance man's concern is with the immediate here and now of events and interactions; his emphasis is upon the components of his environment and not the system as a whole.[2] Second, awareness may take the form of a *long focus* where man stands back or distances himself from the particulars of his environment and is concerned with the whole or unity of the system. This act includes within its power an awareness, as Merleau-Ponty has described it, that 'cultural objects would not be what they are if the activity which brings about their appearance did not also have as its meaning to reject them and surpass them' (Merleau-Ponty 1963).

The long-focus awareness provides that critical and transcendental function that the short-focus awareness cannot, yet man actively uses both forms, oscillating between them, to enrich his awareness both of 'what is' and 'what ought to be' in the world of people and processes. The 'what is' question represents man's concern for epistemological awareness of his environment and events and has a measure of objectivity, while the 'what ought to be' question can only be asked in awareness of his ontological stance and is a purely personal search.

---

[2] One may note briefly here that this adaptation to existing cultural norms represents freedom from 'alienation' for Abramson (1972), Bullough (1967), Fischer (1973) and Scott (1965); while writers like Touraine (1971) and Mills (1973), who are concerned with the lack of awareness of alternative cultural forms, see immersion in the short focus as an example of false consciousness, 'alienation' or conformity.

The epistemological 'what is' question

Man's action in grasping the 'what is' corresponds to a form of model building where his psychosystem is developed through forming, dissolving, and reforming links between entities whether those entities be outwardly manifest (people, processes, and events) or inwardly felt (thoughts, beliefs, ideological structures) thus creating a web or system through which he leads his daily life. The structure that this web imparts to man's psychosystem then allows him to relate other entities to it until he builds up a system with, for instance, one common theme and many sub-themes. As our awareness develops we perceive that we cannot fit all entities into one main structure so we set up another one which in turn can allow us to incorporate yet further entities into our scheme of things. It is to be realized that in exploring awareness of 'what is', man is not actually *constructing* reality, or himself, in a Berkeleian fashion, but is ordering the many entities that face him to give them a personal meaning. Following the construction of a number of main themes the individual may then realize that these themes themselves have a certain unity and can be drawn together – thus there develops a hierarchy of themes, the more general ones being the most abstract.

The individual has, through this accumulation of themes, produced a taxonomy of analysable or perceivable entities, based on a series of archetypes, which will provide the foundation for his actions. Simpson, a taxonomist, calls this a system based on 'idealist morphology' (1961:49), where there is the belief, at any rate implicit, that the archetype is in some way the reality and the entities that are actually perceived are the imperfect embodiments of that transcendental reality. This being so, constant effort is required to enhance and enrich one's perception to come closer to the ideal reality.

The alternative form of epistemological 'what is' awareness arises, Simpson suggests, not in the construction of archetypes, but through a focusing on the *relationship* between each entity. Studying their inter-relationship indicates that awareness is always to be in terms of the entities themselves and their reciprocal changing and dialectical interactions, thus suggesting that the individual does not seek to impose his personal order on the entities as he would do in an 'idealist' frame of mind.

Although distancing one's Self from entities and formulating core themes is to run the risk of constructing an idealist morphology, there are those, for example, Husserl, who believed that distancing can actually remove ideological assumptions. Husserl's (1931) phenomenology wished to abstract awareness from idealist assumptions and purify it into a state of 'awareness of being aware'. That is, he argues that one can experience 'experiencing something' as a conscious act, one reflects on experience itself; an act of distancing which heightens the awareness of the experienced. He points out that man is accustomed to concentrate upon the matters, thoughts, and values of the moment, and not upon the psychical 'act of experience' in which these are apprehended. Instead of the matters themselves man regards the subjective experiences in which these 'appear'. These 'appearances' are phenomena whose nature it is to be 'consciousness-of' their object. He uses the word 'intentional' to denote the essential 'reference' character of the phenomena and contends that all consciousness is intentional. The intentional objects of consciousness are the entities of the perceivable world, but attention could equally be turned to ideal objects: the fundamental concepts of a science, the ideal laws of logic are two examples.

The study of phenomena in this way was, Husserl believed, to produce a descriptive science of the essential structures of conscious experience purified both of interpretive constructions and all of the merely factual ingredients that are studied by the empirical sciences. The method by which this aim was to be fulfilled was through eidetic or phenomenological reduction, or as I have called it, the break from sincerity. The eidetic reduction begins with the suspension ('ἐποχη') of consciousness: a withdrawal from the natural attitude of everyday life in which the individual is accustomed to go about his business into a state of abstract thinking awareness. 'For me the world is nothing other than I am aware of and what appears valid in such *cogitationes*. The whole meaning and reality of the world rests exclusively on such *cogitationes*' (Husserl 1960:9). The procedure was supposed to isolate the field of pure phenomena where 'units of sense' were given with absolute certainty: thus, by attempting to produce a description of the noetic or 'experiencing', and the noematic, the 'experienced', Husserl's phenomenological descriptions are rooted in Cartesian dualism (which Ryle (1973) has rightly damned for its artificial splitting of mind and body). Hence, the more earnestly Husserl sought to avoid subjective idealist interpretations of 'reality' the greater became the split between mundane reality and eidetic reality: a dichotomy which by its very nature was itself ideologically founded. The focus of Husserl's phenomenology was thus on pure experience itself, regardless of the object experienced. Awareness became an end in itself and consequently objects were only authentically experienced in abstraction. The Hegelian conception of estrangement, as we shall see in the next chapter, allows us to understand that this act of abstraction is but *part* of a movement towards a possible mode of authentic experience and one which must be superseded before man's alienation can end.

Merleau-Ponty, in some sympathy with Hegelian views, has a version of phenomenology which avoids the necessity of reducing objects to sensations to be able to perceive them as they really are. His discussion on the contrast between 'classical' and 'new' psychology make this clear: the former failed to progress until it gave up the distinction between mind and body, a dualism which forced psychologists to attempt to unite information from intro- spective thought with physiological data or sensations. The 'new' psychology 'revealed man to us not as an understanding which constructs the world, but as a being thrown into the world and attached to it by a natural bond' (Merleau-Ponty 1964: 53), a bond that is a relationship of concrete immediacy rather than abstract remoteness. He develops this point, showing that although it is clear that awareness of the world was to be found in the relationship between Self and the objects it encounters in the world, the old psychology failed to grasp that the Self is the key aspect in all these transactions and that awareness was to be understood and analysed from the stand-point of the individual's being-in-the-world – his psychosystem, as I call it. That is, awareness and hence knowledge is *metaphysical* because it lies beyond the mere analysis of physical sensations, because 'we apperceive the radical subjectivity of all our experience as inseparable from its own truth value' (Merleau-Ponty 1964: 93). This is Hegel's point too, but he went one stage further as his authentic awareness, in the state of Absolute Knowledge, is remarkably close to that awareness favoured and sought by the followers of Zen enlightenment, although the mechanisms used by each to achieve authentic awareness are quite different.

Awareness in the Zen mode is a complete contrast to that of Husserlian or Cartesian dualism, because it is dependent on an immediate relationship between the Self and the objects it observes, that is, without the presence of a mediating awareness. Thus, instead of attempting to gain further awareness of 'what is' by distancing or dissociating oneself from the knowable, the alterna- tive is to become absorbed into the knowable, allowing the Self to merge and enhance the known as much as the known enlivens the Self. The action of immersion here is not simply to be understood as a phase of awareness taken from Merleau-Ponty's phenomenologic- al system of metaphysics, because Zen aims to use this awareness to realize a form of unification in one's everyday life of lived actualities and not to treat life as any sort of metaphysical exercise:

'Zen deals with facts and not with their logical, verbal, prejudiced and lame representations. Direct simplicity is the soul of Zen: hence its vitality, freedom and originality ... logic is self-conscious. [Zen] has nothing to do with abstractions or with subtleties of dialectics ... nor with ... the act of building up and destroying, the art of discussing all things and accomplishing nothing ... Zen wishes to ... show that we live psychologically or biologically and not logically.'   (Suzuki 1969: 61–4)

That is, there are two camps of thought on how the emergence of awareness of 'what is' occurs. Their differences may be sketched out as in Figure 2(1).

Figure 2(1)   Two forms of awareness

(a) Awareness through reduction to sensation (Husserl, Descartes)	(b) Awareness through reciprocity (Merleau-Ponty)	(Zen)
Awareness is knowledge of the duality between mind and body, Self and Other	The self is the locus of awareness in the presence of metaphysical existence of objects and Others	The relationship *per se* between Self and object or Other is the locus of awareness.
Analytic logic is used to discover awareness in the process of eidetic reduction – the ideal form of perception	Dialectical knowledge is used to discover awareness of Self's relationship to objects and Others	Knowledge of enlightenment is used to discover awareness – occurs by insight not logic
	Perception is immediate, and has no ideal form	

Consequently, the 'art' of eidetic reduction, essential to Husserl as the means whereby the world is revealed in its 'reality' as a preparation for understanding the Self in that world, is condemned vigorously by Zen for breaking down the essential relationship between the person and his environment. The value of the Cartesian basis of phenomenology is heartily rejected too, and in the place of eidetic reduction and logical analysis Zen emphasizes that awareness emerges through the illumination or enlightenment that is revealed to one through *'prajna'* or essential wisdom. This is akin to Christian revelation in the awareness of Christ, a revelation that goes beyond the duality of subject and object, beyond

'I–Thou' even into the realm of 'no-mind' (*Wu-hsin*). This is not just a state of awareness, but a way of action instilled into the psychosystem of man. The doctrine of no-mind was put forward by Hui-neng (fl. c.700 A.D.) on the realization that contemplation of an object in meditation was, during his time, being carried out as if it were the act of viewing an object or contemplating an idea from the vantage point of an observer, thus revealing a duality between 'pure mind' and the fruits of its awareness.

Hui-neng contended that meditating was to be pure seeing; observing the reality is not enough, one must *be* the reality. Awareness thus transcends ideological barriers. *Satori* (enlightenment) arose on the realization that one was reciprocating directly with the object, or the environment generally, a reciprocity from which all aspects of wishing and desire have been banished. To wish is to attempt to perceive according to one's needs and fears and this introduces distortion in the mediation between Self and objects. It is interesting to note that despite these differences, the phenomenological reductionism of Husserl and the Way of Zen enlightenment do have similar intentions: to perceive objects in their purest form devoid of ideological or normative associations. Husserl may be less successful in this endeavour because by splitting the noetic, the subject who experiences, from the noematic, the object of his experiences, he can only achieve an abstract unity within man's psychosystem by eidetic reduction, before man can be said to act authentically; while Zen seeks to show that the subject acts authentically when he 'loses' himself in the reality of the world. That is, for Zen the act of meditation is to bring the subject and object closer through mutual empathy, while the act of eidetic reduction in phenomenology seeks to perceive objects as abstract sensations. As a compromise, the theologian Martin Buber suggests that the former state of awareness, gained by involvement, can arise out of the latter, acquired through analytic distancing. To clarify this point he describes the act of looking at a tree:

'I can assign it to a species and observe it as an instance, with an eye to its construction and its way of Life, ... the tree [thus] remains my object and has its place and its time span, its kind and condition. But it can also happen, if will and grace are joined, that as I contemplate the tree I am drawn into a relation, and the tree ceases to be It. The power of exclusiveness has seized me. ... What I encounter is neither the soul of a tree, nor a dryad, but the tree itself.'

(Buber 1970: 57–9)

Thus the reciprocity vital to Zen has a function similar to the use of a feed-back loop in cybernetics. The subject actively involves himself in the object to unfold its rich details which in turn enhance the awareness of the subject, thereby allowing for further appreciation of the object, and of the subject – object interaction by the more-aware subject. It is, as Gibson (1966) has described it, a perceptual learning process, each step establishing the increasing complexity of the object in the subject's perceptual field.

To sum up so far, the desire for authentic existence must take into account the presence of, and interaction between, the different types of awareness; that is depending on one's conception of how 'reality' is to be attained, the search for authenticity may be directed *either* through the immediacy of reciprocity between the subject and object *or* through the ability to reduce to sensations the pure form of the object: both acts of awareness, although quite different, strive to produce what each considers value-free perceptions, devoid of the wishes, intolerances, fears, and assumptions of the perceiver. Figure 2(2) summarizes the main forms of awareness and authenticity discussed so far in the 'what is' mode of awareness, and links them with their ontological counterparts as a preliminary to discussion on the 'what ought to be' mode of awareness.

The presence of ontological awareness of 'what ought to be' as a further factor influencing authentic life

Mention of 'what ought to be' immediately takes us away from the relatively clear-cut area of 'what is' because it is no longer possible for one's awareness to be limited to what one encounters in the perceived world, one must take up a psychological stance. This means that the analysis of awareness simply for its self-preservation value is submerged by a new force. As Habermas has said:

'. . . society is not only a system of self-preservation. An enticing natural force, present in the individual as libido, has detached itself from the behavioural system of self-preservation and urges towards utopian fulfilment . . . what may appear as naked survival is always in its roots a historical phenomenon. For it is subject to the criterion of what society intends for itself as the good life.'
(Habermas 1971: 312f)

Moreover, personal desires and wishes, together with social and moral issues, immediately clamour for attention within the

Figure 2(2)   Forms of awareness and associated modes of behaviour

AWARENESS OF WHAT IS (Preferred Self-Object Interaction)	AWARENESS OF WHAT OUGHT TO BE (Preferred Ideological Stance)
Locus of Awareness Short focus awareness (by immersion) ↕ Long focus awareness (by distancing)	*Locus of Awareness* Other-willed (non-autonomous) ↕ Self-willed (autonomous)
Mode of Behaviour Awareness through reciprocity (participation) ↕ Awareness through being conscious of awareness (abstraction)	*Mode of Behaviour* Being as striving to attain Being: 'Essensism' (determinate), CLOSED (Demands negative liberty) ↕ Being as becoming: Existentialism (indeterminate), OPEN (Permits positive or negative liberty)
Knowledge of the World EPISTEMOLOGICAL AWARENESS	Being-in-the-World ONTOLOGICAL AWARENESS

Arrows indicate a cyclical process between the two poles.

psychosystem: the inert momentum of cultural forms that confront man can demand his allegiance in the manner a master requires a slave to carry out his caprices, yet the individual himself may have firm ideas as to what he expects or requires in his life. Herein lies the main difficulty facing any meaningful assessment of 'alienation'. Not only is it necessary to understand what society has intended or determined what ought to be, but the individual wishes and expectations also must be taken into account. Thus the only appreciation of the *nature* of what ought to be rests firmly in the source of determination, that is, who and under what authority can one decide that either an individual is 'alienated' from society, or that the society itself causes 'alienation' by its very structure and influence on its component individuals.

'WHAT OUGHT TO BE', AND SOCIAL OBLIGATION

Whether an individual can determine and decide what he desires, in complete freedom, or absence of constraint from the Other, or must select from and adapt to a range of 'desirables' approved by the society in which he lives, is a well known, well worn issue in philosophy, usually discussed in terms of the presence or absence of individual free-will in the face of societal, cultural, or historical inevitability. That is, in the terminology developed in the preceding chapter, either the Self dominates the Other (to be seen in this instance as the accumulation of past events, cultural forms and ideologies, society's accretion of the *praxis*, or directed activity of the individual), or the Self is subordinate to the Other, whereupon society, as the Other, establishes a moral code to which the actions of the individual must accord, thereby negating his autonomous free will.

Thus, as we saw in Chapter 1, Erasmus was able to refute Luther's notion of predestination by showing that if the Other (as God) predetermined man's actions and thus stripped them of their autonomous free-will, He naturally could not then superimpose a moral system that attributed blame or praise to those actions because He, in fact, controlled them *ab initio*. The argument can be extended to the Other as society. If society determines man's actions then his response, for example, as 'alienated' behaviour, is neither blame- nor praise-worthy, merely reactive. Because it is important to appreciate the variety of positions tenable in asking 'what ought to be', let us first explore the notion of personal freedom and its variants in more detail to reveal the social pressures that man faces before the ontological ones can be appreciated.

It will be recalled that Luther saw personal, absolute, free will as an affront to God's Will; one must obey the Divine Will, and by doing so man was then truly free, not a puppet to the whims of the blind goddess Chance. Hobbes (1885) was more lenient on this issue, asserting that the liberty of man in doing what he wills is accompanied by the necessity of doing that which God wills.

These forms of liberty fall into the categories of non- and semi-autonomous forms of existence, and are thus opposed to the fully autonomous state of existence, where liberty is, in principle, unfettered by the Other. Isaiah Berlin (1969) has used the terms 'negative freedom' and 'positive freedom' to elucidate the distinction between freedom attained through common constraint by forms of social contract, and freedom which is gained through personal liberty. The objections raised by some writers to this dichotomy emphasize that freedom *simpliciter* is an unhelpful concept and can only have a meaning if given a focus: that is freedom, or lack of it, *from something*. While this may be a way of localizing the issues surrounding the nature of personal autonomy it is in fact re-presenting the very problem Berlin sought to overcome and which I, in the quest for the nature of authentic awareness, have attempted to clarify; namely the nature of *what* is to be desired as authentic freedom, if such actually exists. Failure to do this would be to resort to a solipsistic interpretation of freedom in order to define it – and that in itself is assuming a positive freedom perspective. Berlin's dichotomy allows us to see that if man appears as determined in and by the world he can be said to live in negative freedom through lack of choice, but if he can determine his own actions through a transcendence of the lived-in world he may be seen to be ascribing to the notion of positive freedom. Yet the determination of his positive freedom may only be fulfilled in negative freedom, that is, having established the nature of his relationship to the world as an active rather than a passive being, he may choose to live within the general will of society in order to use the power of his ontological existence (established by positive freedom) to aid the general will. Moreover, like adaptive awareness, positive and negative freedom have either short or long focuses, depending on what one sees as desirable in the interests of 'humanity'. Thus, in posing the question 'what is *absolutely* desirable?' philosophers present further (false) difficulties over which the terms 'authenticity' and 'alienation' have to clamber fruitlessly.

One must instead question the *relative* ontological value of a particular stance: Nietzsche, for example, desired positive freedom; for him it meant leaving behind the sludge of ordinary humanity to attain the goal of 'superman' while Buber found such an act selfish and ultimately ontologically restricting because close involvement with other men provided, for him, true personal freedom and growth.

However, as we have seen in Chapter 1, if the individual is confined solely to an awareness of negative freedom both in the short and long perspectives, his ontological strength is never derived from within himself, but rests in the shadow of the Other. If the nature of the Other is called into question, this at once weakens the ontological support it provides for an individual who had depended on the permanence of that Other to counterbalance his own impermanence. Durkheim's analysis of increasing suicide rates in times of uncertainty illustrates the consequences that the ontologically weak person endures when the support of the Other is removed. He suggested that the solution to this problem lay in establishing more closely the bonds that linked people to each other and society in an effort to affirm their mutual support; a suggestion that unquestioningly accepts the desirability of negative freedom. Merleau-Ponty proposed a parallel solution, emphasizing the need for 'radical subjectivity'; a category that has positive freedom connotations, although rather than seeking to transcend the Other's presence the individual actively *relates* to it, thus the relationship has many aspects of negative freedom. His argument runs as follows. It is through ceasing to live in the shadow or the existence of the Other, that is by developing a *metaphysical* framework of existence in the world, that one bypasses the need for the formal distinctions between positive and negative freedom, because the matter that *is* important is the nature of man's *ontological life*. Metaphysics in this sense is not simply a Knowledge to complete the edifice of all other knowledges but is used by Merleau-Ponty to indicate the appreciation of the sheer contingency of all things, an awareness that comprehends the limitations of the worth of specific structures of knowledge. His metaphysical system has as its centre man's dynamic interaction with the world, thus establishing that his system is radically different from that of classical metaphysicians, e.g. Plato and Hegel, with their devotion to Absolute Ideals. It is to be seen not only as a rejection of monistic, absolute categories and systems, but the advocacy of a pluralism of ideas, values, and cultures together with the presence of *choice* that permits the individual to establish the nature of his authentic existence. For Berlin this description of existence contains the most sophisticated and desirable version of negative freedom, one which avoids depriving men in the name of 'some remote or incoherent ideal of much that they found to be indispensable to their life as unpredictably self-transforming human beings' (Berlin 1969: 171).

'WHAT OUGHT TO BE', AND ONTOLOGICAL NECESSITY

The self-transformation proposed by Berlin, it is argued, further requires an awareness of the possible forms of ontological existence facing the individual through his relationships with the Other, yet there are those who regard both Berlin's arguments and those akin to my own as irrelevant because they assume prepotency of the individual over the social structures in which he lives. Althusser, for example, has argued at length that all such subjective interpretations of 'reality' are entirely unacceptable.

He believes that it is unnecessary to discuss the presence of individual choice because men behave in the way they do largely as a function of the inevitable praxis, or active movement, of their class as a whole through history. Specifically, man works within the existence of the social relations of production, which includes 'labour process, division and organization of labour, process of production and reproduction, class stuggle, etc.' (Althusser 1976: 95); that is, men are agent-subjects, but not the *Subject* of history: the latter belief has as its basis that man as an individual is the origin or essence of events, while the former emphasizes that the events of history, culture, and indeed all activities of the Other are processes without either a Subject or Object, without originators or goals. While this, so far, is valuable in pinpointing the nature of open-ended systems with the indeterminateness associated with them, Althusser superimposes a determination which, as we shall see later, is only slightly better than an arbitrary one – that is, class movement. History's significance, he believes, is to be found in the analysis of classes struggling against each other for power, or, expressing his point in my terms, to show its narrowness, authenticity can only be achieved in the full awareness of one's class and one's antagonistic relationship to other classes. Althusser then argues that because man is an agent-subject within the class movement, his awareness of the world is found only in epistemology, rather than in his ontology (see Figure 2(2) to recall the distinction). By abandoning a concern for ontology, Althusser hopes to remove all traces of ideological presuppositions and be able to establish a 'science' of history and man's relationship to it. The näivité of this hope will be demonstrated more thoroughly in Chapter 4, but to take Althusser's work and its implications to heart would require us to consider authenticity, awareness, and consequently 'alienation' solely at a socio-political level. This, while admirable in many respects, represents a failure to appreciate the significance of the individual's ontology to the class structure itself and how he perceives society is ordered. Althusser would do well to take Kierkegaard's advice; he thought the worst way to live was to impress the world through one's discoveries and cleverness in explaining 'scientifically' the whole of nature, and yet not to understand oneself and how one interacts with events and occurrences. Kant, too, warned men to treat themselves and other people as an end, never only as a means. Althusser forgets this, seeing men as but the means to promote class stuggle: their inner psychology and ontological existence only has importance, for him, as they affect the antagonism between classes.

Any serious attempt to understand 'alienation' must break away from Althusser's excessively sociological 'black box' approach to man's behaviour and to see how the awareness of 'what ought to be' has particular significance for the individual in his encounters with the constituents of his daily life. While concepts of positive and negative freedom reveal the social and moral pressures man faces in his dealings with other men, his actions in response to those pressures cannot be said to be authentic unless he is fully aware of the ontological possibilities that also confront him. Any movement concerning itself with 'class struggle' and ignoring this human factor can at most alter the superficial aspects of life without affecting the psychological attributes that sustain the very structures they abhor.

Moreover, such movements must be aware that it is possible to see two clear forms of ontological life to which I drew attention in Figure 2(2). I have called these forms *open*, or indeterminate, and *closed*, or determinate – in the language of philosophy they correspond respectively to *existential* and *'essensistic'* concepts of ontology, but my terms cover a wider area, as will be seen, and are less tongue-twisting.

The second two forms of awareness, open and closed: the ontological basis for man's awareness of his psychosystem

There is a double importance in understanding the significance of these polar forms of ontological awareness; first, it completes the discussion on awareness and hence on the different possible forms of authentic life, and second, it gives us the first clear insight into the different uses of the word 'alienation' as understood by Hegel and Marx.

Figure 2(3) Forms of awareness and man's authentic state

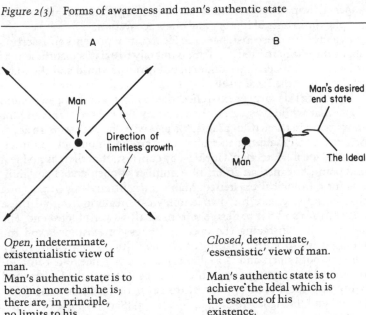

A

Man

Direction of
limitless growth

B

Man's desired
end state

Man

The Ideal

Open, indeterminate,
existentialistic view of
man.
Man's authentic state is to
become more than he is;
there are, in principle,
no limits to his
'becoming' (Allport 1955).

Closed, determinate,
'essensistic' view of man.

Man's authentic state is to
achieve the Ideal which is
the essence of his
existence.

Figure 2(3) will serve as a guide to the discussion that follows.

In the closed system, man's existence in the world is one of
striving for fulfilment by attaining the Ideal end-goal. The Ideal is
metaphysical, in the normal sense of the word,[3] that is, man is
compelled to reach beyond himself and his immersion in the world
of Self to achieve unity with the Ideal; guiding one's life to acquire
this union is evidence of an authentic awareness of the nature of
one's ontological existence. The system is closed because the Ideal
is a given immutable presence. In some ontological forms of awareness the Ideal is a supreme deity and man's union with it can only
occur in a metaphysical heaven wherein lies authentic existence;
for example, man's sincerity in leading his life in a 'godly manner' is,
for non-Calvinists, the way to achieve that authenticity. Alternatively, the Ideal may be a philosophically desirable state of awareness, as it is in Hegel's writings: here the Ideal state is earth-bound
and is to be reached through the acquisition of Absolute knowledge,

---

[3] We saw above that Merleau-Ponty used the term metaphysical in a different context
and with a wider non-philosophical meaning.

a special form of heightened awareness of one's relationship to other people, the events of history and one's ecosystem.

Evidently in these instances the Ideal state represents an assertion about the *authentic* nature of man; merely to exist is insufficient as it leads to an inadequate understanding of the world and the manifestations of the Ideal itself.

Opposing this form of existence, the advocates of the open system argue that while it is certainly necessary for man to transcend his immersion in the world, that is, his passivity, he does so as an act of *Self*-realization and not to realize or aspire to an outside or Other-founded Ideal. Here man's ideal is, by contrast, that there is no Ideal end-point, but instead an infinite number of open-ended possibilities for ontological existence. Man's *authenticity* lies in grasping that he must create his own ontological meaning from all these possibilities and not to derive it from an all-powerful Ideal end. His *sincerity* lies in facing the open-endedness of existence, and the possibilities it offers, with fortitude, as Tillich has argued (1952). Thus in both open and closed ontological existence, our being-in-the-world has two aspects, which may be distinguished as 'factual being' and 'ideal being' (Kierkegaard 1954), or 'being-in-itself' (*être-en-soi*) and 'being-for-itself' (*être-pour-soi*) (Sartre 1966). Common philosophical usage designates the first in each case as 'being' and the latter 'Being'. The former is simply existence, while the latter is considered to be a way of describing authentic existence. Thus, the common theme behind 'essensistic' or closed views of ontology is that we compare our being with Being and aim to make up the deficiency of Being in our being. For the existentialists, or the advocates of the open system, Being is becoming: that is, as we actively emerge from the shell of being we *are* Being; our own essence and hence authenticity is to be found within the act of exploring the many different choices and issues that face us. Thus, any constraints in becoming, for example, the presence of an Ideal, will hamper Being for that individual, consequently what is authentic life for open aware existence is quite the opposite for that of the closed mode.

THE SEARCH FOR THE IDEAL AS THE MOVE FROM BEING TO BEING

If Being, or authentic awareness in the *closed* form, is the attainment of a distant Ideal, we need to know how the individual comes to understand that there is a state other than being immersed in the world, or merely passively existing. That is, how does one as a being *learn* about the 'gap', the lack in his awareness, formed through the presence of Being ((x) in the diagram) and how does he attain that new awareness?

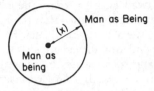

The key to 'essensism' is that one may live authentically only when everything about being is learnt, understood, and taken to heart, that is, intellectual awareness is the necessary percursor to an intuitive appreciation of Being. It is interesting to note that the Greek word 'ειναι', ordinarily translated as 'to be' can mean each of 'existence', 'reality', or 'truth' (Lee 1955: 236), implying that ontological existence and epistemological reality are one and the same: they were apprehended as truth, Being revealed in the act of being. Thus one might have expected that for the Greeks, truth, as a manifestation of the Ideal, would be akin to a state of existential Being (as becoming). However the immediacy of the connexions between existence and truth were not appreciated by the most influential of Greek philosophers, Plato. He argued, as an 'essensist', that truth must somehow be learnt or more precisely, uncovered: existential intuition was quite insufficient as a means of attaining that truth. This point provided the basis for much of Plato's philosophical edifice. He realized that if this distinction between existence and truth (or authenticity in our terms) is a valid one, then the learner faces a dilemma, which Socrates expresses in the 'Philosopher-Ruler' section of the *Republic*: either he does *not* know what he is learning – so cannot begin to learn, or he *does* know, so there is no point in learning it again! This apparent problem is overcome through Plato's doctrine of Recollection, which up to the time of Descartes was widely accepted. This states that the learner, man as being, already holds latent in his being all learnable knowledge, and has, in fact, only 'forgotten' it. Living serves to recollect it once more; learning is thus an intellectual exercise which reveals Being for the individual by allowing the factual being to come closer to the Ideal Being. Writing about 2,000 years later, Descartes considered that Plato's emphasis on the recollection of objective knowledge as the way of attaining Being was inadequate, and proposed instead that the subjective awareness of the individual must be the locus of knowledge of both the Self and of objects in the world. This knowledge was derived from God and not simply recollected from abstract existence (Descartes 1968: 157). Kant also considered the nature of the genesis of awareness of the existence of Being out of being, but broke away entirely from the idea of recollected or divine-originated truths. He argued that the individual constitutes his knowledge by virtue of his own intrinsic resources. Truth is to be found in the 'transcendental dimensions' of the human spirit itself, and the task of metaphysics (the uniting of being with Being, subject with object) turns from a search of *how* we learn about Ideal Being in order to live authentically, towards a realization that the subject, as being, is *himself* the force behind the creation of Being, that is, Being is objectified being.

'Hitherto it has been assumed that all our knowledge must conform to objects. But all attempts to extend our knowledge of objects by establishing something in regard to them *a priori*, by means of concepts, have, on this assumption, ended in failure. We must therefore make trial whether we may not have more success in the tasks of metaphysics, if we suppose that objects must conform to our knowledge.'   (Kant 1933: 22)

This was a distinct advance on Plato's teaching because it allowed the search for authentic awareness to take on the nature of a scientific inquiry by endeavouring to establish truths about the world rather than simply recollecting them. Authentic awareness in this perspective comes to be associated with the ability to apply the appropriate method to discover Being through knowledge. These discoveries according to Kant depended on the individual making synthetic, *a priori* judgements about the world. Synthetic, because knowledge about the objects under consideration is not implicit in reason alone, it requires knowledge of facts derived from experience (*a priori* knowledge) synthesized into a newly created unity. This was contrasted with analytic knowledge based only on reason, which Kant took to be fundamentally tautological in nature.

Thus, while philosophers had previously considered knowledge as the conformity of mind to the given structure of objects, now, following Kant, they could see objects as those entities that conform to the structure of the mind. Equally important, by showing the weakness of pure analytic reason against that of synthetic *a priori* judgements, Kant was able to establish a system of authentic behaviour based on moral judgements. Echoing Erasmus, Kant argued that without freedom personal obligation does not exist; if there are no independent causes (for example, when we say God wills everything) it is meaningless to talk of responsibility. Consequently there can be no occasion to praise or blame one's actions. What was required, he believed, was a morality that arose only from a rational will's obedience to self-imposed universal laws. Moreover, he saw that metaphysical discussions on the existence of God were merely founded on a mystification which prevented man from establishing himself more effectively within the real world: worshipping and other religious activities he saw as being 'fetishes' that allow the person to evade responsibility for his self-growth. Handing over to a religious practice one's personal autonomy and rational integrity, he argued, was an act that did violence to man's conscience. Although he was quite correct in rejecting religious beliefs as a source of *epistemological* authenticity he failed to realize the supportive significance religion has for the closed form of authentic awareness in the ontological mode. One could not, as Kant appears to have believed, establish full ontological awareness solely on the basis of the epistemologically grounded reasoning process he advocated. It was not until three years after Kant's death that Hegel published his *Phenomenology of Mind*, thus founding a philosophy that went a stage beyond the subjective constructivism of Kantian philosophy by examining the nature of ontological authenticity in terms of the metaphysics of subjective Being as it develops in awareness of a unifying immanent presence, Spirit. Subjective awareness, in the ontological mode, was the aim of Hegelian philosophy, whereas seeking for truth in the abstract as the key to authentic life was the intention of his philosophical predecessors. By this I mean that Hegel appreciated that the development of being's growth towards Being has two distinct phases. The first is the realization that the Self, in its subjectivity, at first finds itself and its demands in an alien world; this he saw as the consequence of the Self's release into particularity or explicit individuality of consciousness and will. At this stage, he argued, the Self lives in a way that is estranged (*entfremdet*) from what he called the Universality of Spirit – the Ideal authentic whole. The second phase is the supercession or transcendence of man's self-estrangement through a surrender of his desire for an insular Self to allow the union between him and the world of people, processes, and events. This surrender, through a special act of self-alienation (*Selbstentäusserung*) and the resultant unity enabled man to know, in Absolute Knowledge, that Spirit is the force of reciprocity between the Self and the world, which in turn permitted the full realization of authenticity as Being. It is unquestionably unrealistic to present the core of Hegel's thought in so short a paragraph, so a large part of the next chapter will be used to develop a more detailed critique to show the little appreciated relevance of Hegel's ideas to organization theorists' views on 'alienation'.

THE OPEN FORM OF AUTHENTIC AWARENESS: ARGUMENTS FOR THE TRANSCENDENCE OF THE NEED TO STRIVE TOWARDS AN IDEAL; BEING AS BECOMING

Lest it be thought that philosophical endeavours in the search for authentic awareness move exclusively in this closed, metaphysical way, there do exist alternative movements which seek to question many of the assumptions that lay behind the reasoning of the post-Platonists and their efforts to establish an exclusively episte-mologically based system of authentic awareness. The work of Heidegger is one such example. He contended that the search for authenticity went astray by viewing being and Being through the language of subject and object, that is, as separate entities. This, he said, necessitated a development of a metaphysical philosophy to bridge the gap posited by their difference. The history of metaphy-sics can be seen as the progressive domination of the object by the subject, a futile conquest Heidegger believed, and the fundamental error western philosophy has made from the time of Plato onwards. This flaw was that Plato's theory of Ideas splits apart *truth* and being, whereas in the pre-Socratics' thought, truth belongs in-timately to the very essence of being. We have already seen that the Greek word for 'to be' ($\epsilon \iota \nu \alpha \iota$) means simultaneously 'being' and 'truth'. Heidegger developed this theme of the word's unity from another angle, by showing that the Platonic Greeks distinguished being and truth through the terms 'Physis' and 'Logos'. This division allowed truth as 'unconcealedness', or the awareness of things emerging as a direct consequence of being, to degenerate to mean a mere declaration or statement about a thing *per se*. Heidegger then pointed out that 'logos' (truth) originally meant a 'gathering' or 'putting together', where being is collected or gathered up as a revealing of the truth. His discussion on how 'logos' acquires the modern notion of 'speaking' or 'saying' is fascinating. The basic theme is that formerly the use of logos involved one pointing out to someone that which lies in unconcealment, this 'pointing to' then became a 'saying to' to reveal an awareness of the being of things. This 'saying to' became further corrupted to a description in words of the thing, which *itself* becomes the truth.[4] Being (as physis) then

---

[4] See G. Seidel (1964) for an excellent detailed account of the interconnexions between Heidegger's thought and that of the pre-Socratics.

evolves to become the basis for Plato's Idea, while truth (logos) is absorbed into Aristotle's system of categories which assist philosophers to look at the being of a thing. 'The transformation of *physis* and *logos* into idea and statement [respectively] has its inner ground in a transformation of the essence of truth from unconcealment to [mere] correctness' (Heidegger 1959: 190). Kirk and Raven, in another context, offer a similar view of logos when they suggest that the 'logos was probably considered by Heraclitus [a pre-Socratic] as an actual constituent of things, and in many respects it is coextensive with the primary cosmic constituent, fire' (Kirk and Raven 1975: 188).[5] They go on to point out, somewhat disapprovingly, that pre-Socratics tended not to make a distinction between modes of existence, 'and that what to us is obviously non-concrete and immaterial, like an arrangement, [for them, possesses] the assumed ultimate characteristic of being, that is concrete bulk' (1975: 188–89). The 'obviousness' of the difference between material and immaterial 'arrangements' is only evident when being and truth are themselves divided; as I have emphasized, an arrangement is precisely what is established by ontological awareness of the person in order to comprehend the world and his interaction with it. Constructive ontological awareness establishes full material existence for the person, as concrete as any rock or tree, and yet like those apparently solid entities, the arrangement can change and reform in the flux and fire of existence. Indeed, existentialists demand that the arrangements are never to be seen as static but always open-ended and changing.

The degeneration of logos in the philosophies of the post-Socratics is the consequence of a 'forgetting of being', with which all non-existential philosophy has concerned itself. This in turn has caused the emergence of a philosophy based on epistemology (the study of what is the nature and ground of experience, belief, and knowledge) to the detriment of the study of ontology (or the nature of being) because this dichotomy between knowledge and being required increasingly complex metaphysical systems to reunite them, the most comprehensive of which is Hegel's. Existentialist thought, on the other hand, sees the two as inherently united because the act of the logos pointing out that which lies in unconcealment is none other than the primary act of perceptual differentiation of growing

---

[5] Heraclitus believed that 'this world-order did none of gods or men make, but it always was and is and shall be; an everlasting fire kindling in measures and going out in measures' (Heraclitus Fragment 30 in Kirk and Raven 1975, note 220). The world and its beings all exist in this state of flux and change – a surprisingly modern-sounding view, akin to existentialist thought.

awareness which directly allows us to be aware of being as the basis for truth or authenticity.

Heidegger has a particularly interesting way of making this point by highlighting the pre-Socratic link between language and being, as a connexion that can be established through the logos. It revolves around the metaphor[6] he uses of man 'listening' to being: that is, logos is effortlessly attuned to being, not just by agreeing with but through belonging to that which it 'hears'. Heidegger writing in German can make the linguistic connexion between one who 'hears' (*hört*) and that which belongs (*gehört*). By questioning existence authentically one goes beyond mere sincerity: through the logos, the truth of being, one 'hears' or is attuned to one's belonged-ness in that authenticity, that is authenticity is *itself* the act of hearing, being aware; and not to be found in seeking for an Ideal, or closed Being. As Heidegger summarizes it: 'beings *are* in the abandonment of Being' (Heidegger: 86). This act of relinquishment opens man's ontological awareness to a new form of authentic life, one which seeks to reveal that the Platonic reduction of logos to 'reason' is allowing one's ontological life to become subordinate to an abstract impersonal authority. Moreover, man maintains this abstraction because he is exhorted to *use* logos as if it were an attribute or property, to master it in order to be aware of the nature of authenticity and hence the key to his Being. This foolishness is compounded by philosophers who add a further falseness, that of hunting for Ideals for exclusively epistemological reasons. It is not surprising then that Whitehead was reputed to have remarked that western philosophy could be seen as footnotes to Plato's work: the entire issue of epistemology and the pushing of ontology into a metaphysical category had been accomplished under the assumption that a meaningful set of problems were being dealt with in the most appropriate way.

What we have seen so far, then, is that within the 'essensistic', closed mode of authenticity the main philosophical emphasis has been, up to Hegel, on the achievement of authenticity through epistemological means; that is, the attempt to understand through reason alone the real nature of man's lost state of Being. Consequently, the movement from being to Being, having been created as a necessary process to overcome man's lack of attunement with authentic life, was considered as a process of accumulation of factual information, which was then synthesized by the action of the subject to uncover the universal laws that form the Ideal.

---

[6] Heidegger's use of metaphors has special symbolic value: they are for him a way of approaching the issue of authentic existence.

In fairness to Plato's successors, this emphasis on the epistemological aspects of authentic awareness was pardonable in many respects because those philosophers sought to gain an understanding of man's relationship to the world, one which did not depend on a mystical, transcendental force, God, upon which the theologians were basing their analysis of authentic ontological awareness. Theology had, to the philosophers' disgust, merely used allegory, rather than analysis, not only to explain the mechanism of reuniting being with Being, but also to justify how the distinction arose in the first place. This allegory, as we have seen in Chapter 1, was that of Adam and Eve in the Garden of Eden. Thus, Adam, representing the archetypal Self in his life before the Fall (the loss of authenticity), lived in an innocence of united, non-autonomous existence with God, that is, in a state of Being. Adam's Fall, through the actions of the snake, is characterized by fear and mistrust of God, as the archetypal Other, and represents the regression to being. However, because Adam purportedly retains ontologically the nature of Being in his disgrace – the child in his innocence is the ontological father of the man, to recall Wordsworth – this awareness creates a primal tension that drives him towards the re-attainment of Being. This union is not established epistemologically but only can be acquired through God's approval of his having led a sin-free life, unsundered from the Will of God. Thus the individual's attempt to regain his authenticity provides the basis for an elaborate moral system which was derived through reason and sustained by epistemological awareness.

In the next chapter it will be seen how Hegel was able to unite epistemological and ontological forms of awareness to create a new authenticity but one still within the closed 'essensistic' mode of existence. But now, bearing in mind Heidegger's criticisms of the questionable origins of that closed form of existence, I shall explore further the second main aspect of authenticity in 'what ought to be', that of *open* or existential awareness.

The special significance of open or existential awareness highlighting the internal psychological traumata man must face to achieve authenticity

The primary aspect of existential awareness, as I have suggested, is the redundancy of the need to establish how the individual becomes aware of Being in his being-in-the-world. Therefore, we do not require elaborate mechanisms based on recollection of, or a Fall from, some previous authentic state. Man's becoming aware of the

world and his actions in it is itself his authentic act; the concern
now becomes in what manner does man gain this awareness and
how does its force incorporate and transcend the presence of reason
as the primary source of authentic life. That is, the emphasis of
existential awareness lies clearly in the ontological mode rather
than the epistemological one. There are two aspects to this: first,
existentialists argue that to assert the primacy of epistemological
awareness over that of ontology is to assume that the Self's existence is merely a moment of the world's, an assumption

> 'always both naive and at the same time dishonest because [it
> takes] for granted, without explicitly mentioning it, the other
> point of view, namely that of consciousness, through which from
> the outset a world forms itself around me and begins to exist from
> me.'   (Merleau-Ponty 1968: IX)

The perception of the world forming 'itself around me' occurs
through a ceaseless series of acts of differentiation that create form
and meaning for the individual out of the chaos that faces him, not
just in his childhood but throughout his adult life. The act of
perceiving this chaos in the world is *itself* the beginning of awareness of the individual's Being; hence his authenticity lies in facing
the alternatives and possibilities of action evident in that chaos, and
in living them, rather than avoiding them or striving to derive a
closed unity of form, an idealist morphology from them. The word
'chaos' is used deliberately here, because as understood in the
cosmogonies, the theories of the origin of the universe, of the
ancient Greek writers (e.g. Hesiod), the word 'χαοσ actually meant
the gap that arose out of the first act of differentiation, that of the
separation between sky and earth (Kirk and Raven 1975: 29 and
Cornford 1952: 194). It is this gap that permitted all further forms of
differentiation, and as such is closely paralleled by Sartre's notion of
Nothingness (*néant*) which is to be understood as the unfillable gap,
the differentiation, thrown up by Being-for-itself in the consciousness of the existence of objects other than itself; and which continues to force the individual to face the endless permutations of
forms he may abstract from it (Sartre 1966: 56 ff). Thus, Being as
authenticity is the maintenance of the open-ended differentiation
for existentialists, while for 'essensists' it is the act of reducing the
gap, the chaos, to its former undifferentiated unity.

The second aspect of existentialism's objection to 'essensism' is
that post-Cartesian subjectivism is unacceptable because, whilst
emphasizing man's subjectivity, in itself a step forward, it is in the

context of a union with an all-embracing Spirit, or reciprocity, that abstractly unites all individuals together thereby ignoring the significance of man's ontological freedom as he faces the world. The existentialist argues that the curtailment of human potential and possibilities, either by reducing man to an object or treating him as part of a rational, abstract, absolute system, is a dehumanization of man because it forces him to lead an inauthentic life in order to reach an Ideal. Existentialists see man as not just a thing in the world or in terms of a pure subjectivity, but as, in principle, a free individuality presenting itself to other people and facing the surrounding chaos with open awareness. While the less extreme advocates of existentialism see that, in actuality, the presence of free individuality in other people presents serious problems to the freedom of the Self, Nietzsche in his optimism could over-ride this apparent difficulty by developing the idea that all phenomenal reality is the manifestation of a will to live in the notion of the primacy of the will to power (Nietzsche 1966, 536).

Nietzsche, by seeing man as a power-seeker, meant that power is not only concerned with knowledge or politics, but has ontological significance. One's ontological strength permitted one the courage to Be, by over-riding the obstacles including, inevitably, the presence of the Other. Naturally, as all men are but Others to one another this must precipitate a war by all against all; a war that has its value, Nietzsche proposed, in allowing the primacy of the will to become manifest as the self-assertion of an individual who then, through his moral strength, can claim the 'death of God', the death of the Other. By so doing, Nietzsche explicitly rejects absolute truth and values, not just for epistemological reasons but for ontological ones, to be able to assert his independent reality as a will to power. For him, this represents the ultimate authentic act. Nietzsche's arguments have aspects of both good and evil about them: the good is his enthusiasm for ontological strength, without which man cannot sustain an open ontological awareness. Man must not live in fear and trembling of the Other, forever hoping for external salvation; this is the existence of the ontological coward. But, and this is the evil aspect, ontological strength must not be simply self-assertion, the will to power, for that is too crude, too selfish an existence; the man who *has* to assert himelf often does so to hide his insecurity in the face of the Other. Real ontological strength, I shall argue in Chapter 4 in the discussion of Marx's thought, does not thrive on assertion and power but on mutual trust and reciprocity between the Self and the Other. It may even take the form, unpleasant as it may sound to Nietzsche, of Berlin's negative freedom.

The individual, having the strength not to be dominated by the Other, can then use that 'power' to sustain mutually supportive interaction between himself and that Other. This perspective of ontological strength is not some utopian fantasy. Marx, for instance, has argued that in certain 'alienation'-free situations, man can live with fellow men in a society based on mutual trust and awareness rather than self-assertion. The so-called Age of Aquarius movements, the basis of which is that people try to relate to rather than antagonize each other, ought to give us some hope that people are actively seeking for a form of ontological strength that can both create and is created by mutual trust. That this supportive ontological stance can apply to the organized work context as currently envisaged is much more problematical.

Sartre's views on existentialism are more pessimistic and less Dionysian than are Nietzsche's, because he sees the constraints that operate against the Self in his endeavours to gain ontological strength. These constraints are both external and internal. The external arise both when the Self becomes aware of the consciousness of the Other, how one sees and is seen by other individuals, and how one faces the institutions that man has created. My analyses of Hegelian and Marxian theories of 'alienation' and estrangement will pinpoint in detail the ontological consequences of external relationship of the Self and the Other so I will not pursue them further here.

Appreciating the *internal* constraints that man faces in attempting to establish his ontological strength in the face of existential openness allows one to understand why it is easier to seek for authentic existence in a closed form of Being. In existentialism, because the individual is compelled to find his authenticity 'through continuous leaps in existence' (Kierkegaard 1954) he may live in a state of anguish, the anxiety which emerges when the nature of the Self is understood as a complete freedom to be, a freedom which urges the individual to develop his self awareness by facing the possibilities lying in the nothingness, or the void of existence, that lies before him. This complete freedom may prove too much for the individual who then shies away from open authenticity to the much less ontologically stressful closed form of awareness. However, if he does wish to continue to face the existential, open, mode of existence, he must realize that his awareness gained from the void continuously compels him to make choices about how he must act. Because the consequences of choosing in an open-ended situation have, by definition, no external criteria by which the validity or 'correctness' of his choice can be measured, the

Self realizes that the entire responsibility of his existence and hence his authenticity rests within himself and not on some external God or Ideal. Sometimes, this thought or realization is too much for the individual to bear, and he feels unable to cope with the multiplicity of choices confronting him. In the language of machine intelligence, this inability to cope is known as 'robot's cramp'. Here, too many possibilities of equal merit face the machine so it fails to respond to any of them, and emits 'disturbed' signals to tell the operator to restrict the possibilities to a more manageable level. In an open system, the human being lacks the presence of an obliging operator to aid him in his choices to help him overcome his 'nausea', the individual's disturbed feeling when the constraints on his own existence, by his very existence, confront the contingency of that existence. He then may feel it necessary to restrict those choices by living in what Sartre has called 'bad faith'. This is the Self's act of hiding from Being-for-itself, or as I have described it, living inauthentically by refusing to be aware of the choices that appear through the presence of ontological contingency. This contingency is not based on the whim or Will of God or the presence of an Ideal which one had to, by trial and error, learn about before one could attain authenticity, as it was in the case in 'essensistic' existence; but is founded on the realization that man is not completely determined by a system of laws or causally linked events.

Merleau-Ponty argued that man should not seek to explain things in terms of something outside and beyond himself (the basis of classical metaphysics) because he alone renders possible all meaning, explanation, and value. Moreover, those meanings and values are made when one's consciousness is *in* the world, not, as Husserl believed, suspended from worldly existence nor, as Proust hoped, to be found in the recollection and reconstruction of one's past.

Proust's life offers us a classical example of the force of existential anguish in his searches for meaning and permanence in his world. He believed, as his biographer tells us, that as time passes we lose entirely our previous selves and acquire new ones, 'The successive "selves" are so different from one another that each ought really to have a different name' (Maurois 1962: 173). This lack of permanence was horrifying to Proust, he was frightened even of moving from familiar to strange surroundings. Permanence and certainty could only be found, he believed, when time ceased, on death. Sartre, while he would not agree with the mystical value of this final stage, does see that each choice taken is a form of living death: by choosing our 'project', or way of Being, we establish our finitude, we make ourselves particular by excluding other possibilities each time we state a preference. This finitude is added to our facticity thus constraining even further the nature of our authenticity: at this stage both internal and external constrictions on authentic existence become united.

How the individual responds to the combined pressure of these forces in making a choice, together with his commitment in holding to that choice is a measure of his ontological strength, and hence open authenticity. We have seen that if he fails to match up to the strain of openness, he regresses to an existence in 'bad faith', the goal of which is to 'put oneself out of reach, it is an escape' (Sartre 1966: 110). In extremis this is the action of the schizophrenic who strives to put his Self out of reach of the Other's presence, and his look, to prevent the destruction or petrification of his inner hidden Self. Sartre has also pointed out the important links between sincerity and 'bad faith'. Sincerity has the same meaning for him as it does for us: it represents the fixation of the Self to the 'given' reality. By remaining merely sincere, man ceases the search to enhance his awareness of alternatives; instead he consolidates his present knowledge and can be fearful of attempts to question that knowledge, because both sincerity and 'bad faith' are based on the Self's desire to become immersed in being-in-itself. In both cases the Self seeks merely to mirror itself in its present immediacy and to justify its inadequacies by sheltering in the protection of the already given nature of its ontological world. However, 'bad faith' is only possible because, in sincerity, the Self by its very nature has already resigned itself not to achieve any objectives other than those already within its existence. 'Bad faith' then compounds this by actively ensuring that the Self sees itself as something which it is not. 'Bad faith' in Heidegger's terms would be the consequence of an individual out of tune with authentic existence, struggling through sincere reasoning to justify his refusal to face the unconcealedness of existence in being as truth.

Summary

To allow one to appreciate the impossibility of abstracting the awareness upon which authentic life rests and hence the pointlessness of finding one form of 'alienation', I have presented and discussed the two main modes of awareness, epistemological and ontological, and how they each have their particular value in the way whereby Being is revealed to being through short and long focussing in conjunction with the open and closed form of awareness. We saw that awareness in the short focus form is that of the individual immersed in the existing framework, organization, culture, or society. The individual who is aware in this manner has chosen to adapt to the immediate demands of his environment: this is not simply a passive process, but an actively chosen decision by the individual to be involved in exploring existing Ideals as he perceives them in their richness. On the other hand, the individual who adopts a long-focus awareness is more sceptical of the value of immersion into the immediate social world so he stands back, as it were, to seek the presence of alternative goals or frames of reference. In fact, normally one would use both forms of awareness in a cyclical manner because each have their special advantages. The Zen awareness, which is the immediate immersed reciprocity between Self and Other,[7] gives one insights that distancing awareness cannot: similarly the latter awareness may show the undesirability of full reciprocity with the Other by revealing the Other as something to be avoided.

Thus, to understand the nature of authenticity is to appreciate that it involves for each person a decision over which form of awareness is to be given priority within the further contexts of an open or closed perspective, a point first made in the discussion on possible forms of autonomous existence, presented in Chapter 1. There, it was established that an individual's authenticity could find expression in his choice of one from either non-, semi-, or fully autonomous existence in the presence of the Other. If I now juxtapose in matrix form the two major types of awareness discussed in this chapter: the 'what is' type (epistemological) with the 'what ought to be' type (ontological) it becomes possible to illustrate the links between the different forms of awareness and the possible modes of authentic life (see Figure 2(4)).

The connexions shown here will reappear in Chapters 3 and 4 when I show that what may be 'alienating' for someone in one situation is quite the opposite for either the same person in a different setting or another person in the same setting.

Figure 2(4) shows in a compact form the relationship between the individual's *epistemology*, or the method he uses to understand the world in terms of type of awareness (the 'what is' question), and his *ontology*, or how he interprets his existence in the world in terms of Being (the 'what ought to be' question). Equal weighting is given to both epistemology and ontology following Heidegger's critique of the Platonic emphasis on epistemology. Furthermore, in line with our previous understanding of awareness and Being, it presents each

---

[7] It is to be recalled that the Zen awareness works readily with Objects, but for that awareness to be of an Other, that Other himself must be in a state of Zen awareness already otherwise the mutual reciprocity breaks down.

Figure 2(4)   Forms of awareness and possible modes of authentic life

ONTOLOGY EPISTEMOLOGY	*'Essensistic'* Awareness of Being as an Ideal (Closed)	*Existentialistic* Awareness of Being as becoming (Open)
Short-focus *awareness* (Immersion)	Authenticity as non-autonomous existence	Authenticity as semi-autonomous existence
Long-focus *awareness* (Distancing)	Authenticity as semi-autonomous existence	Authenticity as fully-autonomous existence

type of awareness, short and long focus, and each type of Being, 'essensistic' and existential, as *entirely valid* perceptions an individual may hold. This important point is to be emphasized: if a person selects a preferred state through which another person is to be required to lead his life it is nothing less than an act of coercion on the part of the first person. Because this particular combination of awareness and Being has been chosen by one person as that which is the most acceptable and desirable to him for his existence in the world, it does not automatically mean that they will afford the same value to another person. Both persons must find their own ontologically supportive and epistemologically valid permutation from the four equally authentic types of awareness. It must be noted that authenticity can only arise in each of the four boxes if the individual is fully aware of the alternative forms of existence that prevail in the rest of the matrix, that is, active choice, made in the awareness of alternatives, establishes one's authenticity. This means that to confine awareness to one box is to lead an existence that is at best sincere because one's behaviour is consistent but is not based on any real appreciation of the ontological reason for it. Thus, chosen behaviour in awareness of the different possible permutations forms the different patterns of authenticity within which the individual may live. For instance, an existence within the ontological support offered to an individual by Calvinistic views on the nature of God (top left-hand box) may be as authentic as that existence of complete freedom in the manner of the Nietzschean 'superman' (bottom right-hand box). Both require the individual's transcendence of his sincere but inauthentic awareness through an active choice of his particular form of Self-Other interaction, and both require ontological strength, the courage to Be, but of a qualitatively different kind. The strength of the former is found in the implicit, open-hearted trust of the succour of the Other, while in the latter strength lies in attaining mastery over all forms of the Other to retain one's self-independence.

Readers from organization theory perspectives may have found some of the issues discussed here rather foreign to them, but if they have borne with me it will have become apparent to them that before 'alienation' can be analysed meaningfully it is vital to bring some order to the understanding of 'non-alienated' life. Having found that there exist four archetypal forms of authentic awareness does this imply that there are four forms of 'alienation'? The next two chapters will examine this question and show that the problems of 'alienation' both as term and concept is even more complicated than the search for authenticity because of the presence of two strong contrasting opinions of thought on the meaning of 'alienated' awareness: Hegelian and Marxian.

3

The aetiology of estrangement in a closed form of authentic existence

Approaching a new perspective on 'alienation'

The expression 'alienation from work' has had a varied history. It first appeared in the writings of Karl Marx more than a century ago, was revived by American sociologists in the 1940s, for example in the work of Merton, Mills, Fromm, and Nisbet; and it reached the area of organizational work studies through Seeman's publications in the late 1950s and 1960s. It is not my purpose to dwell upon the rise, and fall, in popularity of the phrase 'alienation from work' as it appears in the sociological literature: Johnson (1973) and Israel (1971), among others, have done this routine exercise quite adequately. Instead, I wish to rejuvenate the phrase's significance by lifting it out of the confines of sociological usage and explore its psychological attributes. My interest is in the possible theoretical forms that 'alienation' may take to alter a person's awareness of his ontological life – his being-in-the-world: this task is interwoven with a desire both to understand the different natures of work and to appreciate the personal significance of 'alienation from work'. This approach allows me to avoid adopting a specific ethical or political approach to the worth of work and instead permits an exploration of its value in terms of the individual's interest in, or indifference towards, establishing a personal authenticity. Thus I intend to link the four theoretical forms of authenticity developed in the previous chapter to the different concepts of 'alienation' as used by social scientists and to show that the writings of Hegel and Marx contain two rather different conceptualizations of 'alienation' that are blurred in the writings of many modern social scientists.

I use the thoughts of these nineteenth-century writers initially to contrast the main differences in significance that 'alienation' has within each of the two broad categories of ontological awareness, open and closed, as defined in Chapters 1 and 2. That is, the plan is to establish the clear importance of understanding the different natures of man's awareness of his world and his fulfilment, in Being or authenticity, as a prelude to clarifying the very specific connotations that the phrase 'alienation from work' can still have.

Because 'alienation from work' is a *social* phenomenon as well as a psychological issue my concern is to explore the individual's relationship with the Other, whether it be another person or the collective socio-political network that makes up organized work-life. Analysis of this relationship reveals that there can be advantages as well as drawbacks evident in the state of 'alienation from work'. At all times the intimate connexion between a person's 'alienation' and his awareness of his environment will be apparent; for instance, it will be seen below that, for Hegel, the growth of the individual's awareness of a possible authentic existence of Being has two phases, both called rather confusingly 'alienation' in some interpretations of Hegel's work (e.g. Schacht 1971). The first phase is *separation*, or in other words, an act of distancing through which the Self's awareness of the Other emerges; and the second is a special form of *surrender* through which the Self overcomes the created distance from the Other. Both these forms of 'alienation' are seen by Hegel as necessary for the full development of the individual in the world.

Marx, on the other hand, argues that the act of surrender, as a form of 'alienation', distorted man's understanding of his environment: when the individual surrendered his labour to the Other he separated himself from his main means of personal creative development.

Over the next two chapters I hope to clarify the foregoing remarks by studying in some detail the points of departure and similarities in these two writers; Hegel as representative of the *closed* form of authentic existence and Marx as protagonist for the *open* form.

It is hoped that the analysis of these two writers' thoughts will allow a firmer understanding of the unwieldy mass of literature on 'alienation from work' that has appeared over the last twenty or so years. Much of the recent confusion in that literature emanates from the indiscriminate use of the term 'alienation' to cover all forms of social malaise; for example, Fromm's remark that 'alienation as we find it in modern society is almost total' (1963: 124) appears to express the tacit assumption, behind much sociological and psychological work on the society-individual interface, that if anything is found to be disagreeable or causes antagonism it must be a source, or sometimes a consequence, of 'alienation'. Glazer's comment is only slightly more helpful when he suggests that a discussion of 'alienation . . . is an analysis of psychological disturbances having a similar root cause – in this case modern social organization' (1947: 380).

Generalities of this order may well reveal some truths but are entirely unhelpful, in their lack of precision, to anyone seeking to understand the form and nature that 'alienation' takes in an organization. The nearest Fromm comes to discussing possible forms of 'alienation' is when he points out that 'the alienated person is out of touch with himself as he is out of touch with any other person' (Fromm 1963: 120). This remark of Fromm's leaves unanswered two questions: by what means does he *become* out of touch and, then, what are the consequences? Both Hegel and Marx gave very specific answers to these questions, as we shall see, but it was Seeman in 1959 who initiated a revival in the term 'alienation' by breaking away from the generalizations of earlier social scientists and specifying what he saw as the five variants of 'alienation'. A sixth was added in 1972 and the categories revised in 1975 to become:

(1) Powerlessness – the individual's sense of low control versus a sense of mastery over events.
(2) Meaninglessness – the sense of incomprehensibility versus understanding of personal and social affairs.
(3) Normlessness – high expectation for, or commitment to, socially non-approved means versus conventional means for the achievement of given goals.
(4) Cultural estrangement (or value isolation) – the individual's rejection of commonly held values in the society in which he lives versus commitment to the existing group standards.
(5) Self-estrangement – the individual's engagement in activities that are not intrinsically rewarding versus involvement in a task or activity for its own sake.
(6) Social isolation – the sense of exclusion or rejection versus social acceptance.

Seeman's aim was to 'translate what was sentimentally understood into a secular question' (1959: 791) in order to be able to subject the general ideas on 'alienation' to specific empirical analysis within a psycho-social framework. Thus, he focuses on the expectations of individuals as they face a given situation, and argues that to consider what is *really* 'alienation' is to make unnecessary value judgement. While I agree with the sentiment, the emphasis on expectations mistakenly by-passes the significance of false consciousness as used in Marxist writings, for example those of Touraine (1977): that is the expectations themselves may be sincerely based in a false awareness of the given situation. We have attempted to surmount this clash of priorities between 'objective' consciousness and 'subjective' expectations by giving them equal importance through my matrix of epistemological and ontological awareness. Seeman, with his interest in psycho-social expectations, is more concerned with ontological awareness, while Touraine emphasizes the epistemological, or knowledge about the world and its influences over people. I contend that to treat 'alienation' as either epistemologically *or* ontologically founded will reduce the term once again to a meaningless catchphrase. Marx saw the difficulty particularly clearly, and devoted considerable effort to show that to alienate one's labour to another was not only the basis for the accumulation of profit but at the same time it brought about the destruction of the personality, the humanness, of the alienator. However, instead of being able to locate the 'alienating' situation in the specific fashion that Marx (and Hegel) were able to do, in terms of the relationship between the Self and the Other, Seeman found it necessary to use his categories of powerlessness, normlessness, and so forth to define what the subjective feeling of 'alienation' was and then 'filled in' what were seen as common 'alienating' situations. Although this could have led him into the assumption that Fromm made about the all-pervading nature of 'alienation' in society, Seeman was able to be more specific, emphasizing that an 'alienating' situation was present where people either felt a general disenchantment with their circumstances, or there was some breakdown of connexions between an individual's actions and their consequences. He believed that this was close to Marx's understanding of 'work alienation' which he interpreted as the 'engagement in work which is not intrinsically rewarding' (Seeman 1971: 736). Seeman, in equating physical *cause*, the 'alienated' relationship between worker and work activity, with the psychological *consequences* of that 'alienation', seriously oversimplifies Marxian[1] theory of alienation. He would have done better, perhaps, to have avoided any associations with Marx's work and simply stated his case for choosing the term 'alienation' on the basis of being able to categorize its popular use.

[1] Conventionally, 'Marxian' denotes work by Marx himself, while 'Marxist' is that of his adherents.

Seeman's error, as Marx would have seen it, lay in collecting a very wide range of problems encountered by people and arranging these problems into a number of headings under the term 'alienation', and then assuming that they *define* 'alienation' and that these people could be deemed 'alienated'.

Although these headings were chosen to define 'alienation' and were seen to be associated with each other through factor analysis, we still are no closer to understanding what binds the categories together, that is what fundamental psychological problem is being encountered and labelled as 'alienation'. Seeman himself admits this by seeing that the categories still

> 'Ought to become the investigation of a steady search for a better grounded theory of alienation, . . . one that can rationalize more satisfactorily why these six categories have emerged, what ties them together and how their sources and consequences should be conceived.'   (1975: 115)

The matrix model of authentic forms will, I believe, go a considerable way toward answering Seeman's difficulties, because by focusing both on the individual's awareness of his situation *vis à vis* the Other, and the organization and the nature of the Other itself, the emphasis of 'alienation' studies is shifted away from simplistic 'objective' or 'subjective' statements about what is or is not 'alienating', that is, statements based on an arbitrary choice of what is socially acceptable or unacceptable, true or false, and move towards an analysis of the *nature* of the relationship between the Self and his environment and his awareness, or lack of it, of that relationship. The emphasis here will be on unfolding the aetiology of the individual's estrangement, his separation from the Other; this should give us a clearer understanding of the exact nature of the different forms of behaviour subsumed under the heading 'alienation'.

'Alienation' in the closed form of authentic existence

Work organizations, as I have argued, are closed systems, so it will become apparent that Seeman's 'alienation' (and consequently much of the literature in organization science on 'alienation', which is derived from Seeman's studies) bears very little relationship to Marx's writings on the term, but has close affinities with Hegelian thought. Thus, it is to Hegel we direct our attention to discover the nature of the relationship between 'alienation' and authenticity in its closed, 'essensistic' mode.

Hegel's system and its methodology is worked out in its most sophisticated (and complex) form in his first book, *Das Phänomenologie des Geistes*, published in 1807 and translated as *The Phenomenology of Mind* (or *Spirit*), while his later works concentrated on expounding the significance of his system. I shall, therefore, focus on the *Phenomenology* which covers in detail the aetiology of estrangement and alienation. Many of Hegel's arguments in this book have a special depth and subtlety to them (not always evident in his later works). A detailed critique of them and all their ramifications would be well beyond the scope of this book, and not necessarily helpful to our understanding of 'alienation'. Moreover, such critiques do exist, for example Mure (1965), Kojève (1969), Kaufmann (1978) and Findlay (1958). However, I shall spend some time on Hegel's analyses of awareness, self-consciousness, and Being as these are immensely valuable to an understanding of the significance of the terms 'estrangement' and 'alienation'.

While the complexity of Hegel's thought in the original German can pose problems, appreciating its subtleties in an English translation presents an added difficulty. Let me try to show how the word 'alienation' itself is exposed to certain ambiguities in meaning based on mistranslations.

'ENTFREMDUNG' AND 'ENTÄUSSERUNG' AND THEIR MEANINGS

That one would not find many explicit references to the use of the word 'alienation' in Hegel's thought in the English studies mentioned may seem surprising, because if one reads Hegel in German, on first impression the words *Entfremdung* and *Entäusserung* – both of which could be translated very loosely as 'alienation' – occur frequently. Indeed, a number of modern English-speaking writers, whose work is likely to be accessible to organization theorists, *have* translated both '*Entfremdung*' and '*Entäusserung*' as 'alienation'; for instance, Schacht, who distinguishes them by calling the former 'alienation 1' and the latter 'alienation 2' and then, evidently inaccurately, argues that Hegel had two uses for the word 'alienation' (Schacht 1971: 35).

Baillie, the translator of Hegel's *Phenomenology of Mind*, translates '*Entfremdung*' as both 'estrangement' and 'alienation', and '*Entäusserung*' as 'relinquishing, surrendering, or divesting', in line with the usage recommended by Grimms' *Worterbuch* (1862). On the other hand, Knox, the translator of a number of Hegel's other works, uses the word 'alienation' to translate '*Entäusserung*', in the section of *The Philosophy of Right* on *Entäusserung des Eigentums* (alienation of property) (Hegel 1964: 65), for the excellent reason that 'alienate' in its English legal sense means the surrendering or divestiture of one's property to another, a usage that accords exactly with Hegel's discussions of property – and, as we shall see, with Marx's too. A certain consistency can be established in the translation of Hegel's *'Entäusserung'* as 'alienation', to recall its English legal sense, and the use of 'estrangement' to translate *'Entfremdung'* to avoid confusing it with alienation as surrender. However, it is more difficult to do the same for Marx's writings.

Marx's work, it may be mentioned at this stage, presents added difficulty to the translator because he occasionally uses *Entfremdung* and *Entäusserung* in such rapid succession (for example Marx 1975: 324, 330) as to be confusing to the unwary reader. The translators of the 1975 edition of Marx's *Early Writings* do distinguish between the terms, using 'estrangement' for *Entfremdung* and 'alienation' for *Entäusserung*, in contrast to Bottomore, the translator of another edition of the *Early Writings* who alleged that Marx's use of the terms lacked 'systematic distinction' (Bottomore, in Marx 1963: XIX).

Faced with this confusion over the choice of words in English to cover the two German words, it is understandable that some doubt should exist, in English texts, over interpretations of the Hegelian and Marxian use of 'alienation'. I shall use *alienation* in the sense closest to its legal sense following Knox's translation of Hegel and the 1975 edition of Marx's *Early Writings*, to signify the surrender, or relinquishment to the Other, of something belonging to the Self (i.e. *Entäusserung*); and *estrangement* to signify 'making strange' or 'distant' the relationship between the Self and the Other. In doing so, it becomes possible to lift the term 'alienation' out of its overworked and misunderstood senses and give it a significance that it had lost. The distinction between *Entäusserung* and *Entfremdung* is crucial not only for linguistic precision; it allows us to appreciate the stages of ontological awareness of the individual because each term represents a form of Self-Other interaction.

To be specific, Hegel has argued that philosophy, the basis of knowledge, is born of the estrangement of man and is the way of understanding the actions of that man as the awareness of his estrangement develops. This estrangement is then transcended *(aufhebung)* into a higher awareness when the individual surrenders or alienates his isolated Self, realizing that to live thus in estrangement is to live inauthentically because it forecloses his awareness of the inherent unity between him and the events and processes of the world as a whole.

THE NECESSITY OF COMPREHENDING THE UNITY OF ALL EVENTS
AND PROCESSES IN A CLOSED FORM OF AUTHENTIC EXISTENCE

Hegel regarded the world as a coherent unified system, a self-contained process, which maintained its unity through the infinitely diverse manifestations of individuality. What this means, he argued, is that apparent contradictions ought to be conceived as the variety present in the progressive evolution of authentic existence. His metaphor of a growing plant epitomizes his thoughts on the nature of authentic awareness as the appreciation of the underlying unity in apparently discrete events:

> 'The bud disappears when the blossom breaks through, and we might say that the former is refuted by the latter; in the same way when the fruit comes, the blossom may be explained to be a false form of the plant's existence, for the fruit appears as its true nature in place of the blossom. These stages are not merely differentiated; they supplant one another as being incompatible with one another. But the ceaseless activity of their own inherent nature makes them at the same time moments of an organic unity, where they not merely do not contradict one another, but where each is as necessary as the other; and this equal necessity of all moments constitutes alone and thereby the life of the whole.'   (Hegel 1931: 68)

For him, philosophy is a process through which one not only seeks to gain awareness of the ends (the fruit): the intermediate stages (budding and blossoming) are equally important although they appear to be in conflict with the end stage. Moreover, seeking to grasp and retain each stage in itself as being the most significant aspect of a system fails entirely to appreciate that the nature of the process *per se* holds the key to our understanding of it. Hegel then argued, in contrast to Marx, that the awareness of the processual nature of reality was acquired through notional or conceptual knowledge. Conceptual thought, he believed, penetrated the meaning of things in the world and their manifestations, enabling one to make coherent, valid judgements about them. Thought of this kind arose from a break away from the immediacy of psychical animal life that was governed by blind responses to stimuli as they presented themselves; these responses merely represented action without thought. The break from immediacy arises out of an awareness of one's *Self* in the world, this means that *man* is the locus of knowledge in the world, not *God* as Calvin had argued. Hegel saw that man's attempts to find authentic awareness in an abstract God was merely to succumb to a 'belief in the fearful and unknown darkness of Fate' (Hegel 1931: 685), because although both Calvin and Hegel represented peaks of 'essensistic' thought, their views on the nature of awareness are entirely opposed. Calvin, as we have seen, argued that one's authenticity lay in awareness through revelation of the omnipresence of God; knowledge of Him is intuitive and can only come through awareness of His will and His wishes. This awareness in revelation provides the authentic awareness of the processual unity of all things. Hegel implicitly disputes this, seeing Christianity as an anticipation in mystical form of truths unveiled through philosophy, truths which go beyond *revelation*, into *reason* derived from what he calls true comprehension. That is, by removing what is but a form of superstition, the Self can face the possibility of knowing for itself the nature of the world, through his own actions and experiences: this is literally Self-awareness, knowledge which enriches both himself and his interaction with Others. In other words, Hegel knew the desirability of ontological strength for the individual to enable him to exist not as a creature dependent on a transcendental God but as an individual able to enter into a Spiritual relationship with the world.

UNITY IS MEDIATED THROUGH THE PRESENCE OF SPIRIT

An understanding of the significance of awareness, estrangement, and alienation can only be achieved through a comprehension of what Hegel meant by Spirit. As with a number of German words, the translation can be misleading. The German '*Geist*' can be rendered either as 'mind' or 'spirit' but it is not to be associated solely with the Holy Spirit of Christianity, because Hegel's usage had also the profane non-mystical associations found in the poetry of his contemporaries, for example, Goethe, whose work he admired, and Hölderlin, a close friend of Hegel's. As with the English word spirit, '*Geist*' has associations with vitality or wit ('*esprit*' in French), the essence in the liquids of the alchemists (e.g. 'alcoholic' spirit), the force animating a group of people, and so forth (Spalding and Burke 1967: 960). Kaufmann has emphasized that '*Geist*' is close to Latin '*spiritus*' and the Greek '*pneuma*', both having associations with breath or wind, the essence of life in contrast to the more logical meanings implied in the terms 'mind', 'nous', and '*logos*' (Kaufmann 1978: 276). It is interesting to note the similar significance of breath and breathing in Zen thought. One is helped in meditation through focusing on one's breathing. The act of drawing breath draws into one part of the essence of the living world: by such an act one is in harmony with that world in a manner similar to the hearing-is-belonging theme of Heidegger. In opposition to Kaufmann's view, Findlay, in his introduction to a recent reprint of Hegel's *Philosophy of Mind*, suggests that Spirit is more closely associated with the words 'mind' or 'nous' and, following Aristotle, he argues that Spirit is a force 'which in knowing the form of an object, thereby knows itself and which, in its highest phases, may be described as thinking upon thinking' (Findlay, in Hegel 1971: VII). I believe that Findlay is mistaken on this point because Spirit for Hegel was not simply thinking upon thinking but was an animating force that had, as its essence, reciprocity between the Self and the Other. It represented the harmony found 'in the inner being of the world' (Hegel 1931: 86) while Absolute Knowledge, itself the *outcome* of Spirit's action on the world, is closer to thinking upon thinking. Without harmony with the world and reciprocity with fellow men, the individual was forever to lead an estranged life. Thus, Hegel argued, awareness of his Spirituality was alone his source of authenticity. Moreover, Spirit, unlike the Holy Spirit, was not to be treated as an objective transcendental force but that which has its true meaning both within each individual and between each individual. As an animating force, Spirit itself brings the subject out of his merely Self-referential frame of existence, from a state of the denial of Spirit into a consciousness that has the force of Spirit as its referent, thus freeing the Self from its self-imposed one-sided awareness, his estrangement.

There is, however, a flaw in Hegel's notion of Spirit: it is its *abstract* nature. Hegel does not specify what Spirit is in reality; we certainly know its function and its significance: it allows the individual to become aware of his estrangement, and it provides the means of overcoming that estrangement through reciprocity with Others, but we only know its reality in the context of the Hegelian system as a whole, not in terms of everyday life. Marx realized this and in the next chapter it will become apparent that understanding man as a *social* being can provide the concrete source of reciprocity that Hegel sought to uncover in the abstract through Spirit. Yet this is not to reject Hegel's work entirely, because its main significance to us is its analysis of the psychological conditions of the Self as his awareness develops in a *closed* system where authenticity is in the form of Absolute Knowledge. In emphasizing the psychological aspects I shall avoid considering the political implications of Hegel's thought; aspects to which Popper has directed a considerable amount of overwrought attention (Popper 1966, v.2: 27ff).

Simply stated, Hegel's analysis of the growth of awareness proceeds through three stages: being-in-itself, being-for-itself, and being-in-and-for-itself. An analogy may serve to illustrate the differences in these stages. Let us assume the existence of a system A and a system B: further, we assume that they must work together to solve a certain problem. Each system 'knows' its own operational capabilities and no others; each may be said to exist *in*-itself. Now, if system A is presented with the problem it 'realizes' it cannot provide a satisfactory solution. It can be told by an outside observer that system B holds the operations in its system necessary to complete the solution of the problem, so it becomes 'aware' of the existence of that system B, but it also 'realizes' that system B is not yet aware of the potential relationship between the two systems because system B's mode of existence is still in-itself. That is, system A perceives system B as something for-itself, an external force that is not within system A's parameters and yet impinges on them. The next stage is for system B to become aware or to be told of the presence of system A. The co-operation of systems A and B to produce the solution is a result of their mutual awareness, their being-in-and-for-themselves.

Extending this to a consideration in terms of the conscious individual, that is one who becomes aware through experience, rather than being told; the Self as consciousness *in*-itself knows something, this something is the essence or what is *for*-itself, and takes the form of the Other. But it is to be appreciated that Hegel does not see the Other as merely a reflection of consciousness into itself, that is, that the Other exists only through the knowledge of that consciousness of it; because by the very awareness by the Self of the Other it alters itself in the knowledge of the Other, an alteration that eventually, after passing through several stages of self-estrangement, manifests itself as reciprocity between the Self and the Other. This is a theme central to Lacan's (1979) work on psychoanalysis. This awareness reveals the truth to each other of both the Self and the Other by contrasting the antithesis, or what is not (the nothingness, to echo Sartre) of each of them. In my example, system B contained the nothingness of system A and it was the 'awareness' of this nothingness in each of them that allowed them to 'realize' their mutual significance.

SPIRIT, AS RECIPROCITY, DEPENDS ON DIALECTICAL AWARENESS

For the conscious Self, awareness arises through Reason which itself emerges through dialectical thought. This is a form of thinking which, instead of viewing the Self and the Other as end-points in themselves, as windowless monads operating in a mutually exclusive fashion, sees them as opposing moments of the closed system as a whole.

In other words, we have in Hegel's system the principles of a methodology that the individual may employ to progress from sincerity to authenticity by breaking out of his estrangement, his existence in Self isolation and engaging in inter-action with the Other through dialectical reciprocity. This methodology, one of exploring the psychology of the individual, will be of particular value in informing the dialectical analysis of the individual's behaviour in his ecological system and in his relationships with others. For example, studying his behaviour in a work organization, it would be inadequate to focus only on his role, his motivation or the lack of it, his interpersonal competence, and other areas familiar to organization theorists, all of which represent the treatment of man as a 'black box'. Instead, we should try to uncover the way he perceives his being-in-the-world, his ontological structure, because I believe that to study those well trodden aspects of organizational life without investigating the ontological structure of the individual and his chosen form of authentic existence is rather similar to analysing the route taken by a motor-car in terms of its responses to traffic-lights, road junctions, other cars, and so forth; that is, its responses to the organized system of roads and other road users but ignoring completely the reasons why the driver is motoring along in the first place, or of the thoughts, expectations, and fears that may be going through his mind. A dialectical appreciation of his activity may aid us to avoid perceiving him as an atom of the genus 'man' by allowing us to particularize our perceptions of his actions in terms of his authenticity and the meaning *he* ascribes to them rather than interpreting them through *our* expectations or in the light of environmental constraints.

Above all, dialectical knowledge is dynamic knowledge, through it one seeks to know the significance of different elements in a system and their interconnexions with each other. Hegel argued that to analyse an element as a concept in a non-dialectical fashion was to make the double error of abstracting it from its familiar setting in an attempt to obtain it in its 'pure' form and then to break it up into its 'ultimate' elements thus producing 'fixed inert determinations' (Hegel 1931: 92). But this act of abstraction merely causes the whole to be self-divided into specific seemingly unconnected elements or moments, a division that loses the coherence of the process, the living whole.

'The action of separating', Hegel contends, 'is the exercise of the force of *Understanding*' (Hegel 1931: 93). This force yields entities with an apparent life of their own over and above the Self. There is, however, a double aspect to Understanding, a form of awareness similar to that described in the previous chapter as awareness through the act of distancing or disconnecting oneself from the perceived object. On one hand Understanding allows the Self to go beyond its immersion with itself in-itself and to appreciate the existence of the Other, but it is to be realized that while this break from one's isolation is essential for Self growth, it is but a *stage* of awareness, that is, it is a part of a dialectical process which has as its other moment the reunion of those separated entities into a whole. Thus, if knowledge is arrested at the stage of Understanding it is a false, incomplete knowledge. The defect with analytic (non-dialectical) knowledge is that it affects the process of knowing *and* the material it purports to know by always maintaining the separation, the estrangement, between the knower and the known. By contrast, dialectical knowledge enables us to be aware of the context of the object known, and the situation of the person who believes he knows it because it treats them as closely related moments of the same 'truth'. A complexity can be added to this point, of interest to organizational analysts because it is valid only in a closed system: dialectical knowledge alone can yield the 'truth' about something. For Hegel, 'truth' is not just the coincidence of the perceived object with the Self's Understanding of it but its accordance with itself as a system of values. Thus we may perceive an object correctly but do we see its truth? The statement 'this leaf is green' may be perceived as correct or incorrect but it is philosophically neither true nor false because there is no criterion of value in it. That is, although one initially may have qualms over the idea of an object having some inherent 'truth', Hegel wishes us to understand that something can only be true or false in terms of the notion or concept[2] of the closed system *as a whole*. This notion, the wholeness of the system and all its parts, can only become apparent through *Reason*, specifically dialectical reason, and not simply Understanding because Reason

[2] The German word is *Begriff*: it is associated with grasping or comprehending something as a whole.

alone reveals the 'truth', the interrelatedness and the end point of the whole system; Understanding merely isolates its moments. The bud, the blossom, and the fruit are revealed as analysable truths-in-themselves through Understanding but Reason sees their uniting notion in the growing tree. 'Truth' thus emerges as actuality from both the possibilities and contingencies inherent in the notion; and it is the Self in its activity both conceptual and practical within the system, that brings about those actualities. So 'truth' is not a static totality of knowledge in the unsubtle sense, it is knowledge of the living totality, the essences, the particulars and their dialectical life in the notion that reveals that totality. That is, 'truth' can only come from existence in the awareness of what Hegel called Spirit, the *reciprocal* force upon which rests an appreciation of the notion of the system as a whole. There are, however, situations where the nature of the notion, the underlying truth of a system, appears to be in question; for example, in work organizations we have what Fox (1966) has called a pluralistic perspective. Thus we, in seeking to comprehend the nature of the organization as a whole, have to ask whether the notion of the organization is based on either a management or a worker perspective or are those simply stages of Understanding, of entrenched perspectives, in a notion as yet unrealized? I mean by this that the ontological relationship of the work-force to the organization may be uncertain even though their function in terms of role or task is quite definite. Thus worker democracy movements are particularly interesting not only because they encourage a long overdue involvement by the ordinary worker in previously management-centred areas, but because they can alter the ontological relationship of the worker to the organizations from that of treating the organization as a transcended Other, which is to be obeyed (a style based on the Calvinistic interpretation of a closed system) and where the Self was given full ontological support by not questioning the superiority of the Other; to a new form of ontological existence where the Self still desires the closed nature of the system but enters into a dialectical relationship with the organization, the outcome of which may change the notion of the organization from a functional one (to fulfil a market demand, to make profits) to a broader psycho-social one. Durkheim, and the many sociologists who followed him, have been aware of the ontological support afforded to the worker in the context of organized labour but only saw this support existing in structures where the Other, as manifest through organized moral laws, existed as an abstract, seemingly immutable, entity. They did not appreciate that a dialectical interaction with an organization in the act of reformulating or uncovering its notion could itself be ontologically supportive, a point I shall return to in the concluding chapter.

The emergence of the Self's perception of the nature of his relationship to the closed system

I shall now turn to show in detail how the Self's relationship *vis à vis* the Other develops from a passive, abstract one to an active dialectical interaction with his environment and Others therein. This is the process of ontological development undergone by the Self in its search for authenticity, or Being – the accumulation of knowledge or Spiritual awareness of the 'truth' of the ultimate notion of the system as a whole; a development which passes through several stages of estrangement and self-alienation. The Self's emerging relationship to the Other passes through three main phases of epistemological awareness, which precede full ontological development: (1) Consciousness, (2) Self-Consciousness, and (3) Free Concrete Mind. A consideration of these three forms of Self-Other awareness will allow me to trace the aetiology of estrangement in the closed form of authentic existence. The terms used earlier, in-itself, or pure generality; for-itself or pure difference; and their union, in-and-for-itself, can now be appreciated as an abstract formulation of the same three stages that must be gone through to allow the transcendence of estrangement.

CONSCIOUSNESS: THE FIRST STAGE OF THE SELF'S AWARENESS
OF OBJECTS-IN-THE-WORLD

Here, initially, the Self has only itself as locus of awareness, its knowledge is immediate and confined to the level of sense-experience of the 'this', 'here', and 'now' of objects. We thus apprehend sensuously rather than comprehend conceptually. When one perceives the world sensuously it certainly seems infinitely rich and varied because all objects are for-themselves, while the Self merely appears as one entity among many. To recall my earlier distinction between being and Being, existence for the Self is simply *being* because 'the I does not contain or imply a manifold of ideas, the I here does not think' (Hegel 1931: 150). That is, the object that the Self encounters simply *is* and merely because it is, it exists and its simple immediacy appears to constitute its truth. But this form of perception poses certain difficulties for the Self, because the certainty of the object's 'truth', immediately apprehended as a 'this', 'here', or 'now', vanishes as soon as another 'this', 'here', or 'now' arises. Our movement and activity in the world, coupled with the inevitable passage of time, means that the 'now' will constantly throw up different 'heres' and 'thises', yet the individual, if he were to remain in this stage of awareness, only sees them as 'heres' and 'thises'.

Thus, the 'here', 'this', and 'now' for the Self cannot reveal any particularity or precise information about the world. Their meanings remain universal because it can be applied to all situations and objects. All that is affirmed is the Self's own awareness of himself as the locus of his perceptions.

However, the demands on the Self to survive in his environment require more than a perception that confirms his own Self-consciousness, an awareness must be developed that enables him to categorize or particularize the 'thises', 'heres', and 'nows', the object of the Self's apprehension and transform them into a rather less evanescent form. Hegel argues that this transformation is the task of the perceptual consciousness through which the object, the 'this', acquires (on observation) a more determinate character by being perceived as the 'thing with many properties' (Hegel 1931: 163); whereupon the object as 'this' also is seen to contain other 'thises' which by their presence seek to negate the 'this' of the object *qua* object. The original 'this' is thus established by the Self as 'not this', as it is superseded by the 'this' of one of its properties, yet, of course, it is not simply non-existent because that would imply the presence of a nothing with a certain property, i.e. the 'this'. This means that the sense-element of an object is still evident, not in the form of immediate certainty, but as that which has a property. This transcendence of the original 'this' and its nothingness into a 'thing' is a dialectical act on the part of the Self, awareness has emerged through the interaction between the object and its nothingness enabling the 'thing' to be identified as the locus of a characteristic set of properties each still with their own 'hereness' and 'thisness' that relates to the Self. Thus the object for the Self has become a set of universals in a simple togetherness. I can illustrate these abstract remarks by quoting Hegel's comments on the interaction between the various properties of salt:

'Its being white does not affect or alter the cubical shape it has, and neither affects its tart taste . . . each is in a simple relation to self; it leaves the others alone and it is related to these merely by being *also* along with them, a relation of mere indifference. This

"Also" is thus the pure universal itself, the "medium", the "Thinghood" keeping them together.'

(Hegel 1931: 164f)

The 'Also' is thus a very primitive form of Spirit. The Self's dialectical movement of awareness is not yet complete, because the 'Also' constitutes a unity indifferent to its contents; that is, the unifying power of the 'Also' lies in its exclusion and negation of other unities. As always with a dialectical movement, awareness of the negation now affords the Self a new connexion between objects because it is a link that reveals contrasts between objects. At this stage then the 'truth' of an object is conditioned through awareness of its self-sameness.

SELF-CONSCIOUSNESS

(1) The Self's awareness of the externality of objects, the first manifestation of estrangement
Now, the realization that the object perceived is defined not only for-itself but also by its own opposite, its negativity, gives consciousness its own awareness of itself. It has become a specific reality on its own account, as Self-consciousness. To the perceiver these pure determinations appear to express the essential nature of the object, as it does not yet realize that the object's existence *per se* is fettered with its existence for another, so although awareness has moved beyond the universality of the merely sensuous it now perceives objects as having unconditional absolute universality; that is, the Self sees the object as something with its own inherent life. The Self is now convinced that its Understanding of the object is sufficient for epistemological awareness and hence ontological action. However, Hegel deprecatingly calls this awareness, or Understanding, 'sound common sense' because through this Understanding the Self is now at the mercy of these apparently 'objective' abstracted entities, a position, I think, that organization theorists put themselves into when they attempt to 'understand' people solely in terms of cultural or sociological systems. The Self is unaware, as yet, that the abstraction of objects is but a moment in the process of awareness that has as its ultimate goal the realization that the Self and object only truly exist in reciprocity, not abstraction. There is, I know, a certain ontological comfort in keeping objects abstracted from us: Fairbairn (1952), for instance, has argued that reciprocating with, or, in his terms, loving an object, has an ambivalent significance. One's love for an object may in fact destroy

it, because love incorporates the object into the Self and the person thereby loses the very object with which he sought to relate. Yet if he keeps it at a distance, the object, Hegel has suggested, presents an external threat to him. Fairbairn believes that this dilemma instigates the schizoid state, and depending on the ontological strength of the person the individual either incorporates or is incorporated by the object. If the individual is sufficiently strong he avoids these extremes by relating to the object in a dialectical fashion, a two-way interaction where both Self and object preserved their independence in their interdependence. If, however, the individual remains in the mode of Understanding this may indicate that his epistemological awareness is insufficiently developed to offer him ontological support. Realizing this, the Self mistakenly may seek to draw yet further abstractions from those objects he Understands in an attempt to try to uncover the underlying laws immanent in the objects: that is, the Self produces a 'science' of the 'objective' founded upon the desire to establish an objectively based unity for all objects. Taylor's (1947) principles of scientific management can be seen in this context as a prime example of this primitive psychological state. In doing this, a non-dialectical activity, the Self's awareness of objects, Hegel argues, moves further away from its true basis. What we have is a Self estranged by this perverted awareness, Understanding, from the objects it purports to comprehend. This is an early indication that Hegel sees estrangement as a primary consequence of living in the world and arising from the inadequate epistemological awareness of mere Understanding. This objective formulation of the origin of estrangement, emerging from *within* the person's relationship to the world, rather than from the social structures that confront him, as Marx believes, has close affinities with psychoanalytic thought on 'alienation': for instance, Karen Horney uses the term 'self-alienation' to indicate a lack of contact between the individual's 'conscious self' and his 'real self' (1950: 155ff). The consequence of this disparity appears in the person feeling that the world and his relationship to it is meaningless. Hegel would agree, saying that his 'real self' can only materialize in the awareness of the reciprocity, the Spiritual force, that ties the Self to the object. The Self, at this stage of self-consciousness, that is, in ignorance of the presence of Spirit, does not yet appreciate the nature of the notion or concept of the system as a whole and thus continues to use Understanding as the basis for his involvement with the world.

I have said that Understanding gives the individual a 'common-sense' picture of his environment or ecosystem, one that assumes that objects are totally independent entities having their meaning outside the Self. In this form of awareness, the individual attempts to establish an analytic approach to perceiving the object's significance, a method that he believes will uncover laws and patterns in the object and reveal the nature of its relationship to other objects, a process seen by him as revealing their 'meaning'. There may be instances where the efficacy of Understanding as a source of meaning is revealed for what it is, an estranged form of awareness; for example, the social science interpretation of 'alienation' as represented by Seeman's six categories – powerlessness, normlessness, isolation, cultural estrangement, social isolation, and self-estrangement (feelings of personal worthlessness) – would then appear to be a catalogue of consequences that the individual experiences when he realizes that Understanding somehow fails to allow him to comprehend the complex interactions and forces present in the organizational system and in the world generally.

It will be recalled that in the previous chapter I argued, in the presentation of the matrix model, that an adequate perception of one's ecosystem required a *blend* of both epistemological and ontological awarenesses. Awareness which emerges through Understanding has the attributes of dissociation, objectivity, and particularity which alone are associated with epistemological and not ontological awareness. That is, Understanding, although a powerful force, limits our perception by focusing on acquiring knowledge of the environment and excluding an appreciation of *how* we use and live in awareness of that knowledge. Alone, Understanding cannot constitute an adequate grounding for authentic awareness because the individual who relies upon it is estranged from the possibility of increasing his ontological self-awareness. Hegel rather more disparagingly equates Understanding, as a source of meaning, with belief in superstition or revelation because it gives us no clue to the dialectical relationships that exist between Self and objects. In fact, he argues that knowledge based on Understanding establishes what he called the belief in a 'priesthood'. The term had a particular emotive association for Hegel, which, in principle, is still applicable to modern contexts. In Hegel's day the use of the term recalled the Church's emphasis on *revelation* of a minority (the priesthood) as the only acceptable method of allowing the actions of God (representing the archetypal Other) to become accessible to the lay majority. This encourages the promotion of an Other-centred ideology which may subjugate the personal Self-centred experiences of the individual; thus beliefs may be generated by a priesthood which produce certain ideals and insights convenient to itself – a modern instance may be the assumption held by certain economists that the poor state of the British economy is due largely to poor worker productivity. The individual in his estranged awareness may succumb to the ideology of the 'priesthood' because their self-assurance lulls the individual into believing that the meaning they attribute to his experiences (in an organization for instance) is immutable and somehow *the* reality.

If he rebels against the 'priesthood's' ideologies and seeks to re-establish his *own* meaning, still in the mode of Understanding, he may adopt what William Reich has called a fascist mentality, the outlook of the 'little man' who is enslaved by the system but craves authority (Reich 1975: 17), in an attempt not just to find meaning in the system but actively to impose his own upon it. The search for meaning in the mode of Understanding becomes equated with the power to control and to comprehend other people's actions in terms of the control that one can exert over them.

In its less extreme form, response by the individual to the power of the 'priesthood's' interpretation or Understanding of 'reality' may cause him to succumb to the authority of the organization and adopt its goals and ideologies as its own. We have seen that the incorporation of the organization's goals into the Self may be active, an authentic act within the non-autonomous existence of the Self in a closed system; or passive, merely a sincere act within the same system. Keniston calls the latter form of behaviour 'autoplastic' (1965: 454) to contrast it with 'alloplastic' behaviour where one questions the 'priesthood's' ideological beliefs by attempting to transform the nature of the organization and its accepted goals. He sees this latter mode of behaviour as an aspect of estrangement that itself is a form of norm rejection. Keniston indicates, quite unlike Hegel, that estrangement's origin lies in the subject's necessary criticism of his culture. Indeed, he also believes that estrangement is an inevitable consequence of sloughing off one's past; every stage of human development, he argues, 'necessarily involves a dialectic between estrangement from the past and growth into a future where past needs must be modified, and new needs, requirements, and satisfactions must be accepted' (Keniston 1965: 457). I suggest that although Keniston's discussions on estrangement and its associated subjects are more sophisticated than many social scientists' work in this area, he ought not to consider rejection of the past or of the established norms of the present as estrangement *simpliciter*: this reduces the term to the commonplace. Instead, both norm rejections and the efforts to supersede one's past can be more accurately described as the action of distancing, dissociating epistemological awareness that itself is the basis for questioning existing cultural norms. This form of awareness is one of the categories present in the matrix of authentic types. When this is appreciated, it can be seen that norm rejection is quite the reverse of estrangement in an ontologically open system, but a good example of estrangement in a closed one. Keniston can ignore this double aspect by focusing solely on the individual epistemological concerns in the present culture. He sees estrangement associated with cultural development – the necessary act of Shaw's 'unreasonable' man, or in Keniston's own terms, the 'uncommitted' man. Contrary to this, we have seen as yet only briefly, Hegel wished estrangement to be analysed in terms of personal development, the growth of the self-consciousness, and reminded us that although estrangement is a necessary moment in the growth of self-awareness, it produces a false perception of the nature of the relationship between the Self and the object in the guise of Understanding.

(2) The Self's reaction to the presence of an Other, either as another person or as an organization
Up to now, still in the stage of self-consciousness, I have considered the Self's relation to *objects* and have shown by way of an example how the individual responds to the 'object-ness' of work-organizations; but it is insufficient simply to treat an organization as an object, something inert, which affirms the Self's own existence through its opposition or attachment to it. An organization's nature is really much closer to that of an *Other*, something having its own self-consciousness, its own life for-itself. In Sartre's language it has its own praxis or self-directed momentum. It also contains other self-consciousnesses and social structures: it is a community. Hegel used the concept of Spirit to argue that a community could be founded properly only on an awareness of the Spiritual unity between its own existence and the life of the self-consciousnesses which it contains. Without this presence of Spirit the community would be one falsely based on Understanding producing an 'alienated' society as Kahler (1957: 40ff) and Marcuse (1966: 102f) have argued. What was required, Hegel believed, was the growth of Awareness of the nature of this Spirit by both the Self and the Other before a true community could exist. Spirit, or as I have called it, reciprocity, as the basis for the dialectical interaction between a community and its constituent parts, incorporates both 'distancing' and 'immersion' forms of awareness; and which allows the Self to realize that treating objects and Others as discrete, opposed, ele-

ments, through Understanding will compel them to remain at the level of estrangement from each other. I have already indicated that Hegel's use of Spirit has been strongly objected to, both by Marx, especially in his early writings, and Lukacs (1975: 357ff), because they believed that Hegel gave this force of reciprocity a life of its own outside the Self: for instance when the self-consciousness is estranged from its object then Hegel believed that Spirit was estranged from itself (Hegel 1931: 509ff). I appreciate that their criticisms are valid in the context of an open system, but if authenticity is specified in an ontologically closed system then the presence of an apparently abstract entity to serve as a unifier is not just permissible but completely necessary. Lacking the existence of a unifying force, God, or Spirit, the ontological meaning of the closed system crumbles. Marx bypassed the problem of the presence of Spirit as unifier by arguing that man's innate nature was as a social, reciprocating being and through his unestranged interaction with other men he confirmed his social existence.

In the closed system, the emergence of the awareness of Spirit, the beginnings of awareness of the importance of reciprocating with the closed system as a whole by the self-consciousness, arises when the self-consciousness faces the Other as another self-consciousness; that is, it becomes aware that its existence in-and-for-itself is dialectically coupled with its existence for another. Buber has made this point by saying that 'man becomes an I through a You' (1970: 80), while the 'detached-I' in its one-dimensionality (*Punkthaftigkeit*) *uses* objects, treating them as an 'It for itself' by refusing, or being unable (through Understanding) to confront them in the current of reciprocity. Hegel has shown how the I and the You, or the Self and the Other, pass through several stages of interacting awareness with each other. These stages represent various kinds of interpersonal estrangement in the closed system, as I shall now show.

(3)   The Lord-Bondsman relationship as an early form of interpersonal estrangement
Initially, when one self-consciousness becomes dimly aware of an Other as a self-consciousness in its own right, the first self-consciousness fears for the certainty of its own existence for itself because it believes that it has, first, 'lost its own self, since it finds itself as an *other* being'; second, it attempts to transcend or annul[3] that other, 'for it does not regard the Other as essentially real, but sees it as Self in the Other' (Hegel 1931: 229). However, to attempt

[3] The German word Hegel uses is '*aufhebung*' which means both 'cancel' and 'preserve'. There is no exact English equivalent but 'transcend' comes closest.

to negate the Other so that the Self can regain its own self-centred independence, is to cancel a source that helps to create that self-consciousness in the first place. The dilemma faces the other self-consciousness as well, until their mutual existence is acknowledged. Before this stage can be reached the self-consciousness formerly as in-and-for-itself now sees itself as in-and-for-Others: hence a struggle must ensue between the two self-consciousness each attempting to assert themselves against the other to establish their ontological certainty. Bateson has discussed the social implications of this struggle in terms of 'symmetrical schismogenesis' (Bateson 1972: 81ff, 293ff) where two people may attempt to outboast or out-drink each other or where a nation may seek to get ahead of another nation in the 'arms race' to prove its superiority. The traditional confrontations between Trades Unions and managements I see as a clear manifestation of this form of ontological interaction. Bateson argues that unless one person gives way and forms a complementary relationship, the symmetrical interaction between the two can only end in some sort of crisis. This, he suggests, is similar to orgasm after the symmetrical action of lovemaking; whereupon a period of calm reciprocity follows. In terms of ontological development the result of the struggles, from each Self's point of view, will either (1) cause it to perceive its existence in the Other as pure existence for itself, that is, it completely dominates the ontological life of its opponent, or (2) it is entirely negated as a self-consciousness by its adversary's actions. Yet, complete negation of consciousness is ontological death, as Laing in his work on 'The case of Peter' has shown (1969: 129),[4] but we get a milder form where negation in (2) changes from the negation of the Self's for-itself into an existence for-another, the submissive part of a complementary relationship. The self-consciousness whose ontological strength negated the other Self, Hegel called the 'Lord'; while the Self whose existence is now for that Lord is termed the 'Bondsman'.[5] The relationship is a dialectical or complementary one because the Lord's existence is no longer that of an isolated self-consciousness but now depends on the acknowledgement of that domination by the Bondsman. The mediation of the Lord with the Bondsman is sustained by their mutual involvement with impersonal objects; the Bondsman labours upon them for the Lord's enjoyment. Hegel

---

[4] Both Laing (e.g. 1969: 87f) and Sartre (e.g. 1966: 319ff *et passim*) adopt their terminology for their own researches from Hegel's writings. Indeed it may be suggested that these modern writers' works can only be fully appreciated through an understanding of Hegel's *Phenomenology*.

[5] Sometimes called 'Master' and 'Slave' respectively, but the terms used here reflect more closely Hegel's intent in using them.

anticipates Marx's point that the Bondsman, working for a Lord, 'cancels in every particular aspect his dependence on an attachment to natural existence' (Hegel 1931: 238). Thus, the Bondsman reverts to the earlier stage of self-consciousness where his concern is, once again to affirm himself over and against the *objects* in his eco-system, having lost in the struggle to establish his existence over the *Other*. As the Bondsman has to bear the brunt of the presence of these objects, his awareness of their independence grows as he works upon them to change them in the manner desired by the Lord. This work has thus a double action; it allows the objects' concrete external nature to become apparent and, more importantly, it gives the Bondsman the basis for the affirmation of his own ontological existence. This ontological strengthening in turn influences the nature of his relationship with the Lord, allowing the Bondsman to shed the ontological fear he lived in through the presence of the dominant Other; the Lord thus loses the ontological advantage over the Bondsman that enabled him to master the Bondsman-to-be in the early stages of self-conscious awareness.

Thus, through his work, the Bondsman has been able to cast off his initial estrangement from both object and Other and has dis-covered that, as I sought to show in the active and passive kittens experiment illustrated in Chapter 1, carrying out his own actions for himself is the way towards a sound appreciation of his relationship to the environment and Others. This growth of the Bondsman's awareness can only occur when, at the same time the Bondsman is regaining his ontological strength, the Lord realizes that he is master *because* he has reduced the Other to a slave, that his self-assurance is at the expense of the Bondsman. When this awareness arises the Lord appreciates that he has not attained the full self-consciousness that transcends crude domination and allows Others to be treated as equals. Marx's analysis of estrangement and alienation has its intellectual roots in Hegel's discussion of Lordship and Bondage because he shows what happens to the Bondsman, the worker, when the Lord, the capitalist, refuses to relinquish control and continues to dominate and assert himself against the Bondsman, by compel-ling the latter to produce for the Lord's self-affirmation. This refusal to relinquish control has two main effects: the more the Lord's estranged existence is protected and affirmed through the com-plementary schismogenic actions of the Bondsman the more reluc-tant he is to face any disruption of the control which gives him his apparent ontological strength and hence the less able is the Bonds-man to free himself of that domination. Secondly, in the act of his self-affirmation over and against the Bondsman the Lord distances himself from his formerly intimate association with the Bondsman and fails to appreciate both the Bondsman's particular connexion with him and his own lack of self-conscious awareness.

Indeed, the Lord may strengthen his dominance by acknowledging the existence and the 'good service' of the Bondsman; or in a work organization context, by giving him a reward, money, security, and status. This severs further the Self-freeing connexion between the Bondsman's activity upon the object and his direct awareness of that object's significance to his ontological existence. The dominance of the Lord, hiding an ontological insecurity, thus produces estrangement for both himself and those over whom he has power and control.

Thus, an Hegelian analysis of the estranged nature of the relationship between capitalist management and worker, to use modern equivalents, in terms of their ontological development, may complement a Marxist critique with its emphasis on the development of political awareness. Thus, I am iterating the point that although it is necessary to study the significance of Marx's political solutions to alienation and estrangement, work in this field of research must be complemented with an examination of the ontological perspectives of those individuals who compose the sociological groups 'workers' and 'management', and should explore ways of transcending the domination of one group by another, not in terms of political warfare but through allowing opportunities to enhance mutual ontological awareness. It is realized that such an approach is not easy because it lacks both the immediate motivating force of a 'them/us' antagonism and its implementation requires considerable ontological strength on the part of the dominator, first to acknowledge the unreasonableness of one's domination and second, to discard it as a means of dealing with Others. As Tillich suggests, the 'power of being' is more important than the power of antagonism (Tillich 1977: 174). Further, he argues that the 'power of being' can lie in the Self's willingness to reappraise its relationship with its ecosystem and change its perceptions of Others and their ideologies. Applying this point to the work context it is possible that the perceived domination of the worker by the forces of capitalism can be reduced through the encouragement of an instrumental attitude towards work. Here work is perceived as being of peripheral psychological interest to the individual who does the job, as it reduces the domination of the Self by the organization (as a manifestation of an Other) to two areas: money and time. Dahrendorf (1959) has observed that this change of attitude towards work is a characteristic of the post-capitalist society:

'In [this] society, the worker, when he passes the factory gate, increasingly leaves his occupational role behind him with the machinery and his work clothes, outside he plays new roles defined by factors other than his occupation. The occupation and the expectation created with it dominate less and less the life of the industrial workers, and other expectations mold his social personality.'   (Dahrendorf 1959: 273)

As the studies of the Cambridge research team under Goldthorpe have shown us these expectations may focus on an aspiration towards middle-class values and the accumulation of material possessions; their instrumentality thus appears as an attempt to use the organized work system for their own end, that is, an evolutionary movement rather than a revolutionary one. It is possible that through an instrumental approach to work, the individual, freed of direct psychological domination, may press for more pay and shorter working hours both of which he can use to affirm himself in his leisure time, provided, of course, that he can cope psychologically with his new found freedom – a point made by Sherman and Jenkins in their book *Leisure Shock* (1981). In turn this may lead to a further questioning of the need to participate at all in organized work with its emphasis on the domination of workers' time and personal attributes, and one has to seek for both socio-economic and ontological structures whereby one's social commitments to other people are balanced with one's personal interests. Although study of the economic structures lies outside the scope and interest of this book, analysis of the ontological structures in their closed system form requires a consideration of the third stage of awareness, free concrete mind.

FREE CONCRETE MIND

(1) The response of the Self to an awareness of his estrangement from both objects and Others
This phase is attainable when the self-consciousness becomes aware of the estranged nature of its relationship with both objects in the world and Others. Here self-consciousness no longer depends upon the need to treat objects as entities in opposition to it to affirm its existence but (1) can attain its *freedom* through the positive acceptance of the Ideal[6] nature of the object, a freedom which is

---

[6] A capital I is used to indicate that it is the culmination and focus of the system as a whole, awareness of which forms the basis for authenticity as Being.

concretely founded, for it depends on involvement with, rather than abstraction from, objects it encounters, and (2) realizes that through rational forms of experiencing objects, consciousness of them is, in a sense, their whole truth and reality. The term *Ideal* has a particular significance in this stage of closed system awareness in recalling that the dialectical movement in the relationship between the Self and an object had its first aspect when 'reality' appeared to the consciousness as having the character of *objective* existence, and its second aspect of only being subjectively for consciousness. The culmination of this dialectical process forms the truth for that which exists or is real in itself, in so far as it is an object *for consciousness*, while that which exists for consciousness is also objectively real. Thus, the Ideal nature of the object is that it belongs to the individual, not as an item of property but as a part of his being-in-the-world. As Findlay clearly expressed it, in awareness of the Ideal 'Objects are all in a deep sense *mine* – mine to understand, mine to experiment with, mine to remould and mine to find myself in' (Findlay 1958: 103). Idealism is not an abstracted view of the object but the consequence of direct dialectical interaction with it; it is neither merely the subject's response to his sure knowledge of the possession of his thought as his own, nor an assumption of the Stoic maxim, 'There's nothing good or bad but thinking makes it so' (Mure 1940: 77). Thus Hegel's emphasis on the objectivity of Idealism at once sets him apart from philosophers like Berkeley who asserted that all objects in the world are but an individual's ideas and sensations having no life other than through that individual. The very concrete test to which Samuel Johnson once wittily put Berkeley's subjective idealism illustrates the weakness in Berkeley's ideas: Berkeley was apparently expounding his views to Johnson and, on approaching the latter's house, Berkeley was invited in to conclude the conversation over dinner. Johnson briskly walked into his house ahead of Berkeley, promptly shut the door and then called out to Berkeley that if his ideas were valid he could will the door away and walk through it. It is not reported whether he swallowed his principles and hence his dinner or walked away. Hegel, had he been alive then, would have had no difficulty in asking to be let in to enjoy the meal, his Idealism being founded on the Self's practical involvement with the world. Likewise, the significance of his Idealism is radically different from that evident in Kant's system of categories or Fichte's own kind of idealism; both saw their categories or ideals as end states but failed to derive their phenomenological basis, by which I mean that although denying it, they were positing forms of abstract idealism and giving them empirical force.

Although the self-consciousness's new awareness of the Ideal nature of objects (in its free concrete mind stage) is one step closer in the construction of the internal unity necessary for the attainment of authenticity in the closed system, this awareness must be complemented by a break away from Understanding as the only means of comprehending the nature of that system. It is at this stage that it becomes possible to see the existence of different forms of estrangement as phases of awareness in the individual's relationship to other entities in the system, the totality of existence.

(2) Scepticism: the end of Understanding; the presence of arch-indifference as a form of estrangement

The general form of estrangement that I have considered up to now arose through the existence of the independent abstract self-consciousness which saw itself in isolated independence of entities[7] and only, falsely, communicated with them through Understanding. The break with Understanding comes when the self-consciousness views the world *sceptically*. Abstract thought, itself the child of Understanding, produces the sceptic self-consciousness; here the reflection of the self-consciousness into the simple pure thought of itself has meant that it believes it sees the entire *externality* of the Other and objects in relation to the Self, forgetting that its origins in self-consciousness lay in perceiving the influence of those entities in the first place.

Furthermore, the certainties of perception together with Understanding as a source of meaning, and the inherent 'truth' of moral values are all swept away into indifferent abstraction by the sceptical self-consciousness but the sceptic is *aware* of his dissolving action upon non-Self entities that maintains his attitude of scepticism. However, this awareness of the act of rejection requires recognition of something that is not even supposed to be acknowledged, and ultimately the pure sceptical attitude breaks down on the realization of the contradiction, the duality, it demands of its self-consciousness to maintain that scepticism. 'In this way, the duplication, which previously was divided between two individuals, the Lord and the Bondsman, is concentrated into one' (Hegel 1931: 251), producing a stressful ontological situation, which Hegel called the *Unhappy Consciousness*.[8]

---

[7] Which includes both objects and Others.

[8] *'Unglückliches Bewusstein'* to which Baillie adds 'Alienated Soul' to clarify the Self's ontological status – I prefer the term 'estranged soul' in line with my usage in this book.

*(3) Unhappy Consciousness: Awareness of the apparent
unattainability of the Ideal through the Self's perception
of his estrangement from it*

Hegel believed that the existence of the Unhappy Consciousness is
to be found at its peak in the expression of Christian devotion, but I
see it is possible also to appreciate it as the individual's response to
the seemingly all-powerful external world. Man in this unhappy
state devotes himself to achieving union with an abstract force, a
union, he believes, or is told, that represents authentic existence;
yet the more he strives towards this abstraction the more he
confirms his own unhappiness at being abstracted from it. This
eternal search for the unattainable is made tolerable in Christian
society when one is told that the more the individual emphasizes his
worthlessness, which he sees as apparent anyway, the more God
will reward that person in an 'after-life', thus justifying both the
existence of an abstract 'ideal' (God) and fulfilling man's need for
meaning in the world. For example, the more one strives towards
abstract, self-maintaining organizational goals, the more powerless
one feels when faced by their abstract power; yet, because organized
work occupies a large portion of a person's life he may believe that
those goals offer him his only source of meaning that is also
intelligible to another; how often one finds that the question 'Who
are you?', elicits the initial response, 'I'm a factory-worker', 'I'm a
manager', at such and such an organization (Mulford and Salisbury
1964). Their role at work is a source of ontological support in the
generalized meaning it offers to Others.

Scepticism and the Unhappy Consciousness: their relevance to 'alienation'

I suggest that an understanding of the nature of both scepticism and
the Unhappy Consciousness can give a coherence to much of the
apparently conflicting material in the social sciences on what
'alienation' is, by revealing that both these aspects of self-
consciousness are the products, the consequences of, the primary
estrangement by the Self from objects and Others. I shall now look at
each aspect in more detail.

Scepticism, the arch-indifference, is the estrangement of those
disinterested in present values, work ethics, cultural norms, and
ideologies. It is possible to see the significance of role-playing for the
estranged sceptic. Conventionally, it is understood as the act of an
individual who desires a form of separation from the world as
protection from personal involvement; thus Bonjean and Grimes

(1970) have utilized the concept of role-playing as an indicator of an individual's 'alienation' from bureaucratic influences.

By contrast, I suggest that role-playing may be the only acceptable way the sceptic can make meaningful contact with the world in which he lives. The use of this form of communication is welcomed by the sceptic because he is able to adopt and discard different roles as it suits him. His actions, as Goffmann (1969) would remind us, constitute a presentation of Self, and his commitments to these Selves are transitory; but, more than this, without them he could not hope to survive, as a sceptic, in organized society. That is, role-playing has a dual purpose for him; as a means of maintaining his estrangement, the detachment of his Self from objects and Others and, paradoxically, the means through which he affirms their existence in order to be able to convince himself of their ephemerality and his permanence. At a more abstract level Heidegger's analysis of the individual's 'self-certainty' and his confidence in the external existence and separation from him of the 'they' (the 'Other' in our terms) adds to the knowledge we have of the nature of the origins of the estranged life of the sceptic. He argues that this Self-Certainty exists through the falling of *Dasein* (Being-there-in-the-world) into a mode of abstracted existence. Falling has a specific ontological significance because it is used to suggest that the Self is estranged by living lost in the remote publicness of the Other which Heidegger sees as the basis of inauthentic existence. Here things are Understood in terms of their 'groundless floating' (Heidegger 1978: 221). The sceptic's existence is thus tranquillized and becomes complacent with the power of his Understanding in an 'estrangement [*entfremdung*] in which its ownmost potentiality-for-Being is hidden from it' (Heidegger 1978: 222). The similarity between Hegel's and Heidegger's use of '*entfremdung*' is further evident when the latter argues that estrangement closes off from *Dasein*, Being-there-in-the-world, its authenticity, causing it to collapse into a form of Being of itself, evident in the sceptic's basic belief of the 'groundlessness and nullity of inauthentic everydayness' (Heidegger 1978: 223). The similarity goes no further, because Heidegger, analysing these concepts from the perspective of an open system of existence, rejects Hegel's 'arduous struggles to conceive the "concretion" of the Spirit' (Heidegger 1978: 486) and criticizes Hegel's inadequate understanding of the nature of time. He fails to realize that in closed systems, such as Hegel's, time is only meaningful in terms of the state of self-consciousness in its progression towards authenticity and is not a crucial aspect of one's ontological existence, as it was, for example, in Proust's case where the analysis of the passage of time and the accretion of events amid memories provided a basis for meaningful actions in the present. The sceptic, by contrast, lives in a timeless world, that is, he is disinterested in its passage because it offers no further ontological support to his existence.

Considering in more concrete terms the nature of the sceptic self-consciousness we may see that it bears a close relationship to certain aspects of behaviour generally subsumed under the broad heading of 'alienation' by those in the field of organization theory and practice.

Neal and Rettig (1967) have argued that two broad themes may be discerned in an examination of this literature, both of which come under the general heading of 'alienation': the first is the

'frequent reference to individual maladjustment, to a negative world view, and to feelings of despair and hopelessness. Yet concurrent with this assumption is the [alternative] perception of alienation as a basis for detached skepticism in science and for creativity in the Arts.'   (Neal and Rettig 1967: 62)

By understanding the nature of the sceptic self-consciousness it becomes possible to articulate *one* of the key themes underlying 'alienation': that of the individual's active *desire* to remain detached from cultural norms and values, that is, free from the influence of the Other. In this context, talk of overcoming 'alienation' can only be based on ignorance of its ontologically protective value. As a sceptic, the individual's response to the Other is not based on despair or frustration, it is an active desire to dissociate himself from that Other, to shield the Self against the Other's values. Nettler, in an early paper (1957), has checked this point by using examples from autobiographies of people well known for expressing their lack of enthusiasm for 'All-American' values. One such example was of the philosopher Santayana, noted for his aloofness; Nettler's subjects were asked whether or not they sympathized with Santayana's proud remark, 'that months would pass without his speaking to anyone except the headwaiter' (Nettler 1957: 673). Nettler found that people who approved of this and similar sentiments were quite sceptical of the desirability of conforming to or of participating in, the culture and way of life common to the majority of the people. Stinchcombe (1964) has also highlighted the scepticism felt by a specific section of the population, high-school students, towards the value of their education and their dislike of bureaucratic authority structures in the school system as expressed in their dislike of conformity. They could not be motivated to work by the conventional rewards offered by schooling as they were cynical about the worth of those rewards (success in a career for instance), when they were more interested in establishing their own personal goals and aspirations. This he called 'expressive alienation' thus failing to question the assumption that it is adequate to define 'alienation' in terms of societal expectations. Indeed some writers, for example Murchland (1971), generalize further by believing that we live in an 'age of alienation', a remark which offers no critical assessment of the nature of that 'alienation'. Specifically, it fails to appreciate that there are certain situations where 'alienated' awareness can give the ontological security that the sceptic needs in his relationship with the Other.

However, this security is, I contend, falsely based. The sceptic, despite his attractive estranged aloofness, has an aspect of cowardice in his self-consciousness, because he refuses to acknowledge the significance to him of the Other and its manifestations (norms, cultural values, prevailing ideologies). Perhaps he forgets, in the pride of being estranged, that the presence of the Other actually is necessary before he can disdain it and that treating the Other as a mere object to be reduced to insignificance is just the act of a person lacking the ontological strength[9] actively to question the nature of the Other's beliefs.

Unlike the sceptic, there are those people who feel intensely unhappy about their estranged lives and devote their energies to finding meaning in the world, a meaning that can establish an authentic ontological strength in awareness of the Other, and enable them to participate more fully with other people. I am suggesting that these people in their unhappy state require more courage than the sceptic because they seek to involve themselves with the Other, for they know that failure to achieve integration has its outcome in feeling even more powerless and anomic in the face of the Other; that is, they fear a reversion to the position of the Bondsman. It is necessary to realize that the estrangement of the Unhappy Consciousness can only exist in a closed system: his unhappiness stems from his striving towards achieving unity with a seemingly unattainable goal, a goal which is seen as the fulfilment of one's ontological existence.

For Christian belief, this fulfilment is found in God, and His unattainability is due to one's feelings of personal inadequacy or unworthiness in His eyes. In everyday life this unhappiness is

---

[9] 'Self-certainty', as Heidegger called the sceptic's self-centredness, is mistaken by the sceptic for ontological strength.

manifest in the individual's struggle to find meaning and order, to establish an epistemological framework of the world upon which he can base his ontological life. In an open system this search must *not* be the source of unhappiness, because the act of searching calls into question one's present form of awareness and is thus the basis of authenticity; but in a closed system authenticity is found in the achievement of a specific state of awareness (awareness of God, Absolute Knowledge, or the Ideal) so one's unhappiness in not achieving it is an early realization of one's inauthentic existence. Thus, the Unhappy Consciousness exists in a state closely akin to that of anomic awareness when he realizes that he cannot understand how to attain the desired goal. Durkheim, like Hegel, appreciated that to

'pursue a goal which is by definition unattainable is to condemn oneself to a state of perpetual unhappiness. Of course, man may hope contrary to all reason, and hope has its pleasures even when unreasonable. It may sustain him for a time; but it cannot survive the repeated disappointments of experience indefinitely. . . . Our thread of life on these conditions is pretty thin, breakable at any instant.'   (Durkheim 1952: 248)

He argued that the individual living in this unhappy state of being, unable to achieve his ideal, may either resort to socially unacceptable methods to acquire it or, because of the metaphysical nature of most ideals, he suffers from a feeling of hopelessness and despair which may lead to suicide. Durkheim believed that to break away from this unhappiness one must accept an outside regulative force, based on a system of morals, derived from the nurturing and supportive structure of society. His belief in the need for the individual willingly to accept societal constraints, through which the individual frees himself of his unhappiness, makes the unwarranted assumption that man's unhappiness must be 'cured' externally by providing him with a structure upon which he can rest his weakness, rather than suggesting, as I do, that while this form of nonautonomous existence is a perfectly acceptable route to authenticity, there is an equally valid alternative approach where such external props are superfluous, and authenticity, the attainment of the Ideal, can be attained (still in the closed system) through one's own ontological strength in one's relationships with the Other in the awareness of reciprocity or mediation of Spirit. Durkheim's strong emphasis on the presence of external ontological supports to counter the risk of anomie led him to develop some curious arguments on the desirability of the division of labour, that is where each person is allotted to a specified, well defined role to be carried out in close harmony with other people in similar roles. For Durkheim, labour *per se* was not the specific process through which one realizes one's intimate links with objects and the Other, as Hegel, and later Marx, had argued but, more directly, was a way of being able to interact harmoniously with other people, an action that both maintained the cohesiveness of society, fulfilled the individual's own need for security, and moderated individual egotism (Durkheim 1964: 56ff). He contrasts the dilettante who 'conserves his original simplicity intact' with the linotyper in whom one observes a 'prodigious assemblage of ideas, images [and] customs', utilized to set up a page of print (Durkheim 1964: 311). He emphasizes the undesirable simplicity of the life of the former in comparison with the full richness of the latter's! He therefore believes it to be a 'real illusion that makes us believe that personality was so much more complete when the division of labour had penetrated less' (Durkheim 1964: 404). While one may have considerable sympathy for this form of societally based work, and note that in principle, Durkheim may be commended for attempting to reduce the burden of uncertainty that the Unhappy Consciousness experiences, his proposals for specialized work are less attractive when one understands the nature of the conditions under which this division of labour was to take place, that is, in the context of a Lord–Bondsman relationship: consequently, the linotyper and his associates merely are grateful but estranged Other-controlled Bondsmen. We shall see in the next chapter the criticisms that Marx levelled against accepting the nature of such a relationship and how, in certain respects, the dilettante's activities, founded on a freedom of choice, are characteristic of one who does not need to seek external factors to provide him with his ontological security.

Because the Unhappy Consciousness emerges from the estranged Self-Other relationship, originating in the Lord–Bondsman interaction, it indicates that anomie, the practical manifestation of the Unhappy Consciousness, is a *consequence* of estrangement, not as Finifter, among others believes, a *part* of estrangement or 'alienation' (Finifter 1972: 56, 189ff). Srole's work in this area has already made this almost forgotten point: when he developed a scale to measure anomie he made it quite clear that what he called 'self-to-others alienation' (Srole 1956: 711) (what I have termed estrangement), was the *basis* for the existence of anomie. In contrast to my approach, however, he emphasized the sociological aspects of anomie, that is, he was not specifically interested in the ontological problems that the subjective feeling of anomie posed for the individual but based his anomie scale on the subject's relationships with society. Srole's interests centred around whether or not the Self felt (1) detached from community leaders, (2) that the social order was fickle and unpredictable, (3) that personal relationships were unsatisfactory, (4) that he was not internalizing societal norms and values (which Srole assumed would indicate to the Self a meaninglessness of life in general), and finally, that the Self was retrogressing from goals already achieved. The main difference between my interest in anomie as the ontological state of the Unhappy Consciousness and Srole's sociological approach is that through the analysis of the growth of awareness between the Self and the Other, I have sought to provide an aetiology of the anomic state. Further, to contend as Durkheim did, that the provision of an externally derived set of moral codes would lessen the risk of anomic existence is to design a sociological cure for a psychological problem. Certainly the presence of anomie generates social problems which may be understood best in sociological terms, but to believe that external corrective measures offer a suitable solution is analogous to putting a fat person into a corset thus improving the superficial appearance but making no attempt to understand *why* the person is overweight in the first place. Similarly, by appreciating anomie as a possible stage in the growth of the Self's ontological awareness it becomes possible to study the 'why' of its existence in society in psychological terms.

Transcendence of estrangement in the closed form of authentic existence

The cessation of the *sceptic's* estrangement in the closed system can occur in two ways. The individual may stop dissociating from the values of the Ideal and re-embrace that Ideal, having perceived its ontological value in a new light, thereby re-establishing the cybernetic loop of awareness and participation between himself and the *closed* system as a whole. Alternatively, he actively seeks to establish his ontological existence in an *open*-ended system of authenticity by breaking out of the existing 'set' of the system and refusing to establish a new set, he questions the validity of the principle of a 'set' or specific perspective as a means of ontological support. Thus, he seeks an authenticity where his existence is not directed towards attaining Being in the specific manifestation of an Ideal, but instead authentic life is signified by his active involvement with Others and their metasystems and institutions.

One can readily appreciate that the open form of authentic existence is more difficult to achieve than the closed form because in openness a person's authenticity depends entirely on his internal ontological strength and not on external goals or ideals to which he may direct himself to give his life a purpose and a meaning. Marx's work on estrangement in the open form of authenticity can be seen, as I argue in the next chapter, not solely as an analysis of the exploitative nature of capitalist economic structures but an exposition of the conditions necessary for a release into open, authentic life through a particular form of ontological development. His error was to assume that ontological strength, the courage to dwell in non-exploitative, unestranged relationships, could arise through political revolution. The analysis in this chapter suggests, however, that those in the sceptic mode of estrangement may be ready to respond actively to a post-revolutionary state but those in the estrangement of the Unhappy Consciousness will have merely the awareness of their anomie and helplessness increased in the loss of the structures and values to which they sought to attach themselves.

The cessation of estrangement in the case of the *Unhappy Consciousness*, I suggest, also can take two forms. The first is a round-about process which involves the individual turning from the unhappiness created by his desire to attain the Ideal and regressing to a state of scepticism where the validity of the Ideal is questioned. This questioning does not necessarily take the form of active criticism, it may manifest itself, as in the early stages of sceptic estrangement, in the form of indifference and withdrawal. Alternatively, the Unhappy Consciousness may successfully attain the desired non-autonomous unity with the Ideal, thus reaching Being or authentic existence. As suggested in Figure 3(1), one may reach Being in the Ideal through either Christian belief in Grace, Hegelian self-alienation, or some form of transcendental logic of which Ouspensky is but one advocate.

In Chapter 1 we saw how Calvin argued that authenticity could only be realized through God's Grace and one's personal self-surrender to His Will: this gives us the key to understand all forms of overcoming estrangement in a closed system – one had, in a special way, to deny one's own particularity. This is not to be misconstrued as an act of self-annihilation, instead one transcends isolation by ceasing to use Understanding to impose one's own particular perspective upon the actions of others or of the system as a whole. By breaking out of a *particular*, unidimensional frame of reference either through revelation, as advocated by theologians and believers in a transcendental logic, or through Hegelian Reason, one comes to see the essential unity in the flux of particulars.

One of Marx's strongest objections to Hegel's work was that the 'essential unity' of the whole system was founded on thought, not action. While agreeing that this objection and all its implications was a powerful basis for a new critique of society, it does not negate the point that awareness in thought, as Reason, can be the *basis* of authentic action; thought is necessary for one to establish one's ontological strength to enable full reciprocity with the Other, without this higher-order awareness one's actions are rooted merely in Understanding with its concomitant estrangement. This point is applicable to Marx's system of *open* authentic awareness too but there is an important difference. In a *closed* form of authentic awareness, thought, in its special form as Reason, enables one to know the 'given', the Ideal of the system; the task is not to change it, because by definition the Ideal is immutable. One cannot know it any better by changing it through one's actions; rather, actions must be guided, by Grace, Reason, or transcendental logic, towards an awareness of the Ideal, an awareness that allows one to see all the interconnexions in the system and sub-systems of which the individual is a part. For example, Hegel argues that if a person believes that action *per se* is the source of truth and reality, he will remain in the estranged structure of Self-Consciousness in-and-for-itself (Hegel 1931: 415). In the *open* form of authentic awareness, however, one perceives the system as having blind, purposeless motion (what Sartre (1976) described as the praxis of the practico-inert), that is, it is a complex interaction of processes uniting and parting, producing consequences both anticipated and unexpected. One can never, by pure thought alone, become aware of all the ramifications of these interactions, one must become immersed in the system so as not to become submerged by it. Immersion is the involvement through one's praxis, one's directed activity, that seeks to cut out shapes to define figure and ground, to comprehend and to act upon the system in order to know a measure of its aimlessness: in fact, one does not desire simply to know it or to master it, one seeks to *Be* in the system. Being is the dynamic act of creating order out of Chaos, the primal gap or division, an ordering that constantly changes through one's very praxis. Active involvement in the *open* system thus creates one's ontological strength through each act of division and ordering because it affirms one's own self-consciousness in the totalizations of all other self-consciousness; while by contrast in the *closed* system such a personal self-willed act leads to estrangement, the separation from the given unity of the

Ideal. This means that in the closed system the individual, governed by Reason, or the awareness of the spiritual reciprocity between the Self and the system as a whole, views action or praxis not as the means to *create* ontological and epistemological meanings but to *affirm* the ultimate meaning of authentic life within the Ideal.

The act of denying one's particularity and one's isolation, for Hegel, was called self-alienation (*Selbst-Entaüsserung*). It has the connotations already mentioned at the beginning of the chapter, of a necessary divestment, surrender, or renunciation of Self-isolation. It is easy to go astray on the significance of *Selbst-Entaüsserung*. Schacht (1971), for instance, believes that Hegel's notion of self-alienation is closely associated with the self-alienation, the self-surrender of the social contract theorists. The idea of a social contract, represented in the writings of Hobbes and Locke, laid great emphasis on the individual surrendering his rights, his personal liberty to the sovereign state to ensure that the community could exist as a coherent whole, and not as a series of warring individuals. This had direct *political* significance for these writers, thus it is far removed from the psychological and sociological emphasis that Hegel put upon self-alienation. He saw it as an act necessary for ultimate personal authenticity: one surrendered or alienated one's self-certainty-in-isolation to gain the spiritual awareness, the appreciation of true dialectical reciprocity with Others in the Ideal; that Ideal took the form of Absolute Knowledge: that is, with Absolute Knowledge one's actions were authentically founded in the awareness of the all-pervading Spirit or reciprocity within all aspects of the system. Self-alienation, then, is similar to the Zen belief in 'letting go' or freeing oneself from one's prejudices in order to perceive the interesting unity of all things. In less metaphysical terms, although these are unavoidable in any discussion of a closed system which has as its *raison d'être* a metaphysical Ideal, self-alienation is the foundation for an authentic relationship with an Other, which in turn means that it permits the inception of a community based upon mutual ontological support and trust, rather than upon the power-relations implicit in the social contract conceptions of self-surrender and explicit in the estranged Lord–Bondsman relationship. Marx's views on the cessation of estrangement, though argued from a very different perspective, lead to a similar conclusion. If man, he said, can divest himself of his estrangement, he may lead a life of interactions with other men based on love and trust. However, for Marx, interaction *in itself* is an expression of man's authentic social nature, it is not based on an interaction in the presence of a closed Absolute Knowledge as it was for Hegel.

Conclusion

In this chapter, I have sought to use the analysis of the forms of authentic existence established in Chapter 2 to explore the meaning of 'alienation', or more accurately estrangement, a concept intended by social scientists to yield insights into the nature of man's relationship to his environment. In tracing the aetiology of estrangement within the closed form of authentic existence, I have argued that it can have an objective, epistemologically based origin: that is, incomplete awareness of the nature of, and need for, unity with the Ideal creates the criterion used to describe the presence of estrangement. In MacKay's terms (1969) the amount of information available to the Self in his relationship with his environment is analysed and found wanting. Specifically I see it is insufficient to stop the analysis at the epistemological level as do those advocates of a scientifically based theory of 'alienation'. This approach, although useful to gain some precision in the academic meaning of the term, approaches the problem mythically, as Wilden (1972) has argued, because it can give us no insight into the ontological relationship that the estranged person has with his ecosystem, that environment which is made up of inanimate objects, animate Others and groups of Others, organizations and institutions. Thus, in the sections on the Self's scepticism and unhappiness the ontological desirability and undesirability of estrangement was considered from the point of view of the individual, and I argued that an appreciation of these two ontological forms allowed one to reconsider more clearly the seemingly irreconcilable variations in the concept 'alienation' evident in a representative sample of the literature. We also saw how estrangement, in the mode of the Unhappy Consciousness, can be overcome, through one's self-alienation, thus achieving a union with the Ideal based on ultimate awareness of its manifestations, allowing one to live in a non-autonomous or semi-autonomous existence. These forms of existence represent the transcendence of estrangement both for the person's ontological existence and for his epistemological awareness of the Ideal. The aetiology of estrangement in the closed form of authentic existence is summarized in Figure 3(1).

As Figure 3(1) indicates, in contrast to the way estrangement is transcended in the closed system, the open system approach appears to involve a further estrangement, estrangement from the principle of an Ideal: here the Ideal itself is rejected, together with the ontological need for any form of Ideal. In this case, through his autonomous action, the person seeks to gain awareness of himself in an open form of authentic existence: that is, complete estrangement from the Ideal could allow the Self to develop sufficient ontological strength to break entirely from the need to strive for authentic existence in a closed form of awareness, and transcend his estrangement by establishing an awareness of his ecosystem through open-ended autonomous action. One of the implications of this study is that it would no longer appear possible to analyse the 'alienation' of man in the abstract, as merely one person among many, in the manner of a sociological examination. It would require further research to understand why the individual has come to adopt his particular ontological stance either as a sceptic or Unhappy Consciousness. I suggest that perhaps the use of some form of projective technique could be of use in this task. Semeonoff (1976) has offered a valuable critical survey of these rather neglected research tools showing that they still can be of use in uncovering how a person perceives the world and the people he meets. Naturally, these techniques require the ability of a skilled interviewer and produce a mass of unwieldy but insightful subjective information; consequently, it is much harder to undertake than an easily administered question-and-answer form which produces readily analysable data but which at best reveals only general trends.

Finally, I have noted that social scientists, particularly organization theorists, like to emphasize their debt to Marx's work on alienation. It is hoped that this chapter has served to point out that the historical antecedents for their work lie within *Hegelian* thought. This is so because their analyses of work organizations are within existing societal structures which they implicitly perceive as a closed system to which the individual must adapt if he desires to participate in 'reality'. Hegel presented one of the best analyses of a closed system (although he incorrectly understood it to be the *only* system) and the individual's relationship to it, so it is to him, not Marx, that they owe their debt. Indeed their attempts to associate their work with that of Marx are usually based on an ignorance of what Marx meant by alienation and estrangement. The next chapter may serve to enlighten them.

Figure 3(1) The aetiology of estrangement in the closed form of authentic existence

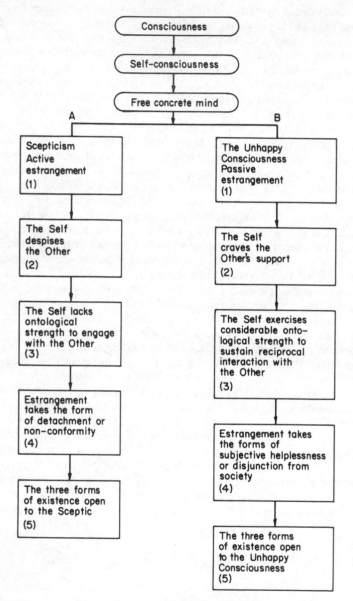

Consciousness: The birth of meaning for the Self through the awareness of form.

Self-Consciousness: Awareness of the Other, based upon the estranged awareness of understanding and culminating in the Lord–Bondsman relationship.

Free Concrete Mind: The emergence of the Self's realization of his independence from the Other and his appreciation of the significance of the Ideal in the closed form of authenticity.

A SCEPTICISM

(1) The individual may appear estranged to observers within the closed Ideal system of authentic existence, but more importantly, the sceptic *desires* his self-imposed estrangement. This state has associations with Hadja's 'rejection of society' (1961), Streuning and Richardson's 'alienation via rejection' (1965), Lowry's 'normative alienation' (1962), Kenniston's 'rejection of American culture' (1965), and Johnson's 'segmental encounters' (1975).

(2) The sceptic protects his Self in awareness of the Other by despising the Other and its ideals: meanings are Self-derived (internal) rather than Other-based (external).

(3) The Sceptic lacks ontological strength to engage himself with the Other to change the nature of the Ideal. The sceptic's sincere belief in his own self-certainty and his unwillingness to accept the presence of an Ideal cause him to reject the authenticity possible within the closed form of ontological life. However, because he does not yet appreciate the nature of open-system authenticity he is content merely to reject the closed system by distancing himself from its requirements.

(4) The sceptic's estrangement can take the form of artistic or scientific detachment (Lakatos and Musgrave 1970), non-integration, aloofness from personal relationship (e.g. Becker 1967 or Milgram 1970). In a slightly more active form the sceptic's estrangement may take the form of non-conformity (Zurcher *et al.* 1965) or 'deviant' behaviour (Dubin 1959). These forms represent the emergence of alloplastic behaviour, i.e. breaking one's estrangement to start criticizing the Ideal.

(5) *The three forms of existence open to the sceptic*
Non-autonomous existence. Here the Self's scepticism is based not on dislike of the Other and the Ideal, but on terror of its influence. The Self's indifference in this case is closely akin to schizoid dissociation (Fairbairn 1952). His existence is non-autonomous because he cannot free himself from the all-pervading influence of the Other – his withdrawal is in fact a manifestation of his attachment to the Other.
Semi-autonomous existence. Here the Self paradoxically requires the presence of the Ideal to confirm his rejection of it: this entails a life of inauthenticity if he continues to remain the closed form of awareness and be disdainful of its ideals. He has dissociated himself only partially from the givenness of the Ideal and its manifestations.
Possible development to full autonomous existence. Here the Self breaks from the givenness of the Ideal having gained the ontological strength through his earlier scepticism to engage and to challenge the Ideal rather than to dissociate himself from it. The beginnings of the cessation of estrangement appear when, in engaging with the Ideal, he either appreciates it in a new light and gains the ontological support it can offer; or he seeks actively to establish his ontological life in the open mode of authentic existence.

B   *THE UNHAPPY CONSCIOUSNESS*

(1) The individual feels estranged, cut off from the means to attain the Ideal. He strives to overcome the undesirable (Durkheimian) anomic effects that estrangement produces. This does not necessarily imply that the individual lives in an anomic society as McClosky and Schaar (1965) suggest. Instrad, his anomie may be ontologically founded. This state has associations with Hadja's 'rejection *by* society' (1961), Streuning and Richardson's 'perceived purposelessness' (1965), Fromm's 'self-alienation' (1963), Johnson's 'reified, projected relationships' (1973), and Tillich's 'estrangement as sinning' (1957), i.e. one is aware of God's Will but falls into sin through a lack of courage to carry out His commands.

(2) Here the person exposes his Self to face the force of the Other in an attempt to gain unity with, or comprehension of, the higher Ideal which could join the Self and Other together in reciprocity (or Spirit), and which will provide an externally based purpose and meaning to one's life.

(3) One requires considerable ontological strength to sustain a reciprocal interaction with the Other. This courage is derived from a belief in the authenticity of non-autonomous existence, or unity, with the Ideal. He does not desire an open authentic existence because of the lack of ontological support associated with it.

(4) The estrangement of the Unhappy Consciousness takes the form of Seeman's (1975) six categories of 'alienation'. These are the subjective awareness of powerlessness, normlessness, isolation, cultural estrangement, social isolation, and self-estrangement (feelings of personal worthlessness). That is, these feelings arise because the Self desires involvement but is denied it, or fails to attain it.

(5) *The three forms of existence open to the unhappy consciousness*
Non-autonomous existence. The Self's unity with the Ideal can arise either through Hegelian self-alienation, Christian devotion, e.g. Tillich's point that estrangement can be overcome through 'Grace' (Tillich 1957 v.2), or through the foundation of a transcendental logic (Ouspensky 1970). Non-autonomous existence gives the Self the full ontological strength to be aware of open forms of authentic life, and yet prefer the richness offered by a belief in an Ideal that fulfils his existence and allows him to transcend his estrangement.
Semi-autonomous existence. The Self uses ontological supports founded on a belief in the Ideal to affirm his own ontological strength. Thus the modern theological view of God is that He is an event in communication with whom one can enter a dialogue to enrich one's life and not simply an object of worship (e.g. Jensen 1969).
Full autonomous existence. Here, in the closed system, this form of existence is not desired, because estrangement of the Unhappy Consciousness produces a state of 'fear of freedom' (Fromm 1960) which can induce anomie and despair. Alternatively, the Self seeing the hopelessness of attaining the Ideal may turn to scepticism – the beginning of an alloplastic activity that questions the validity of the Ideal and can eventually lead the Self out of estrangement.

4

Alienation and estrangement in the open form of authentic awareness

Introduction

I said in the previous chapter that certain social scientists, Seeman (1959) among them, considered their use of the word 'alienation' to be derived from Marx's analyses of the term as found in his youthful, or pre-*Capital* writings, especially the *Excerpts from James Mill's Elements of Political Economy* and *The Economic and Philosophical Manuscripts*[1] both written in 1844 in Paris when Marx was twenty-six years old. In fact, the terms alienation (*Entäusserung*) and estrangement (*Entfremdung*) also occur frequently in his *Grundrisse der Kritik der Politischen Ökonomie – Rohentwurf (Rough Draft for the Outlines of the Critique of Political Economy)* generally called the *Grundrisse*,[2] written in the period 1857–58 and the work upon which were based his volumes of *Capital*.[3]

In this chapter I shall endeavour to make clear first, in what senses Marx himself used the terms alienation and estrangement, and second, what conditions, both ontological and socio-political, are

---

[1] This title was given to Marx's notes by the editors of the Moscow Institute for Marxism-Leninism: not, as Daniel Bell believed, by Marx himself. (See Bell in Labedz (ed.) 1962: 201.)
[2] As McLellan has noted in his preface to an edited version of the *Grundrisse* (1971: 2), Engels, along with many early Marxists, was apparently completely unaware of the existence of this Draft – it first appeared in a published form in German in 1939.
[3] The first volume of *Capital* was published by Marx in 1867.

required before man can exist authentically in the form of open awareness. A theme developed in this chapter is the little-understood point that Marx saw the act of surrendering, or alienating one's activity to another, as the primary *source* of estrangement. Furthermore, I wish to show that Marx had, within his writings on the notion of private property, a fair conception of the ontological significance of this alienation as well as its more obvious socio-political consequences.

The nature of man's actions in the open form of existence

In contrast to my analysis of the aetiology of estrangement in the closed form of authentic awareness, it is not necessary to construct a series of the forms of epistemological awareness between the Self and the Other that predetermine estrangement, because Marx argued that estrangement arose out of one specific relationship; that which we have seen as manifest in the Lord-Bondsman interaction, the surrender to another of one's liberty to act for oneself. Developing this argument further I shall suggest that this surrender is not only representative of an estrangement specific to the capitalist-worker relationship, but is the basis of all forms of unbalanced person-to-person interactions where one individual gains ontological strength by opposing another. Authentic existence in an open system can only occur, I contend, when the individual reciprocates with, rather than oppresses, another. This reciprocity is what Marx saw as the basis for the truly social nature of man, or as he called it in his early writings, man's species-being (*Gattungwesen*).

Marx did not use the expression 'species-being' in his later writings because of its abstract overtones; instead, to make the active concrete origins of interpersonal reciprocity clearer, he chose to describe man as a *social individual*.[4] This term has quite specific connotations for Marx: to be truly social was the hallmark of authentic life, where man interacted directly with other men and not through false mediators which reduce reciprocity to an estranged exchange of social tokens. The most notable of these mediators is money, and in a forthcoming section of this chapter I shall examine how Marx came to appreciate that the presence of money as capital undermines the real social nature of the community by becoming the abstract basis of interaction between people and their activity, their labour. Capital is both the outcome and perpetrator of estranged (*entfremdet*) social relationships, a dialectical interaction that arises out of the alienation, the surrender, of one's

4 e.g. In the *Grundrisse* (1973: 541, 652, 711).

work to another person who then appropriates it and perceives it as his own private property.

However, let me emphasize the complement to Marx's point. Man's behaviour is not simply straightforward activity based on external socially based perceptions, his actions must derive also from an awareness of himself and his inner requirements, or as I call them, his own ontological aspirations. Without this awareness man is less than the animals; even they actively explore the environment and, as I showed in the comments on the responses of the active and passive kittens to the 'visual cliff', they need to link the sensuous perception of events to their own actions. However, if man were to act merely in blind response to the 'givenness' of his environment, physical or social, he would be at the mercy of his senses. He would be as one who:

'Follows his natural desires uncontrolled in the sixfold sense sphere and eats his fill with ravenous delight among the five sensual pleasures . . . all because he is lacking in wisdom and in the knowledge of the truth. He fails to reflect adequately and to understand the experiences of life for what they really are.'

(From the Pali Texts in Ling 1970: 135)

'Reflecting adequately' in the *closed* form of authentic awareness is equivalent to attempting to comprehend the Ideal, awareness of which allows full ontological development; but in the *open* form of awareness this reflection serves to make man's life activity itself an object of his will and consciousness. Awareness of his conscious life activity is not a determination with which man directly emerges, Marx argues (1975: 328). Conscious life activity, the awareness of the ontological significance of his own actions, arises through one's unestranged praxis with Others and the environment. It enables man to become a species-being, a social individual, because his own life is an object for *him*, not for an abstracted Ideal or a Lordlike Other. In this form of awareness Marx believes man is truly creative, and not simply in the manner of animals who produce and work to a biologically determined plan for their immediate needs and their sensuous gratification.

AUTHENTICITY IN THE OPEN FORM OF AWARENESS AND THE IMPORTANCE OF COMMUNICATION AND DISCRIMINATION

Marx's views on the emergence of self-consciousness are similar in principle to Hegel's: both were interested in the processes and mechanisms of the genesis of man's communication with other men and their common environment. Man, as he interacts with the world about him, gains awareness of other beings, together with the recognition of himself as a being similar to those other persons. This two-fold awareness is an inseparable aspect of the same process that allows man to realize his species-being in his self-consciousness. One of the crucial differences between the two ways of perceiving man's relationship to his environment is Marx's rejection of the notion of Spirit, as the force which allows the individual to transcend his self-consciousness in isolation, to attain authenticity. Marx, as a representative of the open form of authentic awareness, argued that man's self-conscious productive activity alone is sufficient to constitute the unestranged reciprocity that founds one's authenticity in species-being. This awareness of his species character as a social individual is not confined to his personal ontological development but extends to that of the species as a whole, the community. Ollman has strongly emphasized this point in his discussion on the difference between labour as productive activity for the individual and labour as creating a 'social relation' (Ollman 1976: 268). Thus in the open form of authentic awareness the power of man's self-consciousness over that of the animals is that he can conceptualize his relationship to his environment and other people as that which enables him to *act* and work as a member of a community, in contrast to the closed form of awareness that uses conceptualization both as the basis of awareness of one's estrangement and as the means of conquering it.

However, this is not to suggest that society produces man *simpliciter*, for, although a superficial reading of some sections of *Capital* may seem to support such a claim, Marx has shown us in his *Economic and Philosophical Manuscripts* that there was a dialectical interaction between the two. Thus, 'just as society itself produces man as man, so it is produced by him' (Marx 1975: 349);[5] an awareness of the dialectical interaction between man and society is essential to avoid establishing 'society' as an abstraction over and against the individual, a tendency evident in the writings of the social contract theorists. Marx repeatedly emphasized that man's individual life and his species-life were not two distinct things however much 'the mode of individual life is a more particular or a more general mode of the species-life, or species-life a more particular or more general individual life' (Marx 1975: 350). This viewpoint has its modern manifestation in the writings of the 'Social Action' theorists in sociology (e.g. Silverman 1972).

The significance Marx attached to man's awareness of his species-

[5] Marx's emphases, of which there are many in his writings, are generally omitted here.

being is thus two-fold: his interaction with others and with the natural environment immediately, without the mediation of an Ideal, enriches both the individual *and* the world he lives in. Marx's concern for man's species-being as a social individual is at heart a study of *perception;* an exploration of how man perceives and acts upon his environment to help us understand how the development of a person's discrimination and knowledge of the interactions and forces around him ensure that he does not become a passive element in a system or environment he cannot comprehend, and which seems to oppose him. Wilden (1972) has seen this key aspect of Marx's work as an attempt to uncover how communication with our ecosystem creates the entities and forms that allow us to grasp the nature of our lived-in world. Similarly Ollman (1976: 87) has pointed out that Marx's studies of sense perception are not merely confined to the interaction of man's five senses with nature, but are based upon a broader theory of man's relationship to all aspects of the social and natural environments.

That the more one is aware of one's connexions with the surrounding natural and social environment, the richer is one's knowledge of that environment and oneself is now a familiar point, but it was an important basis for Marx's subsequent analyses on the significance of alienation (*Entäusserung*), because when this natural interaction between Self and environment or other people breaks down through the act of alienating one's activity to another, one is then faced with man's estrangement (*Entfremdung*) from his fellow men and his species-being. Furthermore, without an appreciation of the different social forces that influence man's perception one could not understand the significance of the concept of false consciousness to Marxian thought, a form of estranged awareness akin to a sincere belief in the validity of undialectical Understanding as a perceptual tool.

In the foregoing sections I have sought to give a brief indication of the nature of existence in an open form of authentic life by way of introducing the reader to the framework within which Marx's early works is set. We shall see, both in the analyses of Marx's critiques of alienation and estrangement and in Sartre's work on the influence of the Other, that there exist powerful economic and social forces which, in their inertia, hinder the attainment of an open form of authentic life. These forces, coupled with the strong ontological need for a guiding Ideal to give one's life a meaning, present almost overwhelming opposition to the attainment of open authenticity. Marx's vision of an open society, I fear, must remain as such both until the elements that inhibit its materialization are understood and until the individual is ontologically secure, or courageous enough to be able to exist without externally based ontological support. This chapter, then, does not seek to prophesy about the nature of open authentic existence, instead it specifies its parameters and tries to clarify some of the circumstances that, intentionally or unintentionally, prevent this form of awareness from emerging. We have seen in Chapter 3 how estrangement and alienation are inevitable consequences of ontological development in the closed form of authentic existence: this chapter shows how their presence represents a direct attack on the attainment of authenticity in its open form, but before the subtleties of Marx's work on alienation and estrangement can be discussed, two important issues should be clarified. The first concerns the relevance of these terms to his writings in his later years and the second centres around the possible confusion arising from the translation of the terms from German into English.

Problems arising in the interpretation of Marx's use of the terms 'alienation' and 'estrangement' in the open form of authentic existence

THE FUNDAMENTAL IMPORTANCE OF ALIENATION
(*ENTÄUSSERUNG*) TO BOTH THE EARLY AND LATER
WRITINGS OF MARX

There are those, and Althusser is particularly to be noted, who argue that the mature writings of Marx, based on his post-1844 work, are the result of a direct epistemological break from his early thinking and writing; the adjective 'mature' indicating the importance they attach to them. These Marxists, mistakenly I argue, perceive the term alienation in Marx's early writings as merely a 'humanistic' concept devoid of 'objective' and 'scientific' truth.

On the other hand, the idea of a 'break' is also held by those who emphasize the value of Marx's 'humanistic' earlier works in preference to the political and economic analysis of his later works (e.g. Tucker 1972). The naivety of the latter perspective can be readily exposed. The distinction emerges between the two periods of Marx's thought, Tucker surmises, as a result of Marx's 'colossal insight' that Hegelianism was about economics and he imaginatively suggests that this revelation must have hit Marx 'with the force of a lightning bolt out of the blue' (Tucker 1972: 119). However, although less sparkling, the reality is that even in his early writings Marx was using his analyses of Hegel's system to explore the modes of man's involvement with the forces of production, money, and the capitalist system generally.[6] Tucker, more remarkably, believes that one could readily interpret Marx's early attempts to analyse alienation and to develop a philosophical system as being subjectively based on his (Marx's) 'urge to be godlike' (Tucker 1972: 74). Mészáros suggests, accurately if unkindly, that to interpret Marx's work as a 'non-social, openly subjectivistic, psychological system is [to believe in] a myth which exists only in Tucker's imagination' Mészáros (1975: 335).

Less easy to dispose of is the emphasis given by those who prefer Marx's later works and who seek to reject their connexions with his earlier writings. Pospelova, for instance, in her preface to Volume 3 of the *Marx-Engels Works* (1975), suggests that the concept of alienation, while distinctive of the initial stages of Marx's work, was

'superseded to a large degree by other, more concrete, determinations revealing more completely and more clearly the significance of the economic relations of capitalism, the exploitation of wage labour.'   (Marx-Engels 1975: XVIII)

She believes that the term alienation was used later as a philosophically generalized expression of the exploiting, inhuman character of the social system. Opposing this view Coletti (editor of the 1975 edition of Marx's *Early Writings*) suggests that those who had been weaned on the mature Marxism with its clear emphasis on dialectical materialism were 'quite understandably vexed by a text [Marx's early manuscripts] treating problems about which "dialectical materialism" had nothing to say' (Marx 1975: 49). The 'mature Marxists' believed that while the use of the concepts of alienation and estrangement were originally necessary to counter the Hegelian use of the terms in their abstract form they were no longer required in Marx's later writings. Indeed, they argue that Marx himself used the term alienation derogatively in the *Manifesto of the Communist Party* (originally published in 1848): in fact, Marx's disdain was directed against the 'German literati' who placed their abstract philosophical interpretations upon the practical ideas generated by the French revolution of 1848; 'For instance beneath the French criticism of the economic functions of money, they wrote Alienation of Humanity . . .' (Marx-Engels 1973: 83). That is, Marx was objecting to the adoption of an abstract form of humanism which turned the concept of alienation into a state of existence without

[6] For example, Marx 1975, *Critique of Hegel's Doctrine of the State* (p. 89ff); *On the Jewish Question* (p. 219ff); *Excerpts from J.S. Mill's Elements of Political Economy* (p. 266ff); and numerous sections in the *Economic and Philosophical Manuscripts*.

analysing its origins or specifying its effects; a point he had made in his discussions on the concrete basis of species-being. To reject the importance of the actuality of the worker's alienation of his own productive activity would be to destroy the foundations of Marx's writings in the *Grundrisse*, where he uses the term 'alienation' frequently, and which was written ten years after the Communist Manifesto was published. Moreover, the significance of alienation in its practical or concrete sense (as surrender or divestment) is implicitly revealed in the Communist Manifesto itself where Marx points out that the working class 'cannot become masters of the productive forces of society, except by abolishing their own previous *mode of appropriation* and thereby also every other previous mode of appropriation' (Marx-Engels 1973: 58, emphasis added). It is to be realized that *capitalist* appropriation can only arise on the alienation (surrender) by the worker to the capitalist, of his right to create himself through his own self-directed activity, a point that is recurrently emphasized in the *Grundisse* (Marx 1973: 198, 515ff, 831ff), while under *natural* appropriation, man, by working on the environment, in reciprocity with others, utilizes it, thus freely developing both himself and his social nature.

Further, it may be noted that Marx's appreciation of the importance of the free self-directed nature of one's work caused him to reject the principle of the division of labour because it directed man's appropriative powers into narrow Other-directed activities. Marx's distaste for atomized functional work gave rise to his notorious remark that man ought to be able to hunt, fish, criticize, and so forth, as he wished (Marx 1965: 44). This comment is not simply an example of an utopian strain in Marx's thought as Eldridge believes (1971: 147). Ollman's analysis of appropriation in its non-capitalist form presents a fairer perspective on this remark of Marx's because he shows that it draws attention to the free self-developing aspect inherent in this range of activity and reminds us that communism as understood by Marx 'is the time of full personal appropriation' (Ollman 1976: 93) where the freedom of choice evident was to be emphasized and not the literal nature of the different activities.

Not surprisingly Marx himself (in v. I of *Capital*) explicitly rejected the idea of a 'philistine utopia' which he saw as the natural consequence of the Socialism of Proudhon (Marx 1974 (I): 161) not of his own writings. Those who prefer Marx's later works to his 'youthful' writings[7] consider that the terms alienation and estrange-

---

[7] Perhaps these people forget that Marx was actually forty when he wrote the *Grundrisse* which may, in time, be seen for what it is, the result of the most fruitful period of his life.

ment were reformulated by Marx under the heading of 'fetishism', a term he used recurrently in the volumes of *Capital*. To believe this seriously would imply an ignorance of the significance of alienation to Marx himself: it is Marx's alienation of his labour, giving rise to appropriation of his product by the capitalist, and precipitating the worker's subsequent estrangement from those products of his labour, that *creates* the fetishism of commodities. A fetish object is an inanimate object 'worshipped by primitive peoples for its supposed inherent magical powers.'[8] Through the use of this term Marx indicates the nature of the relationship of the worker to his product. Under capitalism commodities are reified and perceived in estrangement as external objects with a life of their own and over which the worker has no power or control: fetishism of commodities has its origin, as Marx points out in *Capital*, 'in the peculiar social character of the labour that produces them' (Marx 1974 (I): 77). That 'peculiar social character' is the *alienation* of one person's labour to another, the primary act that produces the commodity as an external object. Thus, the discussions on the fetishism of commodities, which occur frequently in *Capital*, can only be comprehended properly in awareness of the significance of alienation (as *Entäusserung*): failure to realize this is to study the concept of fetishism in its abstract, rootless form. Naturally, exponents of 'mature Marxism' who prefer studying fetishism, rather than alienation emphatically, even dogmatically, deny this crucial connection (e.g. Althusser and Balibar 1970: 17). Rose's article (1977) offers a good example of this sort of thinking: he, like Althusser, firmly believes in the presence of a 'break' in Marx's writings, thus is forced to analyse fetishism by abstracting it from its context in the alienation of man's labour. This method of study is itself a reification of fetishism as a concept and a highly undialectical approach to Marx's thoughts, one that can only be carried out in ignorance of the implications of Marx's writings in the *Grundrisse*.

Despite Mészáros's and McLellan's excellent work in showing that there are many other instances where alienation as a concept, if not a term, is used in Marx's later works (e.g. Mészáros 1975: 217ff; McLellan 1975: 58f), Althusser is one of the few writers still maintaining that there is an important difference between Marx's early and later or 'mature' works.

To devote further attention to this specific area of Marxist thought may require a brief apology to organizational theorists already on unfamiliar ground, but I wish to demonstrate that a consideration of the 'break' and its significance has an important

8 Concise Oxford Dictionary (Sixth Edition).

bearing on further discussions on alienation. If those who use this concept continue to be described as adopting a 'merely humanist' approach to social issues by those advocates of the 'break' then future studies in the field of organized labour and its effects on people may receive the same label.

The valid point the 'mature Marxists' wish to make is that the forces of exploitation and repression that can exist in the work context have an objective, material presence originating in our social history and which transcend humanistic and moral concerns. However, their over-emphasis on the power of these forces often leads them to an unwarranted disdain of the humanistic, psychological, side of work and to the undialectical treatment of man as a purely sociological phenomenon. Thus, Althusser has argued that the terms 'Human essence, Alienation, Alienated Labour', used by Marx in his early works to analyse philosophical issues, are altered and reappear, in objective form, in the *German Ideology* and all his subsequent writings as 'mode of production, relations of production, productive forces, social classes rooted in the unity of the productive forces and relations of production, ruling class/oppressed class, ruling ideology, class struggle etc.' (Althusser 1976: 108–09), terms that reputedly allow one to explore objectively the problems of a capitalist society.

Althusser and his followers see the former terms as applicable only in philosophical or ideological contexts; they are conceptual truths, that is, they have a *general* significance, while the latter are scientific truths, that is, of *specific* significance for an objective examination of the forces of capitalism. An objective science, Althusser argues, is the only adequate way to have a non-ideological, non-philosophical conception of man's relationship to the world, hence it is the only basis for a proper understanding of social history arising from the interaction between classes.

To uphold the principle of a 'break', Althusser argues that Marx's science is born, like any other science, out of an amalgam of ideological, political, and scientific thoughts that form what he terms the pre-history of a science. Once established, it sheds its origins and emerges a fully fledged science. By making this point Althusser hopes to convince us that Marx's early writings represent the foundation of his science, that of Historical Materialism and the supersession of these early works represent the period where this science has established itself and has formulated its postulates.

Rather defensively, he accuses those who object to this distinction in Marx's writings of founding their arguments on reactionary political grounds and suggests that the furore of their rejection of the 'break' indicates their horror at Marxism being called a science (Althusser 1976: 115). He fails to notice that the horror may be a response to his own particular interpretation of Marx's thought processes. He does not appear to realize either that Marx himself, in his early work, where he was already aware of the principle of open system (non-Ideal) awareness, was using the concept of alienation not as a general statement of man's relationship to the world but as a concrete expression, specifying a certain ontological relationship between man and his fellow men (arising from the surrender of one man's labour to another) and that existed in a particular political context.

Althusser is keen to emphasize the scientific as opposed to the ideological foundations of Marx's critiques because he believes, quoting Lenin, that there can be no 'objectively/revolutionary movement' if one's actions are not grounded in a scientific awareness of one's oppression (Althusser 1976: 116). That is, he feels that the presence of a science can counter the 'bourgeois subjective ideality' of the closed 'givenness' of society by establishing an objective analysis of the foundation of the superstructures of that society. However, Althusser's conception of the science of Historical Materialism is not presented simply as an antidote to ideological thought, nor is it based on positivist principles; it has its significance in that it tries to make clear that the history of man is not governed by an Ideal (as it was in the closed form of awareness in Hegel's system) but is to be understood as a 'process without a Subject' (Althusser 1976: 98), a process driven only by the 'motor' of the struggle between the social classes. He ought to have added, perhaps, that motors, no matter how powerful, require fuel, and the fuel of class struggle lies, as Marx's early work makes clear, in man's ontological awareness of the significance of the process of his alienation to another of his own productive, self-creative forces. Althusser's desire to establish the principles of a subjectiveless history is of value to our understanding of the nature of open systems of awareness but his error lies in focusing exclusively at the sociological or socio-political levels. Moreover, attempting to uncover an objective method for the analysis of history is, I suggest, a meaningless exercise; if history is truly subjectless it is, one might say, blind; that is, it is merely the sum of past events produced by many different ideological stances, each seeking to master the others. Their struggle *per se* produces history, but it is not possible to try to understand the causes and consequences of these struggles by analysing them 'scientifically' in a reputedly objective manner because man naturally *attributes* significance to events in order to give meaning to his present circumstances and if this attribution, this perspective, allows him to respond actively to his world then he may continue to believe in the significance he has given to those events.

Von Bertalanffy (1973) has pointed out that to understand scientifically the historical process one must use a nomothetic approach, that is, construct models; these permit deductions, explanations, and predictions, which in turn may lead to the construction of laws applying to the historical process (von Bertalanffy 1973: 116f). Althusser's emphasis on the presence of a motor of history (class struggle) makes the assumption that an understanding of this force will provide us with explanation and prediction in the nomothetic manner. However, most historians, von Bertalanffy notes, have rejected this approach preferring an *idiographic* one, that is, where history is simply 'a description of events which have occurred in a near or distant past' (von Bertalanffy 1973: 209). Description offers no ultimate explanation or underlying laws; to seek these is to revert to an ideological interpretation of history. The power of Marx's analyses of alienation and estrangement is that they offer a clear description of their presence as the source and result (respectively) of man's exploitation by the capitalist or Other-based system. To subsume the significance of these analyses into a questionable science of historical processes is to neuter their present-day validity by attempting to interpret them in the context of a narrow, undialectical nomothetic model. In doing this it may be forgotten that history, in the open form of awareness, has no meaning, no ultimate Ideal, in itself; it merely 'is' or rather 'was'. That is, if history is truly subjectless, it is truly objectless too; having no one 'motor' or underlying force in terms of which it can be analysed. It is, instead, the result of a series of interacting occurrences, or many little 'motors' each producing consequences that can only be understood fully in their own terms; and when one 'motor's' consequences interact with another's consequences, there arise meta-consequences until such a complex web of interactions are built up that to attempt to analyse their origins scientifically in terms of one 'motor', as Althusser does, is only to try to replace the 'bourgeois subjective ideality' with a 'working-class ideality', a valuable exercise in its own right but certainly not objective or scientific. Awareness of the conflict between the sexes and different racial groupings, both 'motors' of history, are ignored by Althusser, but as Firestone (1971), Millet (1971), and Martin Luther King (1969), among many others have shown, have profoundly influenced history and our understanding of it.

Thus, my contention is that Althusser's advocacy of the rejection of the early writings of Marx on alienation, through his belief in a 'break' between Marx's early and later writings, itself rests upon three main biases: ideological, sociological, and anti-Hegelianism, biases that are also found in much of the work in organization theory today.

(i) *Ideological.* An analysis of the antagonisms that create history cannot be objective because if an observer (for instance, Althusser) adopts a specific perspective through which the 'meaning' of the past can be reinterpreted (in terms of the interaction between class ideologies) then his awareness of history is itself formulated from a certain ideological standpoint: Althusser might have avoided this difficulty had he adopted a structuralist approach, one which, by concentrating on the conditions of evolution, change and interaction of social structures and sub-structures in all their complexity, could provide a richer basis for his theoretical understanding of the need to analyse the consequences, the history, of these interactions in their subjectless form. Yet Althusser, unaware of the ideological nature of his belief in one 'motor' of history specifically rejects the much less ideological approach of the structuralists (Althusser 1976: 129).

(ii) *Sociological.* If history is seen as the struggle between the ideologies of the oppressed and those of the oppressor, any attempt to analyse them at an exclusively sociological level is to abstract them from their personal origins, the same act of abstraction, as Marx has warned us, that led to the studying of society as a reified entity.

Antagonism between ideologies, between differences in perspectives, has its roots in the beliefs of the *individuals* adhering to those ideologies. To comprehend their significance and to attempt to understand how one ideology has preference over another it is necessary to complement a socio-political analysis with studies which attempt to understand the nature of the individual's ontological structure, because it is through their ontological attachment that ideologies find their force. If this understanding can be achieved then, as I have shown in the earlier comments on the Lord-Bondsman interaction, the abstract interaction between two forms of belief can be seen as the practical dialectical struggle, on one hand to *defend* an ideological position which provides an ontological protection and hides the insecurity of the oppressor and, on the other hand, to *attack* the same position because it represents ontological subjugation to the oppressed.

In the open system, one must seek ways of allowing both the oppressor's[9] and the oppressed's ontological development to progress beyond attachment or subjugation to particular ideological beliefs and the antagonisms that they produce; this is a task as much for the psychologist as for the sociologist, because if one wants to end conflict of an ideological nature, that is, to be able to live in the open form of awareness, as Marx desired, then each individual must be able to exist without the presence of an ideological prop to give his life a focus and meaning.

In the closed form of awareness the ending of the differences between ideologies can be attained by transcending particular ideologies through awareness of a unifying ultimate Ideal, but in the open form of awareness the opposite is desired, the end of ideology *per se*. Marx argued that this can only emerge through the growth of ontological reciprocity, or *love*. Love, as he sees it, ends antagonisms based on ontological insecurity and terror and where different perspectives are seen in terms of their socio-cultural values rather than as threats to one's ontological inadequacies.

(iii) *Anti-Hegelianism.* Hegel saw the purpose of history as the revealing and attainment of the Ideal in Absolute Knowledge through the awareness of Spirit. History, as a process, revealed itself in the awareness of the Ideal; thus, I called it a closed form of awareness, one's actions were to be understood, along with all history as the actualization of the Ideal. Althusser, an advocate of the open system, was particularly keen to see that the Idealism of Hegel did not extend into Marxist thought and, since he saw Marx's apparent use of Hegel's term *alienation* in the early writings, he (Althusser) appears to have felt it necessary to reject all of Marx's early works, failing to notice that Marx himself used the concepts of alienation and estrangement in a way radically different to that of Hegel, and had specifically criticized Hegel for his 'double error' in their use in an abstract form (Marx 1975: 384). The similarity of terminology between Hegel and Marx need not have misled Althusser and those others like him who believe that Marx's early work on alienation and estrangement was superseded by different conceptualizations in his later writings had they been fully aware that

[9] The ontological terror felt by the oppressed in the face of the oppressor can be alleviated through an awareness of others in the same plight as oneself. This collective force provides a focus for rebellion by offering ontological security.

Marx's early work sets out a programme of critiques based upon what I have called the open form of awareness, in direct opposition to Hegel's analyses in their closed form perspective. In the open form of awareness, alienation was not to be understood in terms of some Idealist humanism but as the origin of a specific ontological relationship between the oppressor and the oppressed.

PROBLEMS IN THE TRANSLATION OF THE TERMS *'ENTAUSSERUNG'* AND *'ENTFREMDUNG'*

One of the sources of confusion about the concept of alienation and, to a lesser degree, that of estrangement lies in the uncertainty over what the terms mean.

It may be recalled that in the previous chapter we saw that the root of the German word *Entäusserung* means literally making something external to one, its usage in German literature has associations of divesting oneself of something, or selling an item of property. The English equivalent, *alienation*, is taken from legal terminology because, as I indicated in the previous chapter, it conveys the German meaning very closely: when one *alienates* a property to another, one transfers the right of ownership of that property. Marx himself has used *Entäusserung* to translate 'alienation' in his *Theorien über den Mehrwerth* (*Theory of surplus-value*) (written in 1862). He first quotes from Sir James Steuart's (1805) work on the *Principles of Political Oeconomy* and then adds his own comments:

' "In the price of goods, I consider two things as really existing, and quite different from one another; the real value of commodities, and the profit upon alienation" [Steuart] (p. 244). *Der Preiss der Waaren umfasst also zwei durchaus von einander verschiedne Elemente: erstens ihren wirklichen Werth, Zweitens den* profit upon alienation, *den Profit, der bei ihrer Entäusserung, ihren Verkauf realisirt Wird*[10] (MEGA 1977 II/3.2: 334)

Thus the use of the term alienation (*Entäusserung*) in this context of divestment or surrender to another of one's labour was not only found in Marx's early works but present even in his thoughts five years before *Capital* was published.

The word *Entfremdung* on the other hand (the root literally

[10] i.e. 'The price of the goods therefore comprises two elements, completely different from one another, first their real value, second 'the profit upon alienation', the profit which is realized on their alienation, their sale.'

means 'making alien'), is a more general term used normally in the context of *estrangement* or separation from something. There is no implication of transferring any right from one person to another as there is with *Entäusserung* (alienation), a point that Milligan made in his translation of Marx's early works (Marx 1959: 11f). It is not yet widely appreciated that this important distinction is made by Marx both in many sections of his early works and in the later *Grundrisse*,[11] yet the difference is a vital one to be aware of, because one can then distinguish, as Marx did, between the profound political and economic significance of the term 'alienation', and the more humanistic implications of 'estrangement'. The blurring of the distinction between the two terms as used in Marx's early works is as much a fault of certain sections of Marx's own writings as it is of his translators. For instance, Bottomore's popular translation of Marx's early works (first published in 1963) became the main English text on these writings.[12] He points out, in his introduction to this book, that he translated

> 'both *Entäusserung* and *Entfremdung* as "alienation" (or, occasionally, "estrangement") since Marx (unlike Hegel) does not make a systematic distinction between them; Marx distinguishes between *Entäusserung, Entfremdung* (alienation) and *Vergegenständlichung* (objectification)'
>
> (Preface to Marx 1963: XIX)

Bottomore is inaccurate in assuming that Marx did not make a 'systematic distinction' between the terms *Entäusserung* and *Entfremdung*; certainly there are sections in the *Early Writings* (e.g. Marx 1975: 324, 326, 330) where *both* terms are used together but this was because Marx himself was convinced that *all* acts of alienation (*Entäusserung*), that is, all relinquishment of one's labour to an Other under the capitalist system, inevitably results in the estrangement and of the person concerned: he uses the terms apart often enough in the *Early Writings* alone to make this clear (e.g. Marx 1975: 169ff, 261, 266ff). The influence of Bottomore's translation is such that numerous writers using it see 'alienation' in the humanistic philosophical light that was only generally intended by Marx for 'estrangement' (*Entfremdung*). Plamenatz, for instance,

---

[11] Unfortunately M. Nicolaus, the English translator of the *Grundrisse*, does not always make the distinction clear. In selections from the text I have added the German words where appropriate.

[12] In fact, the first English translation of excerpts of the *Early Writings* was by H.P. Adams in 1940, with a subsequent complete text by M. Milligan published in Moscow in 1959, but only with a limited circulation – it is now widely available (1970).

uses the term 'alienation' to cover both estrangement and alienation (Plamenatz 1975: Chapter 6) and is thus able to suggest that Marx was uncertain about the causes of 'alienation' (1975: 148). Had he been aware of the distinction in the German he might have realized that the act of alienation *is* the cause, and estrangement its consequence. Ollman, in his otherwise valuable book, makes the same mistake, suggesting that for 'most purposes' *Entäusserung* and *Entfremdung* can be treated as synonymous even though they do have a 'difference in emphasis' (Ollman 1976: 132). Livingstone and Benton, the translators of a recent edition of Marx's early writings edited by Colletti (Marx 1975), *do* make the distinction between the terms, and Colletti himself in his Introduction to that edition draws attention to the importance of keeping them separate for a fuller appreciation of Marx's work of that early period.

Let me now justify my assertions that by the separation of *Entäusserung* and *Entfremdung* we find in the former term not only the basis for Marx's later writings but a key to the door through which one must pass to attain authentic existence in the open form of awareness.

The inevitable presence of alienation in a capitalist or Other-directed system

THE IMPORTANCE OF THE CONCEPT OF PRIVATE PROPERTY AS THE BASIS OF ALIENATION AND ESTRANGEMENT

I shall start with Marx's *Critique of Hegel's Doctrine of the State*[13] in which he seeks to show that Hegel, in applying the principles of his dialectical system founded in the *Phenomenology* to the political context, has mystified the nature of man's relationship to the state and its institutions, by treating the system as 'given' or closed. That is, Marx was objecting to Hegel's efforts to unite individual civil interests with political or state interests through the notion of the Ideal (represented in political terms by a politically neutral, hereditary sovereign). A vitally important aspect of Marx's critique of Hegel (and one that he raises again in *Capital* 1974, v.3: 615ff) centres around Hegel's concepts of *private property* and primogeniture, the principle that continues to ensure that through inheritance, property remains in private possession. Without understanding the sig-

---

[13] Written in 1843. Unless otherwise mentioned these titles are taken from Marx's *Early Writings* 1975 Edition (in English). The German text may be found in *Karl Marx-Friedrich Engels: Historische-Kritische Gesamtausgabe*, published between 1927 and 1935.

nificance of private property to Marx's reasoning it is impossible to grasp the importance of his terms *Entäusserung* and *Entfremdung*. Hegel had argued that under the law of primogeniture the wealth of the land and property among classes is:

'fortified against its own wilfulness, because those members of that class who are called to political life are not entitled, as other citizens are, to dispose of their entire property at will.'

(Hegel 1964, s.306)

Hegel had pointed out in an earlier section (s.65) that 'the reason I can alienate (*entäussern*) my property is that it is mine only in so far as I put my will into it'. If private property is necessary for the furtherance of the political development of the State then it becomes inalienable (*unveräusserlich*).[14] Marx countered that Hegel, in using this curious argument to justify the means (of primogeniture) in terms of its political end, is making 'the cause into the effect and the effect into the cause' (Marx 1975: 167). The reality, Marx argues, is that primogeniture represents the power of abstract private property both over the political state and over individuals who do not inherit that property. This implies that if private property is inalienable then the *right* to dispose of that property is itself alienable. Plamenatz has agreed with Marx that Hegel's defence of private property is 'lamentably inadequate', but cannot understand why Marx is so critical of private property. He suggests that Marx's events look 'like a wholesale attack on the institution of private property as undiscriminating as Hegel's defence of it' (Plamenatz 1975: 121). Plamenatz foolishly goes on to propose that Marx's desire to see the end of private property and his dislike of money as *the* form of social exchange was the consequence of the bitterness of similar 'poor men of great talent who devote their energies to work which brings neither money or worldly success'! (Plamenatz 1975: 122). If one understands the background to Marx's thoughts on private property in terms of the concepts of alienation and estrangement, then Plamenatz's remark can be treated with the disdain it deserves.

Marx, both in the *Critique of Hegel's Doctrine of the State* and in the *Grundrisse* (1973: 475), mentions the contrast between the simple Roman view of private property and that of the legal and political importance it had in Hegelian Germany: the presence of private property for the Romans was simply 'an inexplicable fact

---

[14] '*Veräusserung*' 'means the "praxis" or activity of alienation' (Notes, in Marx 1975: 430). Marx himself said that 'Die Veräusserung ist die Praxis der Entäusserung', i.e. 'Selling is the praxis of alienation' (Marx 1975: 241).

with no basis in law' (Marx 1975: 179). Anticipating my later arguments I contend that it *is* possible to understand the basis of the 'fact' of private property, not in terms of law or its political importance, but through an awareness of the ontological support it offers, a point intuitively grasped by the Romans. Marx never made this explicit, but his critiques of the assumptions underlying private property allow one to see that its abolition, necessary to end the estranging effects of the alienation of one's property[15] to another in a capitalist system, can only occur when an alternative is found to supplant the ontological security that possessions offer to people. As Marx himself argues, an alternative support does exist, through the emergence of man's mutual reciprocity or social interaction. What he did make explicit was that through the alienation of one's property to another a false, inhuman, relationship was established between the people involved, a relationship that had its reciprocity only in the presence of an external mediator, money.

MONEY AS THE ESTRANGING MEDIATING FORCE BETWEEN MAN

In his *Excerpts from James Mill's Elements of Political Economy* (1844) Marx agrees with Mill's comment that money is the medium of exchange but adds that money is not simply to be considered as externalized property; it includes the *estranged* human and social activity of man, his labour, because man has alienated the true mediating function of his activity in order to labour for the capitalist. Through this alienation, money as mediator destroys the natural relationship between things and man's dealings with them, because:

> 'Man gazes at his will, his activity, his relationship to others as a power independent of them and of himself – instead of man himself being the mediator for man. His slavery thus reaches a climax.' (Marx 1975: 260)

Man's slavery is to the god Mammon, because money is seen to have real external power over the dealings and interactions of man, but this power only exists because of the distorted way in which private property is understood and exchanged for other private property through the medium of money. The economists of Marx's day propagated this distortion by seeing society as a community of men having its true existence in terms of trading and exchanging

---

15 One's property includes one's *labour* in the capitalist system (Marx 1975: 287).

goods. Marx argued that they were not aware that this community was one based upon man's estranged relationship to man, that is, estrangement from their species-being; the community only exists in the presence of an external, artificial mediator: money, and relationships were in terms of man as private property holders, not as people *per se*. Further, this means that in their estranged form of relationship the exclusive ownership of something allows a person to 'preserve his personality and to distinguish him from other men', (Marx 1975: 266) an important realization of Marx because it shows, in our language, the ontological commitment that individuals have to private possessions. For instance, one may recall the number of suicides that followed the 'crash' of the New York Stock Exchange in 1929, when many people were suddenly stripped of their paper possessions. Their loss was much greater than the disappearance of the money itself; it represented the removal of a fundamental ontological prop. Without possessions they did not just have nothing, they felt as if they *were* nothing. Marx has shown, given the existence of private property and the strong attachment that man has to it as a source of *meaning* for him, that its alienation to another represents an act of selling, an alienation, of the Self of the possessor, a loss of some aspects of his personality, which then *causes* his estrangement from both himself and his property. Marx's seemingly interchangeable use of the terms in some sections of the *Economic and Philosophical Manuscripts* stems from the fact that *all* acts of alienation, in a system where private property exists, will lead *automatically* to estrangement. However, Marx, making the distinction very clearly, shows how this happens in a long passage worth quoting in full:

'then it follows [from the premise that private property is man's essential support] that the loss or sacrifice of that private property signifies the *alienation of the man* as much as of the *property* itself. We are concerned here only with the latter determination. If I cede my private property to another it ceases to be mine; it becomes independent of me, something outside my domain, something external [*äusserlich*] to me. I thus externalize, alienate [*entäussern*] my private property. I define it as *alienated* private property so far as I myself am concerned. But I only define it as something *alienated* in general; I renounce only my *personal* connection with it, I return it to the *elemental* powers of nature when I alienate it only from myself. It becomes estranged *private property* only when it ceases to be *my* private property, without at the same time ceasing to be *private property*, i.e. when it enters into the same relationship with *another* which it formerly had with *me*, in a word when it becomes someone else's private property.'

(Marx 1975: 266–67, his emphases)

In the capitalist system one is compelled to alienate one's property, which includes one's labour, to the Other, the capitalist, in order to survive, because in so doing one receives money in return for the alienation, which then allows one to enter into a relationship with others already in the system. I have outlined the main differences between alienation in a non-capitalist system and a capitalist system in Figure 4(1). It may be noted that the 'non-capitalist' act of alienation, although an important criterion of existence in the open form of awareness, is treated rather simply in this Figure; this is because I have not yet added the problems, both economic and psycho-social, that exist in the system. The Figure highlights the point that 'all man's advantages over animals become disadvantages when the natural objects to which he is related become the property of other men' (Ollman 1976: 151) and it shows how these disadvantages appear in the forms of estrangement and mutual distrust. Figure 4(1) also illustrates why Marx believed that the presence of private property was a sign of people's 'barbaric stupidity' (Marx 1975: 170) because instead of being able to interact freely with each other, people's relationships were founded on possessiveness and mistrust. Marx, as we shall see, argues that the undesirable presence of private property is rooted in the power that the economic system holds over natural social relationships but I wish to emphasize the equally powerful presence of individuals' ontological needs and weaknesses which are protected by the capitalist system. This protection exists because ontologically the capitalist system has the characteristics of a closed system. This is why it has been possible to designate the capitalist as 'the Other' because, although the capitalist of Victorian England does not exist as such now, the power of organized work systems over the Self still remains; the worker continues to alienate his labour to the organization, that is, it belongs not to himself but to the Other. The capitalist system, as a source of security for the individual, provides an Ideal, private property, which the individual may strive towards, thus *giving* the individual's life an external purpose and meaning instead of allowing him to *find* a truly personal meaning to his existence. Moreover, the system provides both the mechanism (the alienation of one's labour to another) and the presence of a mediator (money, the force that allows people to interact with each other) whereby that Ideal,

Figure 4(1) The nature of man's relationship to other men in open and closed work contexts

Work in a non-capitalist context
(open)
↓
Man's labour is for
himself as a social being
↓
Thus he may freely alienate his product because:

(1) his activity itself is the source of his ontological fulfilment: that is by working upon something he gives both form and personal particularity to that object of his creation, *and* enriches the texture of his Self through learning to perceive, or be aware of the object's subtleties and its possibilities

(2) others do not seek to possess his products, to make them their *own* property to fulfil their ontological *needs* but, instead, freely use them for their ontological *enrichment* as objects with which they can interact to affirm themselves
↓
Man's relationship to the products of his activity is an unestranged, immediate one because they affirm him rather than oppose him.

Having enriched his ontological awareness through his self-directed activity he may relate to other people directly without the need for abstract mediators (money) or distancers (role playing)

|

↓
Relationships are based on reciprocity, or love, between people not exploitation.

Work in a capitalist context
(closed)
↓
Man's labour is for the Other
(the capitalist) not for himself
↓
He cannot alienate his product freely because in the capitalist system his productive activity is for the Other not himself, since he has been compelled, through the power of the system, to alienate his labour to the Other.

Thus he loses an essential source of his ontological development; his activity instead of developing himself, affirms the Other's power over him, because the objects he produces are retained by that Other for its use to dispose of as it wishes, that is they become *its* private property
↓
Thus, because the worker is estranged, separated both from the products of his activity (because they have become the Other's private property) and the activity itself (because it has been alienated to the Other), it becomes vital for him to obtain some *concrete* manifestation of his activity. Money provides this, but cannot restore the worker's natural connexion with his activity: it merely is a substitute; that is instead of being able to relate to people directly through his productive activity he is compelled to interact with them in an abstract form, through trade, exchange and barter. His work is assigned an *arbitrary* exchangeable value by others, rather than having a personal inherent value in terms of his own self-development
↓
Relationships are based on mistrust, each trying to get the best 'value' out of the other.

private property, can be obtained. I suggest that the ontological effort required to break out of the system into open awareness is much greater than Marx realized. Not only must the economic system be changed but man's ontological dependence upon it also must be removed through his awareness of the capitalist system's estranging aspects and a realization of the possibility of open awareness as a social, or species-being.

However, not only has the demise of Victorian capitalism with its attendant, obvious, oppression become modified into the implicit presence of a Lord–Bondsman relationship between the Other, as organized work system and the Self as the individual, it has added a powerful psychological component. On one hand, while employment in an assembly line of a car plant may be seen as our present-day equivalent of working in a mill, can the same be said of other occupations, nursing and teaching for example, where the work itself provides a rich immediate sense of *personal* reward? That is, in these cases, the system offers a means both for self-actualization, to use Maslow's term, and the opportunity to help other people, factors which would appear to counteract the exploitative aspects of cruder forms of capitalist employment. If this is the case, then are organization scientists who attempt to introduce job enrichment and its equivalents to motivate workers in the more mundane jobs overcoming the estranging aspect of capitalism and negating Marx's critique of the significance of the act of alienation?

As an answer, I now consider in detail how the presence of private property, the key to alienation, brings about and perpetuates man's estrangement from his fellows, and we shall see that the introduction of job enrichment and similar ideas is akin to giving inmates of a mental home tasks of basket weaving, painting, embroidery, and so forth in an attempt to ensure that their dissatisfaction, boredom, and desire to leave is kept to a minimum. More positively, the emergence of psychological commitment to a job, for example nursing, and the underestimation by Marx of its significance, will be examined in a later section.

Private property and money as concrete manifestations of the loss of man's social existence or his species-being

Marx has suggested that a person already in possession of some private property may feel that he desires a portion of someone else's private property because some aspects of that other's property, he believes, will fulfil a want or express his existence more adequately. These two people may therefore mutually agree to alienate a portion of their private property to each other for their mutual benefit. Through this double alienation, a relationship is established between the two owners. However, they fail to appreciate, Marx argues, that by relating to each other on the level of their possessions as businessmen their interaction is the complete antithesis of a *social* relationship, because they are estranged from each other as people. This mutual alienation[16] of private property has significance not only for the estranged social relationship it produces but for the fact that it enhances one's ontological dependence upon another person, because each side of the relationship embodies some part of the existence of the self-productive activity, or labour, of the other. In Marx's words the property has lost,

> 'the exclusive distinguishing personality of its owner for the latter has alienated it, it has parted from its owner whose product it was and has acquired a personal significance for the new owner who has *not* produced it. It has lost its personal significance for its [former] owner.'   (Marx 1975: 268)

This loss of its personal significance is its estrangement from its original owner, an estrangement which, once established, is maintained through the presence of money as *exchange value*: that is, social relationships between men are based upon their economic standing, and labour, formerly the means of developing oneself through one's activity on the objects of the world, merely becomes wage-labour, or only meaningful in terms of its monetary value. As Marx points out in *Capital*, when labour is meaningful only as a source of exchange value it is merely 'human labour in the abstract' (Marx 1974, v.1: 46). In *unestranged* social existence,

> 'my labour would be the free expression and hence the enjoyment of life, [but] in the framework of private property, it is the alienation of life since I work in order to live, in order to procure for myself the *means* of life.'   (Marx 1975: 278)

That 'means' is money. I have already mentioned that for Marx, money included the estranged human and social activity of man. This estrangement has two elements: the first is that the presence of

---

[16] For Marx 'mutual alienation' of private property is the *estrangement*, the separation, of private property from its owner. His use of the two terms together is to be understood in this context: e.g. 'Through the mutual alienation or estrangement of private property, private property itself comes into the category of alienated private property' (Marx 1975: 267).

money alters the nature of the ontological relationship of man in the world by distorting his interactions with other men: people come to place more faith in money than they do in each other as people. In the *Grundrisse* Marx reminds us that Aristotle called money 'the dead pledge of society' (Marx 1973: 160) because of the social significance it acquires. In my terms, money becomes the only concrete evidence of his labour that is available to the worker, and as such has to become the substitute through which he seeks ontological fulfilment.

These abstract aspects of the estranging nature of money can produce a very definite form of behaviour, as Samuel Johnson has shown us in his description of London life in the eighteenth century:

'Slow rises worth, by poverty depress'd
But here more slow where all are slaves to gold,
Where looks are merchandise and smiles are sold;
Where won by bribes, by flatteries implored,
The Groom retails the favour of his lord.'

(London: A poem. 1738)

Not only does the presence of money have an explicit influence upon a man's relationship with another person, but it can also have equal, if less overt, power when one person depends upon another for credit. If someone lends money to another he expects to be repaid through the latter's industriousness, his labour guarantees to the money-lender a return on his investment; thus, as Marx points out, the content and nature of the borrower's life activity, the potential source of ontological enrichment, represents to the lender the certainty of his money being returned to him with interest; he merely evaluates his relationship with the borrower of his money in terms of that money, thus reducing the human aspect of the relationship to that of a function of the means that brought them together.

Fox (1974) has extended this point in his discussion of the presence of levels of *trust* between people in the work organization context; he relates trust to a distinction between the prescribed and discretionary elements of institutionalized work. An extreme low-trust situation would be where the worker has no decisions to make in his job and where his role is rigidly defined for him, that is, he is not permitted any personal discretion in how the job is to be done. Closer to Marx's point, he suggests, following Blau's work (1964), that high and low forms of trust are related to types of exchange. Clearly prescribed money-based or economic exchanges are characterized as low-trust interactions, whereas social obligations and interactions are high-trust because they have no abstract mediator (money) to define their parameters.

Increasingly in modern organized work, the presence of low-trust in an exchange relationship is likely to result from a lack of specific technical knowledge between the actors in the situation – where there is no knowledge there can be no 'feeling' either for the job or between the people concerned.

The second element in the estranging aspect of money arises from the traditional economists' belief that labour is *directly* the producer of money (Marx 1973: 225), that is, its self-developing expressive, immediate, aspects are ignored and in their place comes the assumption that one may be said to live only if one's labour is directed towards attaining the Ideal, private property, or its exchangeable equivalent, money. Thus, instead of the worker's estrangement being overcome through his self-directed activity upon the objects in his environment, his estrangement is affirmed even further because he gains no ontological strength to break away from the power of the Ideal either from his product or the act of work, the former having been alienated to the Other, the latter is carried out under the Other's direction for *its* benefit. All the worker receives, instead of ontological enrichment, is a wage: consequently 'his production is the production of nothing, his power over objects appears as the power of objects over him, in short he, the lord of his creation, appears as the servant of that creation' (Marx 1975: 266).

Both in sections of his early writings (Marx 1975: 269f, 327f) and in the *Grundrisse* (Marx 1973: 453f), Marx argued that the presence of wage-labour, that is, work carried out only for its value to the Other and not done as a self-enriching activity, has four consequences:

> '(1) The estrangement of labour from its subject, the labourer, and its arbitrariness from his point of view; (2) the estrangement of labour from its object, its arbitrariness *vis-à-vis* the object; (3) the determination of the labourer by social needs alien to him and which act upon him with compulsive force. . . . (4) the labourer regards the maintenance of his individual existence as the aim of his activity; his actual labours serve only as a means to this end.'
>
> (Marx 1975: 269)

It is the summarizing of the form that estranged labour takes, particularly in the 'Estranged Labour' section of Marx's *Economic and Philosophical Manuscripts*, that is most familiar to organization theorists who claim that their studies on 'alienation' derive from Marx's when at the very most they attend to the estranging consequences of Marxian alienation. Marx's own writings in this particular section (on 'Estranged Labour') are a compressed and powerfully presented set of ideas[17] worked out in more detail both in his earlier works and the later *Grundrisse*. It is in this section above all that he uses the terms *'Entfremdung'* and *'Entäusserung'* juxtaposed in such a manner that unless one was aware of the many instances when he uses them apart quite distinctly, as we have seen, their equivalence could be taken for granted, for example:

> 'So if the product of labour is alienation, production itself must be active alienation, the alienation of activity, the activity of alienation. The estrangement of the object of labour [i.e. the product] merely summarizes the estrangement, the alienation in the activity of labour itself.'   (Marx 1975: 326)

Yet there is a point to this apparent confusion: he is arguing that although he has been able to locate the origins of estrangement in the alienation of the individual's private property (and labour) to another, the present structure of society is the result of a complex interaction between alienation and estrangement and dialectical interaction between the two has meant that private, alienable property is estranged property, that is, separated off from its true social state, and that labour which results in estrangement is alienated labour, that is, where an individual has surrendered and externalized, the personal (ontological) meaning of his labour to another. Thus, private property is both affirmed by and arises anew from alienated labour, yet alienated labour is itself a consequence of private property. Money sustains this cycle of alienation, which in turn maintains man's entrangement from his product, his work, and from others.

The introduction of equal wages proposed by Proudhon, the French political economist, Marx saw as merely perpetuating this cycle by making society a capitalist in the abstract. Calling for the equalization of wages could only be made in ignorance of the interaction between man's alienation of his labour and the wage he obtained for it, and a crude response made in envy of other people's wealth, both personal and financial.

To clarify even further the nature of their interaction, Marx then used his critiques of political economy developed in the early

---

[17] To leave them in their rather truncated form was not Marx's intention: the manuscript is missing just after the point where he says he will take a closer look at the relationships between alienation, estrangement, products and other people.

writings to analyse specific aspects of the relationship between alienation of labour and money. We find many instances of this approach in the *Grundrisse*.

As I see it, Marx in his *Early Writings* had established the distinction between open and closed forms of ontological existence, and had clarified the significance of alienation of one's labour to the Other as the force that maintains both the foreclosure of awareness (through the loss of one's labour activity for *oneself*) and the perpetuation of the Ideal, private property. In his later writings he then turned to a detailed consideration of the interaction between the capitalist and the worker and sought to show that the worker's estrangement, ontologically and socially damaging in itself, was compounded by the actions of the capitalist.

For instance, in *Capital*, Marx drew attention to the capitalists' dislike of labour that was merely self-productive or ontologically enriching: if man's labour did not produce an object of utility, directly exchangeable with other similar objects then that labour was worthless – 'if the thing [produced] is useless, so is the labour contained in it: the labour does not count as labour' (Marx 1974, v.I: 131). Labour only has value in the eyes of the capitalist in terms of its alienability for money.

The presence of money thus adds to man's estrangement in two ways. First, at an individual level it represents a direct denial of the ontological value of man's self-productive labour in the face of the power of capital (accumulated money). The worker 'divests himself [*entäussert sich*] of labour as the force productive of wealth, capital appropriates it as such' (Marx 1973: 307). Thus, the creative power of the worker's labour now establishes itself as the power, the life-blood, of capital, that is as his own power turned against, and alien to, him. Second, at the social level I have already noted that the presence of the circulation of money as exchange value indicates that one's productive labour only has meaning in terms of another person's labour in its abstract, alienated (to the Other) form; but there is a further form of estrangement based on the fact that one's products are made not just to create surplus value but to fulfil the 'needs' of other people: similarly their products are specifically designed to cater to our wants. That is, man's interaction with another occurs at the level of the exchange of estranged products, created through the medium of estranged labour, and transformed in the form of an abstract mediator, money: 'Our mutual value then is the mutual value of our mutual objects. For us therefore man himself is worthless' (Marx 1975: 277).

Money's power, and thus ultimately the power of the capitalist system, together with the forms of estrangement that arise from that power, all derive from man's alienation of his labour to the Other. This connexion expressed pithily, but in places confusingly, in the *Economic and Philosophical Manuscripts* is clearly laid out in many sections of the *Grundrisse*; for example, the section quoted below comments both on the ontological aspects of alienated labour (labour has become a means not an end), and on its social implications:

'(1) . . . My product is a product only in so far as it is for others, hence suspended singularity, generality, (2) that it is a product for me only in so far as it has been alienated [*entäussert*], become for others, (3) that it is for the other only in so far as he himself alienates [*entäussert*] his product; which already implies (4) that production is not an end in itself for me but a means. Circulation [of money] is the moment in which the general alienation [*Entäusserung*] appears as a general appropriation, and general appropriation as general alienation [*Entäusserung*].'

(Marx 1973: 196)[18]

This makes it quite clear that first, alienation is not merely a humanistic term to label discontent as Althusser (1970) assumes, but it is the process, the means, which in the context of private property exchanged through the medium of money gives rise to estrangement, the separation of oneself from products, means of production, and other people; second, it highlights the central importance of the need to understand the *process* of alienation before one can appreciate the implications of Marx's extensive writings on money and, indeed, all aspects of political economy, in the volumes of *Capital*.

THE EXPLOITATION OF MAN AS THE DIRECT CONSEQUENCE OF THE ALIENATION OF ONE'S LABOUR TO THE CAPITALIST

However, the significance of the alienation of one's labour to another is not confined to the estranging aspects produced by the presence of money as an abstract Other-derived 'value' for one's work, a value substitution that cancels out the essential ontological, self-enriching aspects of labouring for oneself, nor is limited to the estranged social relationships that are built upon money as mediator. In the capitalist system, Marx argues, the alienation of one's labour leads directly to *exploitation*.

[18] German text to be found in *Marx-Engels Gesamtausgabe* (MEGA) (1977), 2: 111, p. 126.

Exploitation arises because the labourer does not receive an exact monetary equivalent for the object he has created through his labour[19] for the Other, because the latter uses the labour to produce an object, the product, *and* to create a surplus value, profit. The capitalist creates profit by ensuring that although the worker alienates his labour to him for the whole day, he produces enough goods to pay his wage in, say, half a day's work. Thus the other half-day represents the production of surplus value to pay for 'overheads', reinvestment, and so on. This means, as Habermas has also emphasized (1974: 221f), that the exploitation of labour is not to be considered solely in terms of unpleasant physical or mental conditions as modern organization theorists assume, but is found at the very foundation of the capitalist system. Without economic exploitation, capital could not be accumulated, labour could not be hired, private property could not be acquired, in other words the cessation of this exploitation would affect every aspect of modern western society. To rupture the foundation of our society by ceasing exploitation represents the consequences of moving from a closed system, with its Ideal as private property, to an open system where the power of a person's labour is not abstracted from him, but remains with him for his ontological development and social fulfilment.

It is this analysis of the non-humanistically based description of the exploitation inherent in the alienation of one's labour to the Other that at once sets Marx's use of the term 'alienation' aside from the jaded and shallow application it receives in organization literature. The latter focuses on psychological exploitation: unpleasant work, meaningless tasks, isolation from fellow men, and the frustration, the powerlessness, one feels in the face of the Other. This is but a microcosm of the exploitation that Marx had uncovered. When a person worked for the Other, and received a salary or wage in return, his labour was being used to make money, and no matter how pleasant the job appeared, unless the work was for himself, he was being exploited, used for the Other's ends.

There is thus an irony in that the organization scientists' eagerness to overcome 'alienation' actually justifies the macro-exploitative nature of the relationship between the employer and employee because these organization scientists are, in their efforts, making capitalist Other-based labour tolerable. Certainly, the removal of psychologically unpleasant work is valuable in itself. No-one wants to do disagreeable work, but the desire to 'de-alienate'

[19] Marx used the term 'labour-power' in his later writings, i.e. the power to yield a surplus using 'labour-saving' mechanical devices.

people, quite apart from being carried out in ignorance of the different ontological significances of 'alienation' or more accurately, estrangement, is effectively denying the validity of an open system perspective, because it encourages people to cease questioning the *need* to work for the Other. That is, 'de-alienation' delays the growth of open awareness through the organization scientists' efforts to induce conformity or acceptance of the closed, Other-based form of awareness.

Revolution as a means of transcending alienation and estrangement – the need to consider psychological as well as socio-political consequences of sudden change

Marx believed that the maintenance of the closed nature of the socio-economic system exists at all levels, from the political to the personal, and one of the most effective ways to rupture the self-perpetuating nature of the system was, he thought, through a 'revolution of the proletariat', that is through the direct action of those oppressed by the Other. He believed that this revolution must occur initially at the *political* level to be effective in altering the nature of the superstructure of the system; an alteration which then permits a *social* revolution, by which he means the change from closed Other-directed awareness to open, social awareness. In principle, Marx's desire for revolution is quite logical, because unless their is a high-level political change, the individual in the system will continue to live in estrangement or false consciousness,[20] and as psychoanalytic studies have shown, will continue to use the psychological mechanism, repression, to maintain himself in its closedness. In practice, however, to hope for a revolution based solely on political and social perspectives is to omit consideration of the ontological aspects of those people who create the social whole. Radical change is only truly possible, I contend, when the development of political and social awareness is coupled with an appreciation of the ontological difficulties that radical change implies: to be able to withstand the psychological effects of such a change one requires a considerable degree of ontological strength, that is the courage to live in the uncertainty and possibilities offered by an open form of existence. Marx himself gave an indirect clue to the need for ontological strength as the basis of political awareness by pointing out that 'political understanding is produced by social

---

[20] Or, as I have called it, 'blind sincerity' to avoid the value judgement 'false', and to make the point that from the individual's perspective his actions are sincerely based within the *limitations* of his awareness.

well-being' (Marx 1975: 417). Lest it be thought that Marx's only solution to the exploitation within our system was a naive belief in revolution (as Plamenatz has suggested (1975: 181)), it is worth noting that he did argue in the *Grundrisse* that the bases for radical change were inherent in the capitalist system itself because capital, through its own self-generating momentum, will reach a stage where it creates a 'large amount of disposable time' (Marx 1973: 708). This free time arises from the dilemma that faces the capitalist when he becomes aware of the dialectical interactions between the worker and capitalist; the capitalist realizing that on one hand he must minimize labour costs thus 'presses to reduce labour time to a minimum', yet labour time is on the other hand the 'sole measure and source of wealth' (Marx 1973: 706). If he retains a surplus of labour time to produce more goods, that is, to convert circulating capital into fixed capital (property and other assets), a situation of surplus production may arise, a surplus that cannot be consumed.[21] To absorb this surplus labour time Marx argues that 'the mass of workers themselves must appropriate their own surplus labour' (Marx 1973: 705), that is, they are to use their work for *themselves* instead of alienating it to the capitalist. In this way one's leisure time arises out of the capitalist's inability to absorb all the labour time potentially available, together with the worker's increasing desire for more free time. Marx believes that ultimately a stage will be reached where one's work time is governed by *social* needs rather than economic forces, an issue emphasized by Sherman and Jerkins (1981).

Although it is not my intention to explore the specific aspects of political and economic changes necessary to permit the radical alteration of the structure of the given system, I iterate the contention that their change, no matter how induced, is still subtly coercive to the individual, because, in the language of psychiatry, change based on 'visionary realities constitute threats to satisfactory ego development' (Glass 1974); that is, unless the people who compose those political and social groups are psychologically ready, both to *need* the change and at the same time to *sustain* the openness offered by being aware of its consequences in terms of their ontological perspectives, they simply will be moving from ontolo-

---

[21] Marx did not anticipate the emergence of the 'consumer society' which consumes for the sake of it. Bookchin has pointed out (1974: 37) that here 'immiseration takes a spiritual rather than an economic form – it is starvation of life', while Veblen has emphasized the social pressures that exist to maintain consumption of 'luxury' or superfluous goods. 'Since the consumption of these more excellent goods is an evidence of wealth, it becomes honorific; and consequently the failure to consume in due quantity and quality becomes a mark of inferiority and demerit' (Veblen 1935: 74).

gical dependence upon one Ideal to that of another. Thus, the purpose of radical change to allow ego expansion or self-development by carrying out one's activity for oneself in a social context, becomes distorted to that of directing one's activity towards the maintenance of the new political Ideal, as seen in Stalinist Russia for instance (Nove 1972: 142ff). That is, without a psychological understanding of the significance of change, analyses focused at the political and social levels have to be treated with some caution.

Freud appreciated this lacuna in Marx's analysis of revolution:

'The strength of Marxism clearly lies not in its views of history[22] or the prophecies of the future that are based on it, but in its sagacious indication of the decisive influence which the economic customs of men have upon their intellectual, ethical and cultural attitudes . . . [but] it is altogether incomprehensible how psychological factors can be overlooked where what is in question are the reactions of living human beings.'

(Freud 1973: 215)

Thus it is necessary to understand the relationship of these people involved with the system from their point of view, to study the ontological constructs they use; that is, to see how they perceive their being-in-the-world because economic, political and social changes, particularly of a sudden nature, will cause a profound disturbance to their awareness of the world they live in and take for granted, as both Toffler (1970) and Berger (1966) have testified. Brown (1959) and Ollman (1976) have also expressed awareness of this problem by suggesting that an understanding of people's 'character structure' has to be added to Marx's conceptual framework before radical change can become viable. What I have discussed in terms of ontological structures and the forms of sincerity and authenticity, Ollman sees as aspects of the organized habits in which most people lead their lives and which arise from the influence of societal *mores* and existing political conditions. For him these 'character structures' and habits must be seen as 'exercising a separate influence on how we will respond to future events and conditions' (Ollman 1976: 248). That is, there may be a natural reluctance from *within* a person to encourage radical change if it affects his ontological structure – this reluctance Fromm (1960) has described as the fear of freedom.

---

[22] I have already expressed reservations about the Marxists' nomothetic approach to history, through my criticisms of Althusser's work.

THE IMPORTANCE OF THE ALTERATION OF ONE'S
EPISTEMOLOGICAL FRAMEWORK AS A COMPLEMENT TO
ONTOLOGICAL AWARENESS FOR REVOLUTIONARY CHANGE

I appreciate that some people may not wish a change or disruption in their perception of the world, because they have already established in 'the inner theatre of their mind' a fantasy escape world with a richness that is in contrast to the poverty of their everyday lives. Routine frees their minds to indulge in escape, and any real effort to disrupt their lives represents a threat to their fantasy world (Cohen and Taylor 1978). Berger is less tolerant of these flights from freedom or open awareness and states that while society provides for the individual a gigantic mechanism by which he can 'hide himself from his own freedom' (Berger 1966: 167), this tends to forestall the transformation of consciousness that Berger, like us, believes is the true basis for all revolution. What is desired, he believes, is that the person living in the given structure of society, must experience 'ecstasy', that is, not some sublime experience but a standing-outside (literally *ekstasis*), a distancing from society, not to be seen as an end in itself that would merely represent the estranged state of the sceptic to be used, but as a force that 'transforms one's awareness of society in such a way that givenness becomes possibility' (Berger 1966: 157); in other words, closure becomes openness. The ecstatic act is the equivalent of the individual undergoing an ontological break because it represents a freedom from the structures around which he had constructed his awareness of being-in-the-world.[23] This was how the mediaeval mystics saw ecstasy, as de Guibert (1954) has pointed out; it was equated with the stepping outside, a relinquishment of, the existing structures of the Self to allow the presence of God to make itself manifest. Although I am concerned here with ecstasy in the open form of awareness, it may be noted that it produces the same ontological effects as occur in the closed, God-as-Other, system; namely, the presence of a mixture of joy and fear. Joy, because in openness the Self finds a new self-awareness or consciousness that transcends the limitations of the old; and fear because, before that new awareness can establish itself, the prevailing ideologies and constructs that the Self has used must be changed, thus leaving him without reference points around which he can give his being-in-the-world a meaning. That is, a revolution that can abolish private property together with the alienation and estrange-

[23] Sartre also uses the term 'ekstasis' to describe the method whereby the Self comes to know itself and its presence in the Other; the process is very similar to the development of awareness in Hegel's system except, of course, in the former there is no Ideal towards which awareness is directed.

ment inherent in its presence not only entails a high level of ontological preparedness, but it requires, to sustain the transaction from closed to open forms of awareness, an epistemological revolution or a change in our methods of knowing the world. Our *ekstasis* can only be complete when we have formulated a new, open way of perceiving the world, a perception that is based on awareness of the Heraclitean flux in the system, metasystem, and subsystem interactions, to show that the meaning and the significance of such systems lies within themselves, their praxis and dynamic change rather than in terms of an absolute Ideal which is inherently static. Wilden has summarized some of the changes of epistemological perspectives required in the move from closed to open awareness:

'from stasis to process, from entity to relationship, from atom to gestalt, from aggregate to whole, from heap to structure, from part to system, from analytics to dialectics, from closed systems to open systems, from causality to constraint, from energy to information, from bioenergetics to communication, from equilibrium theory to negative entropy – in a word, from atom to system and thence to ecosystem.'   (Wilden 1972: 241)

The epistemological jolt that is entailed in the abolition of private property, the Ideal of the closed capitalist system, may be such that unless the individual is ontologically prepared for it, a considerable feeling of anxiety and fear may arise. Thus to reduce the feeling of helplessness, the individual actively seeks to reestablish the validity of a closed Ideal. But this search presents a particular dilemma, because if that Ideal has been abolished, his search is fruitless – his actions and unease are now that of the Unhappy Consciousness: that is, he is aware that he is in some way inadequate without the guidance of the Ideal, yet that Ideal having itself been transcended by other individuals now no longer affords him the meaning and social support that it did before its abolition. Yet, if he does reposit its existence he does so by affirming his epistemological framework against those who have developed open-ended epistemologies. Thus, in his efforts to find personal meaning in the world, he has lost contact with his social meaning: a state close to that of anomie. In extreme cases this may lead to the withdrawal of the person to protect his perception of the world against interference from others, as in the case of schizophrenic awareness. Thus, the highest act of social reciprocity, love, is particularly terrifying to these people because they feel that they are being engulfed by the person who wishes to love them. The schizophrenic feels that the lover is

attempting to take his Self into his (the lover's) possession, and if
that happens the schizophrenic feels that he may lose all sense of
self-identity because he lacks the ontological strength to withstand
the lover's intrusion into his Self. This perceived intrusion into the
very being of an individual is not confined to this extreme case. It
may also arise, as Sartre argues (Sartre 1966: 340ff), where, through
the Other's *look*, another person, perceiving that look, has some
aspect of himself revealed to himself. If that person is caught by the
Other at some socially unacceptable task he may feel shame because
the look reveals that 'I recognize that I *am* as the Other sees me'
(Sartre 1966: 302). Perhaps the fear of the schizophrenic is in part
based in an ashamedness that his unusual epistemological structures will be revealed to the Other.

However, if the individual is psychologically prepared to change
from a closed form of awareness to an open one, he can be helped
further to withstand the ontological shock it entails by being aware
of his *social* nature. Thus, instead of viewing other people as Others,
that is as external, powerful forces to which the Self must submit,
an individual comes to realize that, as a social being, his mode of
existence with them is *reciprocity*. I have shown, in the closed form
of authentic life, that the awareness of spiritual (reciprocal) existence is achieved through the knowledge, based on Reason, of the
Ideal; while in the open form of awareness it is founded not on an
essence, 'an internal dumb generality' (Marx 1975: 423), but on
man's unalienated praxis, his self-directed activity which enriches
both his own ontological awareness and his social existence. That is,
it is a *natural* occurrence in his development unless he is forced, in
the alienation of his labour to another, to live in estrangement from
other people through false mediators, for example, money. Thus
Marx's apothegm, 'workers of the world unite' has a double significance: by uniting with each other, people create a collective force
powerful enough to establish their own demands against those of
the Other, the capitalist, and this union will also serve as an
ontological support when the existing props of the capitalist society
are destroyed and when man can live in open unestranged awareness. To summarize my point, Marx himself wanted the joy of
openness and freedom to exist between men: this is the ultimate
reason for his insistence on the necessity of the abolition of private
property. He knew that the removal of private property in itself is
meaningless unless it represents an emancipation of man's senses,
attributes and labour power from the influence of the Other, but
what he was uncertain of was the nature of the process through
which emancipation could be achieved. Because private property

was dialectically related to the alienation of man's labour to another, which in turn led to man's estrangement from his products and his fellow men, he believed that its abolition through socio-political means could free man and allow him to affirm himself by objectifying the specific character of his individuality in an open, natural social context, where one's work complemented that of other persons rather than competing with it. But none of this openness can be maintained unless the individual is able to withstand the psychological trauma that exists concomitantly with a break into openness. By adding to Marx's analysis a psychological level I do not seek to reject the value of his work, particularly on the nature of exploitation; on the contrary, I believe that it increases the possibility of the emergence of existence in open awareness, where, as Marx has poetically phrased it, instead of living in estrangement from each other, my existence can be 'confirmed both in your thoughts and your love' (Marx 1975: 277).

Special constraints that face a revolutionary or radical change from closedness to openness

I have pointed out that to attain open awareness one must be prepared to face both strong ontological and epistemological shocks, the force of which may prevent the individual from being able to make the transition from closed to open existence, but this is not all that man has to confront.

THE INEVITABLE PRESENCE OF THE PRACTICO-INERT

Sartre has shown (1976) that there exists a further force, rooted in man's praxis itself, that can unintentionally create structures or totalities which through their own praxis act against man's attempts to exist in open awareness. Like Marx, he argues that in his directed activity or praxis man works upon inert matter or objects in their natural state, both to develop himself and to enrich and particularize those objects with his meaning and significance. However, this praxis also inevitably leads to the creation of social *institutions*, that is committees, organizations, and bureaucracies, which then appear to have a power or life of their own above and against the praxis of the constituent individuals. This power is located in the *praxis* of the *practico-inert*, to use Sartre's terms; that is in the momentum of the institution as the transcended sum of individuals' praxes.

Sartre's noted illustration of deforestation in China gives a practical instance of where the praxis of the individual can go beyond the expected immediate consequences and actually produce adverse long-term results. He has pointed out (1976: 161 ff) that Chinese peasants have extended the amount of arable land available to them by cutting down trees and then working on the land thus freed: this is the immediate praxis of the individual who only sees its positive value in that it allows him to grow more crops. What the peasant does not see, lacking an ecosystemic picture of his environment, is that it produces an *absence* of trees: this absence causes the extensive flooding to which areas of China are subject, because the trees' presence had acted as a barrier which prevented the silt, drained off the mountains by rain, from collecting in the rivers and their tributaries. Once the trees had been removed the silt clogged up these rivers, causing them to overflow and flood the plains. Thus, this systematic act of deforestation, through individuals' praxes, has produced a counter-praxis that appears as something occurring entirely outside man's own actions and that is yet a direct result of those actions. This counter-praxis is the praxis of the practico-inert, and effectively negates man's individual praxis, because in this case the flooding has spoilt the land the peasant had hoped to use for crop-growing. That is, he has lost control over the consequences of his actions because it produces a chain reaction that occurs when an action passes through a series of steps or transformations each of which is both qualitatively and quantitatively slightly different from its predecessor.

NEGATIVE FEEDBACK AS A PROTECTION FROM THE POWER OF
THE PRACTICO-INERT AND YET AS A FURTHER SOURCE OF
CONSTRAINT AND ESTRANGEMENT

The individual is faced with a difficult situation here, his authentic existence in open awareness depends on his free praxis, yet that activity may precipitate the sort of chain-reaction Sartre has described. To constrain that reaction one requires the presence of some form of negative feedback or restraint operating within the system. However, negative feedback itself can be restrictive of one's own praxis depending on the circumstances: that is, feedback can take either of two forms, following Waddington's (1977) terminology it may be either homeostatic or homeorhetic. The former type of feedback attempts to keep the system stationary or stable – one's praxis is thus directed to provide a *maintenance* function, while homeorhetic feedback ensures the 'continuation of a given type of change' (Waddington 1977: 105); that is, one's praxis is channelled to produce directed *growth*. Sartre has made it clear, as we shall see below, that the competition between individual praxes tends towards the creation of homeostatic states or totalities, as he calls them. These have their own inert power and momentum, which ensure their self-perpetuation by transcending the praxes of their constituent individuals. By contrast, homeorhetic feedback occurs only rarely as in the case where the praxes of the people involved in the system unite or fuse together to produce a given, commonly desired change. However, we face a further problem, the maintenance of that change becomes subordinated to the problem of sustaining the fusion of the group itself, because each individual in the group may come to perceive that the praxis of the group is different to, and hence restrictive of, the aims of his own free praxis. In other words, a *split* emerges between the expectations that an individual has about the consequences of his own praxis and its actual outcome: the dialectical connexion between the individual and the practico-inert is lost and, more significantly, the individual's free, open, praxis is lost to the control of the practico-inert, that is, it now takes on the *appearance* of an Other. This split Sartre sees as *aliénation*.[24] His use of this term is not the same as Marx's; for instance, the latter emphasizes the deliberate but avoidable exploitation of the workers through the alienation of their own labour to the Other, the capitalist, while Sartre argues that although all *aliénation* is inseparable from exploitation, it may be of an unintentional kind, as the deforestation example shows; that is, something that arises through the 'infinite flight of particular relationships' and that takes on the character of a 'passive synthesis of a false unity' (Sartre 1976: 164). Passive, because it was not desired, false because its consequences appear as intentional acts of a unified opposing presence, an Other.

ESTRANGEMENT AS ANTAGONISM BETWEEN PEOPLE AND THEIR PRAXES ORIGINATING IN THE CREATION OF TOTALITIES AS THE IMMEDIATE CONSEQUENCE OF SEEKING OPENNESS

In fact, Sartre asks himself if his use of the term *aliénation* is closer to a Hegelian rather than a Marxian understanding of the concept; the former he sees as capable of being expressed in terms of the 'constant characteristic of all kinds of objectification' (Sartre 1976: 227). Although he gives himself an ambivalent answer, his actual

---

[24] The French term is used for the moment to distinguish it from both Marx's and the social scientists' use of the word. In fact as we shall see below it is very similar in usage to the terms 'estrangement' and *'entfremdung'* but not 'alienation' or *'entäusserung'*.

use of the term (e.g. Sartre 1976: 67, 396, 435, 458, 628) accords closely with that of Hegel's discussions on '*Entfremdung*', or estrangement. Likewise, Chiodi (1976) has suggested that Sartre's analysis of *aliénation* rests on many Hegelian ideas and he sees this affinity most clearly in Sartre's emphasis on the need to understand *aliénation* at the level of the individual's *perceptions* of his interaction with the world, together with an appreciation of how this level relates to other levels, for example, group, class, and political awareness. There is, of course, a very important difference between Sartrean and Hegelian usage of *aliénation* and estrangement respectively; Sartre's analyses alone are based upon an existential, non-Ideal mode of awareness and in this respect his work has the same starting point as Marx's. However, he does not discuss the significance of the origins of *aliénation*, as Marx was able to through his understanding of the dialectical interaction between private property and the alienation (*entäussert*) of one's labour to the Other, because he is more interested in what Marx saw as the estranged (*entfremdet*) existence between man, other men, and their products. Sartre thus interprets *aliénation* not as a specific objective act of selling one's labour to the Other, but as the subsequent breakdown felt by the individual when his own activity or praxis for himself becomes subordinated to the power of the Other, or capitalist. In this he provides a valuable complement to both Hegel's and Marx's work by showing the nature of *aliénation*, or more precisely estrangement,[25] in the open form of awareness and the inert power that exists to maintain the estrangement. Like Marx he agrees that estrangement can be overcome through man's mutual reciprocity based on their shared praxes, but unlike Marx he is much more pessimistic and sees that this reciprocity is a rare, temporary occurrence. Sartre contends that people who are in an unestranged reciprocal relationship with each other are only those who have formed a 'fused group': this special group is at once both the sum of the constituent individual's praxes and a collective force more powerful than each of those praxes. The consequences that the fused group in action can achieve are the results of the desires of each individual manifest as a *whole*. However, the fusion of the group, which ends estrangement, is mediated by common *desires* and not founded on social reciprocity *per se* as Marx had advocated. That is, it does not depend upon mutual love or trust between people; this is particular-

[25] Although the English translator of Sartre's *Critique de la Raison Dialectique* uses the word 'alienation', from now on I will use the term 'estrangement' as the English rendering of '*aliénation*' to avoid confusing it with Marxian 'alienation' or '*Entäusserung*'.

ly borne out by the transitory nature of the group; it is function orientated, to combat the influence of the Other, or that which is outside the group. Sartre appears unable, and this is a direct reflection of his earlier existentialistic work, to accept that mutual trust can be the true human basis of man's behaviour towards others, as Marx and Hegel believed, and he argues that the presence of estrangement appears as a constant threat to destroy the group because this group 'is always in danger of relapsing into the series[26] from which it came' (Sartre 1976: 67). Moreover, the presence of a group automatically signifies the exclusion of those who are not members, the more that exclusion is maintained to avert the internal threat of estrangement the more its members are estranged from those non-members with whom they come in contact (Sartre 1976: 564 ff). That is, what represents the transcendence of estrangement for one man is quite the reverse for another because it is essentially the force of one person's free praxis attempting to overcome another's free praxis in order to be able to control that praxis and make it his own, so preventing himself from being controlled by it. It thus may appear that Sartre believes all men to be fixed at the stage of ontological development immediately preceding the Lord-Bondsman stage of existence in the closed form of awareness, because each man perceives the other as a threat to his existence. But Sartre is concerned with the interacting opposition between men's *praxes*, while in the closed form of awareness each *consciousness* sought the death of the other *per se*, that is their antagonism is an attempt to annihilate the very existence of the Other in order to maintain the insularity of their own existence. In the open form of awareness, however, the opposition between two people ultimately has a positive value because it allows man to assert his own praxis through which he retains his freedom from the Other; the destruction of the Other Sartre sees as incidental 'and the real aim is objective conquest or even creation' (Sartre 1976: 113). This perspective underestimates the creative, constructive aspect of personal praxis, because Sartre is much more concerned to make clear that one uses one's praxis to break down and destroy totalities or inert 'given' institutions so that one negates their power over one's own free praxis. He tended to assume that constructively using one's praxis represented the creation of totalities or closed inflexible entities that have inorganic, inert existence rather than an organic life of growth and decay. Following this point it is preferable to

---

[26] A group of people with a common aim but having no interaction with each other, 'a series is a plurality of isolations' (Sartre 1976: 256). A queue waiting at a bus-stop is an example of serial interaction.

direct one's praxis towards retaining one's freedom rather than to face the risk of creating a totality; for there to be truly open existence man's praxis should materialize only as *totalizations*,[27] as stages of temporary fragile resolutions[28] when the praxis of one group or individual gains the upper hand against that of another group or individual before it is superseded. Hence, a precondition of openness is the presence of flux between two (or more) opposing sets of praxes each attempting to assert its right to openness, to be able to attain freedom for its own self-development, yet which in their very act of assertion are forced to oppose another group trying to assert theirs. The dilemma that faces man (and one that the sociological camp of organization theorists tend to minimize) is that he can never openly reciprocate with others because before he can engage with another person he must have sufficient ontological strength not to be overwhelmed or engulfed by that other person. The source of this ontological strength is found in man's own self-directed (un-alienated) praxis: but the attempt to carry out this free praxis always appears to be at the expense of someone else's praxis, because one's activity has altered the nature of that which he works upon and gives it a particularity, a life for himself. If another person were then to act upon it, his behaviour would be seen by the first person as negating his (the first person's) objectified existence. Thus, if one supports this argument every person's praxis *inevitably* confronts everyone else's. It is necessary to question the fundamental factor upon which Sartre rests his analysis of the antagonism between the praxes of two people or groups, that of the *scarcity* of workable-upon objects, because its reputed presence provides the focus around which are concentrated the arguments for the inevitability of estrangement. Notwithstanding this weakness, undoubtedly Sartre's analyses still stand as insightful interpretations of the psychosocial dilemmas one faces in the attempt to exist in open awareness. If one does exist within circumstances constrained by real or apparent scarcity then confrontations with other men's praxes can be diffused by existing in a 'pledged group'. One example of this is a team or project group in an organized work context. This is a stage that arises following the breakdown of the fused groups; where people who form the group are those who have pledged to each other to join and remain together to achieve a certain end or goal. The

---

[27] A totalization may be described as a transitory stability in a context of ever developing and changing interaction between the praxes of groups or individuals.
[28] In fact, by definition all resolutions in an open form of existence are temporary, otherwise they take on the nature of a totality.

cohesion of the pledged group is provided not by mutual trust or reciprocity as Marx would hope but by what Sartre calls 'fraternity-terror'. This is founded on the 'gradual disappearance of the common interest and the reappearance of individual antagonisms' (Sartre 1976: 430).

This common interest was originally the group's opposition to the Other's praxis; subsequently, if that Other's power has been weakened by the group's actions, in its state of fusion, then the group now lacks a focus against which to direct itself and to give it a meaning or justification for its existence. At this stage the group may dissolve and relapse into estranged seriality, because it was function-oriented, not founded on reciprocity for its own sake. Alternatively, there are good reasons why the original members of the group should remain together. First, it may be subject to renewed attacks from the Other in its attempt to re-establish the validity of its praxis against that of the group: second, and more important, there exists the fear of betrayal from within the group. Each member knows that he himself is capable of leaving the original group to assert the autonomy of his praxis against that of the group so he is fully aware that it is equally likely another member or sub-group of members may likewise break away from the original group and form a new group with its own praxis. This latter group's praxis thus takes on the appearance of a new Other to the remaining members of the original group. Furthermore, the individual may fear that he will be rejected by the group: his desire to continue his affiliation with the other members is seen by social psychologists as simply the desire to maintain friendly and perhaps supportive relations with other people (e.g. Zander 1971: 106 ff) but there is a more ominous aspect to the need for staying with the group, that is, if the person is rejected then that group, formerly the embodiment of *his* praxis now becomes that of the Other's praxis and as such opposes him in his desire for openness. Thus we have an uneasy tension in the pledged group, where each has to surrender, or alienate to the collective, his desire for full autonomy to carry out his free praxis, and instead live in a state of semi-autonomous existence where his actions both govern and are governed by the group as a whole; a state, although undesirable, certainly preferable in an existentialist context to non-autonomous existence, that is, domination by the power of the praxis of the Other.

Reciprocity as the key to un-estranged life in open awareness

SARTRE'S PESSIMISTIC VIEW OF RECIPROCITY AS
ENDS-DIRECTED

This cheerless view of man's relationship to man is based on Sartre's rich psychological interpretation of reciprocity. He saw that reciprocity, which he calls a double totalization of the constituent members' praxes, arises when each person 'makes his body into the Other's instrument to the extent that he makes the Other into his' (Sartre 1976: 114). What is important is that this action is conscious, that is, it is a negation of a real spontaneous unity between the two people, each is aware of the other as an Other and hence as a limitation on the possibility of attaining the totalizations of their individual praxes for themselves. They attempt to ignore the possibility of such a restriction (which of course adds to their awareness of the nature of their uneasy reciprocity) by behaving with a 'kind of influence compulsion . . . each insisting on continuing it [the relationship] out of consideration for the Other' (Sartre 1976: 116), thus the reciprocity becomes a restricting 'crushing totality'. The presence of a third person adds to this totality. He unites the duality of the original pair's praxes through his perception of the product or outcome of their interaction, and can in turn cause the interiorization of that reciprocity, that is, the emergence of a spontaneous unity which is directed against the third person to exclude him and his praxis, but which disappears again as soon as the third person no longer constitutes a threat to the praxes of the first two. The notion of threat used in this context by Sartre reveals that he treats reciprocity as an ends-directed or functional phenomenon, and fails to consider its positive means-oriented values. The dangers of analysing behaviour through the separation or exclusion of one of means and ends has been described by Mead (1942); to emphasize the latter is to have an instrumental view of human behaviour, one that omits consideration of the value of the behaviour in itself.

Sartre, by viewing reciprocity as a double totalization that attains its temporary unity in the face of the Other, can assume that the interaction between the two people will normally proceed along the lines of increasing differentiation of their praxes, thus producing what Bateson (1972) has called 'schismogenesis', of which he describes two polar forms. First is *symmetrical* schizmogenesis (direct competition between two people's praxes), which we have seen can occur as a *precursor* to the Lord-Bondsman relationship where each person seeks to outdo the other. If not restrained in some way, their behaviour can lead to hostility and eventual breakdown of the relationship. Restraint is an agreement, a pledge between the two people to cease antagonisms. The other form of schismogenesis is *complementary* where, as in the fully formed Lord-Bondsman relationship, one dominates a submissive other. That is, the latter person exists in a non-autonomous state where reciprocity is present but is of the closed form. As we saw in Chapter 1, in the Calvinistic view of Christianity the Self willingly yields to the power of the Other, God, in return for ontological support; reciprocity is completely within the context of the closed Other-based totality.

MARX'S VIEW OF RECIPROCITY AS THE NATURAL BASIS FOR MAN'S SOCIALITY – THE REFUTATION OF SARTRE'S PESSIMISM

However, Marx's notion of reciprocity, in its open form, is a mixture of these two forms of differentiation. The relationship between two people is supportive; in Bateson's terms it does not lead to a schismogenic breakdown because it is 'compensated and balanced within itself' (Bateson 1972: 43). Thus, it does not require the mediator of a pledge to allow the interaction to continue; that is, it is based upon awareness of individuals' differences and how they complement each other. Here one person's free praxis is matched by supportive appreciation of that praxis and its interactions with the praxis of another person. This gives me one standpoint from which to question Sartre's assumption that one person's praxis is always restrictive of another's and will, by implication, produce symmetrical schismogenesis or breakdown unless a pledge, based on terror (ontological threats) is arranged between the two. What concerns me here is that the ontologically enriching aspects of social (Marxian) reciprocity are ignored, because Sartre emphasized the 'ends' of reciprocity: to achieve a purpose, to assert one's free praxis *per se* against that of the Other. This is serious, because one's development cannot occur simply by self-assertion through free praxis; one becomes like Mattieu in Sartre's trilogy *The Roads to Freedom*, whose efforts to 'be himself' compel him to reject all human involvement. Mattieu's desire for limitless freedom represents the search for freedom without content, an abstract existence. His life is one of rejection rather than involvement because like his author, he assumes that all involvement is inherently self-destructive. I agree that it is, if one lacks the ontological strength, the openness to accept that other people's praxes are not always threatening but can enrich one's perspective, and in turn one's own praxis. To live, like

Mattieu, as a Sceptic, questioning and rejecting all things, does have a certain value, it questions the validity of the context and meaning of systems, the totalities that one lives in. But questioning alone is not enough, one could equally change that context in a positive manner by using one's praxis as a *creative* force – this is how Marx envisaged it. One creates new possibilities out of the 'givenness' of the old; mere destruction, although appearing to negate the force of the Other, is in actuality completely governed by it, because one's actions are totally directed by its presence and derive their meaning from it. However, Sartre believes, as I have mentioned, that he has one further argument that effectively denies the possibility of social reciprocity or interaction for itself. He argues that reciprocity cannot be affective or emotionally based, that is, for itself, because it is a circumstance of the antagonism between people's praxes which arises directly from 'the relation of the multiplicity of men to the field of action, that is, on *scarcity*' (Sartre 1976: 735, emphasis added). Scarcity may be described as the force of negative unity between people, and is to be considered as a consequence of people's behaviour towards each other rather than a physical lack in our ecosystem. Sartre hints at this by pointing out that it arises because 'man constantly sees his action being stolen from him and totally distorted by the milieu in which he inscribes it' (Sartre 1976: 150). But I have already shown *how* man's action is 'stolen from him': it happens through the compulsory alienation of his action, his labour, to the Other, which then uses it for its ends. This alienation, as Marx had made very clear, both creates and is sustained by the existence of private property. Thus, by seeking the abolition of private property, Marx was also attempting to end the presence of a created scarcity that he knew maintained the estrangement of man from man, or prevented social reciprocity. It is therefore very surprising to read Sartre's remark that 'Marx says very little about scarcity' (Sartre 1976: 147) because Marx's discussions on private property, and its estranging effects, all revolve around how scarcity is created (for the mass of propertyless workers) by capitalistic labour which produces from that enforced scarcity a surplus of worked-on and Other-owned objects which is then concentrated in the hands of the few. As Sartre points out, scarcity is more accurately to be seen as *interiorized* scarcity because it arises from man's praxis which he then claims as his own, whereupon it takes on the appearance of an Other, or an opposing force, to those who do not possess it. If, as Marx strongly advocates, those objects were not perceived as one's own, as personal property, then they would cease to appear as Other-based forces and not represent a threat to those who have not worked directly upon them. Instead, those people could utilize them freely in *their* praxis. This freeing of materials upon which to direct one's praxis, part of the consequences of the abolition of private property, would thus remove the interiorized or perceived scarcity of those objects.

That is, although Sartre has shown us the difficulty of existing in an open society by arguing that one's praxis, the basis of that openness, automatically creates scarcity for another person, Marx, through his insistence on the abolition of private property, has demonstrated that one's praxis need not create scarcity for other people; in one's unestranged praxis one does not seek to make that object a possession. That is, one's praxis does not just enrich oneself, it enriches the community, allowing reciprocity, for itself, to emerge as a primary ontological perspective.

However, even if we see that Sartre has been too restrictive and pessimistic in his assessment of the nature of reciprocity, and his analyses of the nature of small social groupings are incomplete, we cannot question the validity of his point about the continuing, inevitable creation of powerful edifices of practico-inertness through the cumulative praxes of individuals – as we have seen in the deforestation of China example – that act blindly against the freedom of the individual's own activity. Marx believed that these structures, in their manifestation as social institutions, could be broken down through revolutionary change. However, he did not appreciate that they would arise again, in a different form, but still as an inertness, simply through man's cumulative actions. Instead, Marx assumed that a new society would take the form of a massive fused group, composed of social man, and where each aspect of society reflects the direct wishes and intentions of man in his social existence. Sartre more realistically sees the inevitability of free praxis creating meta-praxes which in turn produces consequences, the chain-reactions, beyond that intended by man and which oppose him in his attempt to maintain openness.

THE RELATIONSHIP BETWEEN AUTHENTICITY AND RECIPROCITY

In the face of these seemingly insuperable forces, both ontological and epistemological, how then is one to live authentically in openness? We have already seen that in the closed form of existence, the *attainment* of the Ideal the totality, represents authenticity, or Being; one's progress towards it is characterized by the sloughing off of several forms of estrangement before full union with the Ideal can be achieved. In its ultimate form (for example in Calvinistic theology) one does not overcome one's estrangement completely until death, where one becomes united with the Ideal, God, through a transcendence of one's 'Fallenness'. In contrast to this view, Marx, as an early advocate of open existence, argued that authenticity was found in man's awareness of his *social* nature, that is by living in an unestranged existence; through the use of one's (unalienated) labour one could reciprocate openly with other men and their praxes. However, for Sartre, authenticity is attained solely by continuing at all times to exert the power of one's praxis against that of the Other. It was this attempt to prevent the emergence of any form of totality that *itself* represents authentic open existence. Social relationships ultimately restricted one's authenticity because they amounted to a hampering of one's praxis: thus love, the ultimate form of reciprocity, is not a measure of authenticity for Sartre as it is for both Marx and the advocates of the closed form of ontological existence. I have already questioned the premises upon which Sartre bases his dislike of reciprocity by suggesting that in the long term, Marx's call for the abolition of private property could lessen the presence of interiorized scarcity and thus remove the competitive nature of a social relationship. Moreover if I disagree with Sartre, and view reciprocity in terms of means, commitment, or involvement with other people, then reciprocity can itself be ontologically rewarding. It allows one to use one's praxis *positively*, to supplement another person's praxis, rather than simply as a force to reject the Other. This is not to say that used positively, one's praxis inevitably affirms the existing totality. On the contrary, the dialectical nature of this praxis both cuts through the inertness and the complacency of the 'givenness' of the Other, the act of Other-denial, *and* allows one to progress beyond the Other's limitations, an act of Self-affirmation. That is, I am suggesting that it is one-sided to see that open authenticity only arises through the *assertion* of man's praxis against the Other to negate and destroy its praxis; one can equally use praxis, as Marx understood it, as a creative *productive* force. Through this positive, creative approach towards the Other, man can view it as an ontological challenge and not simply as a threat to his praxis.

RECIPROCITY AS A SOURCE OF ONTOLOGICAL SUPPORT

By sharing in a social context the burden of that challenge, man is able both to question the Other's blind drive towards totality and affirm his own ontological awareness of his positive relationship towards other men by realizing that in their praxis lies an inventive power, not just a destructive one. Thus, this affirmation of himself, and of his relationship to other men, gives him the authenticity, the courage to be in openness: simply, he gains confidence by valuing his praxis as a source of creative adaptation and change, instead of sinking into the hopelessness and despair that results from the ultimately futile effort (as Sartre saw it) of devoting all his energies to the attempt to deny completely the Other's praxis with the distant hope of being able, at some stage, to assert his own.

In turn, this self-affirmation allows him to interact further and in an increasingly rich manner with other men, because instead of fearing the influence over him, he comes to know that he is confirmed both in their 'thoughts and love'. That is, he can welcome the active presence of other men as a source both of ontological support and the creative enrichment of his own praxis. This perspective ought to be to the fore of social scientists' thoughts as they examine organized work structures.

Conclusion

Having considered the natures of alienation and estrangement in a life based on openness we have seen that the transcendence of the latter requires changes at both the ontological and the socio-political levels of awareness; both through the growth of self-affirmatory behaviour and the cessation of the alienation of one's labour or activity to the Other. However, organization science literature on 'alienation' has tended to emphasize its subjective nature in the given socio-political context, hence its similarity to Hegelian estrangement, and has underestimated the significance of man surrendering his labour to the Other. Schacht (1971) commits this error through a particularly muddled interpretation of Marx's own writings:

'In conceiving of this alienation in terms of a separation *through surrender to another*, however, Marx obscures its basic character, and encounters problems of both over- and under-inclusiveness. It would seem more fruitful to drop all reference to the mediation of an "alien will" in the explication of the concept of such alienation itself, and to focus solely upon the relation of labor to the individual. It might of course turn out to be the case that this alienation very frequently *does* involve the surrender of labor to the direction of another man; but this would be a factual correlation rather than a matter of definition.'

(Schacht 1971: 92)

It should be clear by now that Marx's analyses have provided that factual correlation, but Schacht's blunder may, in part, be excused because what he is really talking about, along with most writers in this area, is *estrangement*, which he then unthinkingly equates with *alienation*. We have seen that estrangement arises in the open form of awareness when one's praxis is not for oneself, and one's actions affirm the power of the Other instead of enriching one's own life. This focus on estrangement (even if it is incorrectly called 'alienation') has special significance for organization theorists who, because of the nature of their interest, tend to accept the 'givenness' of the socio-political system of which organizations are a part, and instead treat estranged labour as the *converse* or negative aspect of work that furthers the 'dignity of the human individual' by permitting 'autonomy, responsibility, social connection and self-actualization' (Blauner 1964: 15).

In attending to the self-actualizing[29] aspects of man's existence, organization theorists, almost unwittingly in their misinterpretation of Marx's notion of alienation, have provided the necessary focus through which the abolition of (Marxian) alienation may be achieved. We know that these factors of self-actualization, autonomy, and social connexion were desired by Marx too but, as I have argued, they will not materialize simply through a revolution that ruptures the 'givenness' of the system. One must be ontologically strong enough to withstand and, preferably, to desire, this rupture. Only then can one cope with the associated paradigm shifts (to use Kuhn's (1970) terminology) that occur in the transition from closed Other-based existence to that of open-ended growth.

Ontological strength, as I emphasize, is not only the source of the ability to negate the praxis of the Other but also allows one to affirm both oneself and one's interaction with other people. The organization theorists' interest in self-actualization strongly reflects the importance of ontological growth for the individual. However, to deal with these factors in their negative form under the rubric of 'alienation' not only distorts the long-term socio-political significance Marx gave to the term, but perhaps more seriously, diverts attention from attempts to discover the positive aspects of work and existence, to that of simply removing the negative ones.

Undoubtedly it is easier to remove problems rather than to see how one could promote open-ended growth or self-actualization; by nature the latter is undefinable, because it is a matter understandable only in the context of each individual's ontological awareness, a context all too often ignored by organization theorists. The reasons

[29] Self-actualization is to be understood as a facet of generalized ontological growth.

for their reluctance to handle this key aspect of working life may in part be due to the sort of sentiments expressed by Argyle (1972) about self-actualization, when he wrote: 'This concept of self-actualization is popular with existential psychologists, but is regarded as mysterious and unmeasurable by their more scientific colleagues' (Argyle 1972: 97).

One surely hopes by now that the labels 'scientific' and 'measurable' no longer indicate a concept's superiority, but merely reveal the insistence of the observer to close off and categorize what he is studying instead of allowing the factors under observation to retain their relatively amorphous subtleties. Craik's comments (1967) on hysterical conduct mirror uncomfortably closely the behaviour of Argyle's 'scientific colleagues'. Hysterical conduct, he suggested, consists

'in adapting oneself by excluding all parts of the environment to which one's powers and attitudes are inadequate: a form of adaptation is thus achieved by narrowing and distorting the environment until one's conduct appears adequate to it, rather than by altering one's conduct and enlarging one's knowledge till one can cope with the larger, real environment.'

(Craik 1967: 90–1)

Measuring narrows and distorts the environment into one given perspective (for example, behaviour as related to output levels at work), and ignores a consideration of other perspectives, for example, self-actualization and hence ontological life in all its variety.

The concept of self-actualization has a double significance for this essay: first, to many organization theorists it represents man's authentic nature in opposition to 'alienated' life, and second, because of its close connexion with the notion of ontological awareness and growth, it can play a vital role in both person-to-person and Self-to-Other interactions. I am aware that considerable confusion does exist in organization literature over the significance of self-actualization because the use of the term does not always indicate whether the actualization occurs in a closed, that is, organization-directed context, or in an open or self/socially directed one. Thus, I shall now consider in more detail, in a brief concluding chapter, the *nature* of self-actualization; this will also serve to particularize into an organizational context both my somewhat abstract discussions of ontological awareness in the open and closed forms of existence and to indicate the significance for further research of the terms 'alienation' and 'estrangement'.

5

The transcendence of alienation and estrangement in organizations: the quest for self-actualization

Introduction

Throughout this book I have pointed to the importance of self-productive activities: ontological development, love and reciprocity, courage, authenticity, and the transcendence of alienation and estrangement. In each case the terms make a statement about man's nature and his relationship to the world; they emphasize his growing out of and superseding the limitations of his mundane existence through a praxis, or directed activity, based on his ontological awareness as it is manifest in the three forms of Self-Other relationship (non-, semi-, and full autonomous interaction).

In the context of the literature on man's activity within the organized working environment these themes appear in embryonic form under the term *self-actualization*. The essence of this concept is that through his activity man seeks to fulfil himself and to grow beyond his present limitations. The writings of Maslow (e.g. 1954, 1968, 1969, and 1976) on the concept of self-actualization are widely known to organization scientists, but as we shall see, are treated by many of them in a mechanistic or functional manner, because although understanding that self-actualization presupposes a different form of work, they misunderstand its nature and purpose. Gadalla and Cooper (1978) have argued that organization scientists approach the issue of self-actualization from a perspective of *in-*

strumental humanism that is: 'from an epistemological point of view the core theme of this literature is one which exemplifies the split between subject and object. In this case, man as subject is raised above the environment as object.' (Gadalla and Cooper 1978: 351).

This split between man and his environment was quite contrary to Maslow's own understanding of self-actualized work. To clarify the connexions between his thinking and my own views on authenticity a brief synopsis of Maslow's work is appropriate here.

Understanding self-actualization as an expression of the individual's psychological growth: the work of Maslow and his associates

Maslow sought to re-establish the union between the Self, as subject, and the environment, as Other, not by reducing the Self to the service of the Other but by exploring man's potential in the context of a mutuality of interaction between the Self and the Other. He found a number of insights for his work in Goldstein's (1939, 1947) views on the psychopathology of the individual. The latter had argued that the tendency to actualize oneself is the 'drive by which organism is moved' (Goldstein 1947: 140). He made clear, as did Allport (1955: 66), that his conception of a drive was not that of an urge to reduce tension as Freud had believed: this is merely the response of a sick individual who strives to avoid tension present in situations with which he cannot cope: 'For the sick person the only form of actualization of his capacities which remains is the maintenance of the *existing state*' (Goldstein 1947: 141, emphases added). In the language that I have been using, the sick person's drives are towards the maintenance of his present ontological structure in the face of a changing epistemological framework. The normal person, by contrast, actualizes by using his skills, experiences, and personal knowledge to grow psychologically, not just to reduce tension by avoiding the unexpected, but to express his 'joy of coming to terms with the world' (Goldstein 1947: 112). He responds actively and creatively to the novelty and uncertainty of situations, thereby enriching his perspective on the world. Maslow (1954) specified the pre-conditions necessary for the emergence of this active creativity by proposing that the individual must first have satisfied his 'lower needs' before the 'higher' desire for self-actualization can manifest itself: self-actualization is seen as a high-level need because unlike the other needs it can never be fully consummated, because of its open-ended psychological nature (Alderfer 1972). The presence of higher and lower needs suggested to Maslow the existence of a hierarchy of these needs. 'These are, from the lowest: physiological, safety, belongingness and love (or social), esteem and ultimately, self-actualization' (Maslow 1954: 8off).

The appearance of these needs in a developmental hierarchy is one of the less significant aspects of Maslow's work. He used it simply to prepare the path for an understanding of the primacy of self-actualization, yet organization scientists have subjected the validity of the hierarchy to their scrutiny. Having shown that it is not always possible to discern the presence of a clear-cut hierarchy in man's needs they readily dismiss the rest of Maslow's work as 'unscientific', (e.g. Cofer and Appley 1964; Lawler and Suttle 1972).[1] The criterion of validity used by these writers is that the application of Maslow's theories to the organized work setting does not necessarily motivate the work-force to work harder. These organization scientists seem to have forgotten Maslow's argument that self-actualization is related to *personal* satisfaction and growth and not to organizational labour. In fact, the organization scientists who reject Maslow's work probably do not really forget that he had emphasized the psychological aspects of actualization, but they deliberately turn away from his writings because they cannot incorporate his more advanced ideas on man's desire for psychological growth into the functional, role-playing business environment where the growth of the Other has precedence. Maslow (1968), in his later writings, made more explicit that real personal satisfaction and self-development arises in the transcendence of such Other-based forces through the individual's practice of Being-cognition or B-cognition. This form of cognition he believed to be the richest that one could attain, because through it the person comprehends and acts in the awareness of the inherent unity in all things by perceiving the world about him through a 'second self-actualizing innocence' (Maslow 1976: 246). The attainment of this second innocence does not signify a regression towards the blind sincerity of pre-Fall awareness, nor to a child-like state of naïveté based on ignorance of the world's sordid aspects; these are expressions of a first or primal innocence. On the contrary, it is the *incorporation* and transcendence of the deficiencies of the world, or as Maslow called them, the D-aspects – its 'vices, its contentions, poverties, quarrels and tears' into an awareness of one's active reciprocity with the world and all its particularities, where people, events and processes are seen as

[1] From another perspective, Gratton (1981) has questioned the validity of the measures used to test Maslow's hierarchy and has found them to be rather 'unscientific' in themselves.

they are and not through a veil of personal desires, needs, inadequacies, fears and weaknesses. It is 'unmotivated perceiving': people in this mode of perception specifically *reject* behaviour oriented towards 'striving, doing, coping, achieving, trying, purposiveness' thus allowing the individual to achieve an awareness closely akin to the Zen perception of the 'suchness' of objects.[2] However, this perception presupposes one's harmony with an Other whose presence is supportive or unobtrusive: without this relationship between the Self and the Other the former resorts to the motivated perceiving and acting that precedes psychological actualization. Thus the functional efforts of organization scientists to use the principle of self-actualization as a motivating force to achieve goals in the Other-dominated context of the working environment are quite contrary to the spirit of true Maslovian self-actualization.

It is hardly surprising then that those in the system of organized work have embraced with some enthusiasm other need theories of motivation that avoid emphasizing the attainment of self-actualization. For instance, Herzberg's (1959, 1966, 1968) two-factor theory of motivation, despite all the criticism it has received on methodological grounds,[3] is a straightforward attempt to incorporate the enriching aspects of self-actualization into the closed system of organized labour by emphasizing that work which apparently allows or encourages self-actualization usually leads to personal satisfaction and increased productivity. A person in such a job can derive feelings of wellbeing and confidence in himself through his success at his work. Herzberg saw these feelings as necessary to one's mental health, while I see them as indicators of emerging ontological strength. Valuable as this strength is, and I shall return to this point shortly, the emphasis is on the enhancement of material Other-controlled resources first, and personal needs second. Opposing this, Maslow desired the prepotency of mental or inner resources and wished to see the nature of the Other's influence upon the Self altered to allow the self-creating aspects of work to emerge. He understood, like Marx, that work directed by the Other and for the Other's reward was in essence a self-estranging activity: the more it appeared to affirm the Self the more in reality it affirmed the Self's dependence on the Other for the continuance of actualizing opportunities.

---

[2] That is, seeing the object 'not only in itself, but in the situation as it finds itself – the situation in its broadest and deepest possible sense' (Suzuki 1957: 102).
[3] e.g. Dunnette, Campbell and Hakel (1967); Behling, Labovitz and Kosmo (1968), and King (1970).

I have already pointed out (in Chapter 1) the origins of this emphasis upon the use of material resources to the detriment of man's psychological wellbeing: the sixteenth-century business man ignored Calvin's plea to remember the spiritual force that gave work its particular personal meaning in the face of God the Other. One sees the living proof of the failure to heed Calvin's warning expressed in North American business culture which, as Maslow noted, is dominated by purposefulness and striving for Other-defined ends. Other cultures, whose origins are not in Judaic-Christian theology, for example the eastern tradition of Taoism, place importance upon the *non*-emphasis of being-for-something or striving towards something. This tradition views such directed behaviour as a striving to make up deficiencies in oneself and not real self-actualization. The personal effort required to attain the latter, though less obvious, is no less intense. Maslow made this point in a reference to Allport's work when he said that Allport

> 'stresses strongly and correctly that "being" is as effortful and active as is striving. His suggestions would lead us to contrast striving-to-make-up-deficiencies with striving-to-self-actualize rather than striving with being. This correction also serves to remove the too easily acquired impression that "being", un-motivated reactions and purposeless activity are easier, less ener-getic and less effortful than coping with external problems.'
>
> (Maslow 1954: 292)

The effort is of a psychological nature, part of which is to perceive afresh one's environment and part is a struggle to develop and express one's potential to 'be' rather than to succumb to a preoc-cupation with the need to respond to the demands of the 'busyness world'.

Although Allport uses a different term for self-actualization – that of 'becoming' – the principle behind his work in general accords with that of Maslow. Becoming, he argues, is not a mere matter of actualizing oneself within the given context; it 'involves the shift-ing of dominance from segmental systems to comprehensive sys-tems or from one comprehensive system to another' (Allport 1955: 87). Thus while he would not have agreed with Sartre's pessimistic view of man, Allport's understanding of becoming is akin to that of Sartre's in that both see freedom in terms of the utilization of all one's possibilities. Allport's optimism arises because he believes that a person's religious convictions can support him in his en-deavour to become, because man's courage to 'be' gains ontological support through his semi-autonomous reciprocity with the Other. Religion can be a positive support permitting authentic growth because it is not merely a protective fortification for the individual against anxiety or despair, it also enables him at each stage of his becoming to 'relate himself meaningfully to the totality of Being' (Allport 1955: 96). He views the totality of Being not as a fixed force in the manner that Sartre saw totalities but as an inherent interconnecting and developing reciprocity between people, events, and systems. Thus, we see that for Allport, man can derive his strength to be himself and to go beyond his present Self by perceiving Being as a spiritual force which, like De Chardin's (1970) view of God, is an immanent rather than a transcendent presence – found in the immediacy of the here-and-now rather than in the abstractness of the out-there.

De Charms (1968) has, following Maslow rather than Allport, sought to particularize self-actualization into the specific forms that man's actions should take, by suggesting that man's active, creative projects are rooted in 'personal causation'; that is, the 'initiation by an individual of behaviour intended to produce a change in his environment' (De Charms 1968: 6). His point is that by initiating change man disrupts the givenness of the system in which he is located, thereby encouraging him to be an active actualizing agent rather than a reactive one. Because causation rather than freedom *per se* is, for De Charms, the prime focus of man's actions, his beliefs lie closer to Marx's views on the active, creative nature of man's species-being rather than to the isolated existential becoming advocated by Sartre. The contrast is evident in De Charm's discussions on whether one perceives the influence of outside forces as either a threat or a challenge to one's existence. In the former case one responds to the outside force by desiring to *master* it, thereby resecuring one's freedom from its will, while in the latter instance one is not intent on domination but, in a way, *yields* to its presence by using it as a challenge for the stimulation it provides and for the enhancement of the awareness of the efficacy of one's personal causation that emerges from this activity. In other words, responding to the challenge of a situation gives man the confidence or ontological strength to act upon and influence further situations as they appear and, in turn, permits the expression of man's actualization in the complexity of his responses and actions upon the world. This is expressive behaviour rather than coping activity: it signals that one's acts are metamotivated, as Maslow (1976) called them; motivated to *Be*, rather than simply motivated to overcome a need. A facet of responding to situations expressively is that it shows the inadequacy and unsubtlety of asserting one's Self, one must be able to *give* one's Self too as May (1953: 227) argued. As we have seen, this free giving of the Self is the essence of the reciprocity at the base of Marx's view of man's truly social existence.

Problems in the application of self-actualization to the organized work context

THE DOMINATION OF THE SELF'S POTENTIALITIES FOR ACTUALIZATION BY THE ORGANIZATIONAL OTHER

An appreciation of self-actualization as understood by Maslow should cause one to question the belief that self-actualization is possible in the context of the competitive and aggressive business environment and has its outward expression in the form of higher productivity. Its implementation could lull the individual into believing that his full potential for becoming or self-actualizing can be obtained within that context alone, whereas the omnipresent force of organization *mores* and goals ensures that man's potential is arrested and contained within these Other-based parameters. The individual who concentrates on actualizing himself at work forgets that its successful manifestation in that context (expressed as competitiveness, drive towards pre-defined goals, ambition, ruthlessness) are the very antitheses of expressive Maslovian self-actualization. The result is that even in his private non-working life man's efforts to actualize himself are tainted with the characteristics that hinder its emergence. Indeed man's private existence may be consumed not by his endeavours to actualize or grow psychologically but by his efforts to prevent further encroachment into his inner life of the repressive qualities of the organization as a self-engulfing system. These qualities as Marcuse (1964) has pointed out, ensure the systems survival by excessive repression of man's *instinctual energies*. Thus the application of the principle of self-actualization to the work context can be seen as an effort to *utilize* these energies, and the measure of success of this redirection and repression can be seen by observing that for many people, working in the organization context is the richest and most challenging activity that they can experience. It appears to absorb all aspects of their person because it intentionally strives to 'utilize the useless parts of self, by redefining these as not being useless' (Gouldner 1969: 350). Gouldner had seen that the worker's desire for involvement may be more immediately connected with the fear of the 'unemployed self's sense of life wasted', because although the *man* is employed, in many jobs he feels that his *Self* is redundant. This fear arises, Gouldner reasons, because society treats men as utilities who simply perform functions that are marketable. That is, man's actions are channelled by the system of organized work in accordance with the system's Ideal of the maximum utilization of material resources. This ensures that not only must the efforts of organization scientists to increase self-actualization at work be to the advantage of the Other, or organization as a totality, they must fall within the technological and economic parameters of the system as a whole. Moreover, efforts to make work interesting, actualizing, or whatever pseudo-psychological term is used is only judged worthwhile if it is cost-effective in terms of reduced absenteeism, increased motivation and commitment.

THE POTENCY OF TECHNOLOGICAL AND ECONOMIC FACTORS OVER PSYCHOLOGICAL VALUES

A number of writers have criticized this functional approach of the application of the principle of self-actualization to job design (e.g. Argyris 1957; Cooper 1974; Blackler and Brown 1975). Blackler and Brown (1978) have further suggested that self-actualizing or 'enriched' work can emerge as a *fortuitous* spin-off from technological or economic changes which create a demand for a new style of work. The interaction between technological and economic forces and those of self-actualization may, I suggest, be represented in a Venn diagram, thus:

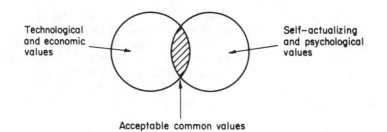

Technological and economic values → ▨ ← Self–actualizing and psychological values

Acceptable common values

The shaded area represents the 'acceptably desirable' human values, that is, acceptable because they accord with existing knowledge of profitable technological systems and, in some cases, can be publicized by a company as the key factor in its decision to introduce technological change. Blackler and Brown (1978) argue that the

Volvo job redesign programme (outlined by Gyllenhammar 1977) can be seen as a case in point.

The aspects of self-actualized life which are outside the prevailing values are ignored because their inclusion would represent a value *transformation* with subsequent loss of comprehension and control by those within the dominant technological frame of reference. Control is lost or weakened because the precision of given material values is now diluted by unknown and unquantifiable human values. F.W. Taylor (1947) appreciated that it was crucial to remove these latter elements to give 'Scientific Management' its validity and the appearance of objective impartiality. More recently, the introduction of self-actualization has suffered the same indignity in the attempts to tie its presence to the dubious values of scientific respectability and an increase in the utilization of material resources. The comments of Herrick and Maccoby reveal this crude approach rather well:

'A number of factors support the possibility of humanizing work at this time. First is the pressure of international competition. The cost per unit production in the United States increased 22 per cent between 1965–1970 as opposed to only 3 per cent in Japan. Thus industry in America has to search for more productive ways of organizing work, re-examining assumptions about the productivity of the old mechanized system. The need for higher productivity also encourages greater automation, requiring better educated workers who must understand machines and be alert to problems before they develop.'

(Herrick and Maccoby, in Cherns and Davis 1975: 67)

The redirection of the principle of self-actualization away from a real concern for psychological growth towards an obsession for organizational efficiency rests, in part, on an issue that many organization scientists have taken for granted, namely that their research work is simply to find the optimum social and educational environments that permit attainment of the system's functional goals of higher productivity and efficiency.

THE ASSUMPTION OF ORGANIZATION SCIENTISTS THAT THEIR
RESEARCH IS DIRECTED TO MAINTAINING THE SYSTEM

This state of affairs arises largely because organization scientists believe that their research work has credibility only when they can produce a change that can be measured either through productivity increases or assessments of the individual's attitude improvements.[4] This bias in research work can be seen in its more explicit form in McGregor's (1960) development of what he called 'Theory X' and 'Theory Y' approaches to work. 'Theory Y' holds what he believes to be a 'humanistic' perspective of work; by researching into this area he believes one must seek to create conditions such that the members of the organization 'can achieve their own goals best by directing their efforts towards the success of the enterprise' (McGregor 1960: 49). There is no mention of research into the nature of a generalized spiritual or psychological enhancement that may be afforded by altering the *nature* of the enterprise.[5] Likert's (1961, 1967) 'participative management' model of human relationships, which he grandly believes to be founded on science-based theory, in fact rests on the same assumptions as McGregor's work, but is developed in a more complex fashion. Perrow (1972) has demonstrated effectively the numerous methodological weaknesses in Likert's 'science' and has cynically commented that those items of Likert's which indicate good participative management are nothing more than 'motherhood ideas . . . drawn from a boy-scout creed for organizations' (Perrow 1972: 125). I may add that this creed (of working hard and playing hard) is the juvenile version of the sentiments associated with the Protestant Ethic. Likert takes it for granted in his research that this is the only acceptable attitude for management to have if the system or organization in which they are located is to remain viable and productive, that is, self-perpetuating in its closed totality.

As I have indicated, this type of research into the application of self-actualization is based on a misunderstanding of Maslow's own conception of actualized behaviour, the premise of which is to allow one to *transcend* the need to achieve given goals, yet the majority of organization scientists believe, or what to believe, that their research can be directed to ensure that self-actualizers are motivated goal-getters or, in McClelland's (1961) terms, that they have a high achievement need ('n Ach').[6] McClelland took it for granted that achievement, to be significant and satisfying, must be manifested through external, material, and competitive forms rather than in spiritual or psychological ways. Myers (1970) speaks for many of these organization scientists when he claims that the two express-

---

[4] I know of at least one large American-based company whose use of a five-point attitude scale, rated by supervisors, plays a very significant part in promotion within the firm because the correct attitude is associated with high ability.

[5] Maslow (1969; 1976: 274ff) has added 'Theory Z' to McGregor's categories in an effort to lift McGregor's work out of its functional context.

[6] I see that the reduction to chemistry-like cyphers is a symptom of the desire to show that their research is 'scientific'.

ions, self-actualization and motivated behaviour, are actually synonymous and that, further, a self-actualized, hard-working person is a satisfied individual (Myers 1970: 11).

These views rest on the unquestioned belief that the principle of self-actualization is rooted in an essensistic rather than an existential framework of being, that is, one's actualization or ontological growth can only be achieved through attainment of the essence or Ideal of the closed system. This in itself could be acceptable if that essence allowed for full reciprocal unestranged interaction between people (this, it may be recalled, was the ultimate outcome sought for by both Hegelian and Christian essensistic systems) but, as our analyses on alienation ought to have made clear, the system of capitalist work, with its foundation in man's exploitation of man, is a perversion of the principle of essensistic reciprocity. Therefore to seek to implement a programme of actualization that has as its explicit purpose the furtherance of the perversion is to reinforce the alienation to the Other that the Self already experiences.

THE QUESTIONABLE CONNEXION BETWEEN SELF-ACTUALIZATION AND PRODUCTIVITY LEVELS

There is, however, even in the USA, a counter-current to the general tide of pragmatic literature seeking to equate self-actualization with increased productivity. Twenty-five years ago Brayfield and Crockett (1955) suggested that

> 'it is time to question the strategic and ethical merits of selling to industrial concerns an assumed relationship between employee attitudes and employee performance.'
>
> (Brayfield and Crockett 1955: 418)

March and Simon (1958: 58) noted similarly that the variables of worker morale, satisfaction, and cohesiveness (or reciprocity)[7] did not have a consistent relationship to productivity. Vroom (1964) carried out a comparative analysis of twenty studies which used the interaction between satisfaction and performance as a focus of their research. He found that the correlation between the variables ranged from minus 0.31 to plus 0.86 with a median of plus 0.14, that is, only a faintly favourable connexion between satisfaction and performance. Despite this long-established evidence, as Fein (1973) has remarked, it has not prevented those within the system from continuing to believe that connexions do exist between self-actualization and the motivation to achieve a high performance.

---

[7] Factors which self-actualized jobs were supposed to be high in.

Indeed, some organizational scientists, for example, Lawler (1973), having been alerted to the lack, or the uncertain nature, of the links between these variables, have attempted to join them explicitly through 'mutual goal achieving packages' which have as their 'selling point' the belief that opportunities for good performance will *cause* satisfaction: in other words, Lawler takes for granted McGregor's (1960) research assumption that the ontological perspective of the individual at work is firmly within a closed Other-based system and that fulfilling the Other's desires will simultaneously fulfil the individual's. Tausky and Parke (in Dubin 1976) praise this assumption of Lawler's by stating that the application of his expectancy model to the literature on behaviour in work organizations makes it 'one of the most promising *reinforcement* models'. Clearly its attraction is that it purports to *train* workers to respond favourably to the system's goals in preference to their own inner goals or desires.

However, these efforts to rechannel self-actualization into the work context face criticism from another direction: Strauss (1966) and Gross (1970) suggest that the desire for self-actualization is inappropriate for the majority of workers in their jobs because implicit in it are strong value judgements (individual dignity, creative freedom, and self-development) with all the hallmarks of its academic origin. I would not disagree that strong value judgements are present *if* self-actualization is confined to the job-context because this assumes that a self-actualizing person will be more productive, but to suggest that actualization, as the search for psychological openness, is simply an academic desire, is to miss entirely its general ontological value to all types of people.

It should be now readily apparent why an authentic existence in what I have called the non-autonomous and semi-autonomous Self-Other interactions is not possible in an organized work context: the context itself is a mono-thematic (productivity-oriented) Other, which unlike a spiritual, godlike Other, cannot provide the Self with the complex psychological support necessary to ensure ontological growth. However, recent developments in the USA seem at first glance to redress this balance. For instance, Pascale and Athos (1981) argue that work organizations need a 'spiritual awareness' infused into their management philosophy and practice, to reunite the split between man's personal and productive aspects by creating an organization that plays a complex supportive role in the individual's life. Although this sounds an interesting step forward, the worker still has to alienate his labour to the organizational Other, because the whole basis of the drive to 'spirituality' is in response to

American businesses' desire to be more productive than their Japanese counterparts. The Marxian cycle of estrangement and alienation is thus unbroken, merely obscured further.

THE LACK OF DEVELOPMENT IN ORGANIZATION BEHAVIOUR LITERATURE TOWARDS UNDERSTANDING THE PSYCHOLOGICAL PROCESSES BEHIND SELF-ACTUALIZATION

In sum, the efforts of organization scientists to encourage commitment to organized Other-based work under the guise of encouraging self-actualization are, I suggest, no more advanced or psychologically rewarding than the sort of incentive scheme devised about 120 years ago by the philanthropist Robert Owen for use in his mill in New Lanark. This was the

'contrivance of a silent monitor for each one employed in the establishment. This consisted of a four-sided piece of wood, about two inches long and one broad, each side coloured – one side black, another blue, the third yellow and the fourth white, tapered at the top, and finished with wire eyes, to hang upon a hook with either side to the front. One of these was suspended in a conspicuous place near to each of the persons employed and the colour at the front told the conduct of the individual during the preceding day to four degrees of comparison. Bad, denoted by black and No. 4 – indifferent, by blue and No. 3 – good, by yellow and No. 2 – and excellent by white and No. 1.'

(Owen 1858: 111)

Work quality and quantity improved very considerably and his employees reported that they now got greater pleasure from their work. He goes on to say:

'Never perhaps in the history of the human race has so simple a device created in so short a period so much order, virtue, goodness and happiness out of so much ignorance, error and misery'!

(Owen 1858: 189)

These, to our eyes, amusing remarks echo the importance that some organization scientists attach to their much more recent, and must more complicated, attempts to introduce 'goodness and happiness' into work within the system. Less amusingly, their efforts are nothing more than palliative exercises which clearly aim to minimize or conceal the estranging aspects of alienated Other-based labour, and which fail to remove the basis of that estrangement through attempts to change the nature of the system itself. Their approach also reminds me of the notable passage in Tolstoi's book *What Then Must We Do* (1925) where he says: 'I sit on a man's back, choking him and making him carry me, and yet assure myself and others that I am very sorry for him and wish to ease his lot by all possible means – except by getting off his back'. The inability of organization scientists to help the individual to get the organizational Other off his back is not solely due to their own immersion within the capitalist work ethic but that there is no driving force from *within* the system to act as a catalyst to stimulate a reaction to Other-based work. Perhaps this should be the role of the Trades Unions.

THE LACK OF A REAL FOCUS FOR RADICAL CRITIQUE OF THE SYSTEM

The Webbs in 1920 hoped that a fully established Union structure could provide the critical force necessary to ease the workers' lot, not just by improving the circumstances of the *employment* through demands for higher wages and better conditions but to enrich their working *lives* (Webb and Webb 1920: 1). Hyman (1972) has described the Unions' role in blunter terms by stating that the Unions' purpose is to react against the 'more glaringly brutal accoutrements of managerial control' (Hyman 1972: 96). Unfortunately, however, the potentially radical nature of Union activity has been minimized through the bureaucratic activities of present-day Unions. This bureaucratization, as Wall and Lischeron (1977) suggest, is one of the factors that has led to a strong preference for *personal* participation over Union or representative interaction with the management. Arguing from results of their field studies on nurses and blue-collar workers, they say,

> 'The relative lack of support based on trade union representation is noteworthy. Among nurses this may be expected, but for blue-collar workers (especially those in the industrial sample who were all union members and active in this respect) it is less predictable. Nevertheless, the explanation is straightforward. To most of these workers, pay security and disciplinary issues defined the normal limits of their shop stewards' and trade union activities. Consequently . . . [the workers] looked to other forms of involvement of a more personal nature.'
>
> (Wall and Lischeron 1977: 145)

That is, because the Unions' functions have become remote and indeed Other-like, their role as constructive critics of Other-based work has disappeared. In fact, it is possible to argue that their existence now depends on the maintenance of organized Other-based work without which they would have no immediate function.[8] The ironic result of the Unions becoming Other-like is that workers are generally not seeking to question the nature of their work activity but are attempting to become *more* involved in the context of their jobs.

The disappearance of sources of potentially radical reassessment of the work context encourages man to mould himself around that context since he sees no viable, alternative form of self-growth.[9] The result is that the Self may acquire tent-like qualities: impressive and useful in appearance but its hollowness ensures that, if the organizational poles are removed, collapse is inevitable.

Understanding the nature of man's interaction with work organizations requires an exploration of the psychological aspects involved

The disinterest in the effect of capitalist Other-based work on the person's psychological attributes is partly due, I believe, to a predominantly *sociological* approach towards the work context. This tradition, emanating from a Marxist perspective of capitalist work, is certainly necessary for a sustained, long-term critique, but its demotion of the psychological aspects of work[10] exposes it to the risk of generalizing the particular experiences felt by each individual. Perrow (1972), as an advocate of the sociological approach, argues that a concern for man's psychology can never satisfactorily 'explain organizations by explaining the attitudes and behaviour of individuals, or even small groups, within them' (Perrow 1972: 143). I can counter this claim by contending that one of our aims, and that of the followers of the British 'human relations' school of thought is not to 'explain organizations' but is to specify the nature of man's relationship with organizations by understanding the influences, both good and bad, that organizations can have upon man's ontolo-

---

[8] But this is *not* an argument for the introduction of self-actualization or similar schemes despite Jones's (1971) naive belief that by 'humanizing' jobs one can render unions and their negotiating functions redundant because workers with satisfying jobs would not need to ask for increases in pay as compensation for monotonous tasks.

[9] This is obviously not a new phenomenon: Lafargue, imprisoned in France for his revolutionary views, often accused the workers of blindly accepting that work must dominate their lives and argued that they, as part of the proletariat, by 'betraying its instincts, denying its historic [revolutionary] vision has let itself be perverted by the dogma of work' (Lafargue, 1971: 13).

[10] A demotion which, as I sought to show, is quite alien to Marx's own work and thought.

gical existence. By this act of specification an awareness may
develop through which people at work realize more clearly the
nature of the profound contrast between their daily actuality and
their spiritual or psychological possibilities. Efforts to 'explain
organizations' *qua* process face the danger of assuming that people
within those organizations are simply sociological entities to be
handled quantitatively rather than qualitatively. As Argyris (1972)
notes, it is necessary to remember that:

> 'generalizations are made about processes . . . [which] are, in fact,
> developed from responses made by *individuals* which are then
> aggregated. Once having summed them up they become
> "sociological" variables where the individual as a causal explana-
> tion can be ignored. The conceptual process by which they go
> from individual processes to sociological processes is not expli-
> cated.'   (Argyris 1972: 69)

Argyris (1973), in a subsequent article, argues that sociologically
oriented theorists (he lists Blau, Perrow, Dubin, Goldthorpe, and
Lockwood) justified the treatment of man as a black box because
they rejected the 'need to have an explicit model of man'. As
Argyris's model of man shares many characteristics with Maslow's
concept of the actualizing individual, he does not find sympathy
with Crozier (1964) who, although lacking such a model, was still
able to conclude from his research that inhumanity of the work
organization towards individuals was not confined. How, Argyris
asks, can one define inhumanity without a concept of man? By
seeking to understand man's behaviour at work through 'Personality and Organization Theory', Argyris can study possible sources of
inhumanity by analysing man in terms of what he is capable of, not
only how he actually behaves. This approach can only be adopted
meaningfully at a level where man's psychological make-up is the
central issue of study, as is the case in this book. However, comparison between man's behaviour and his psychological potential can
reveal a gap so large that any meaningful form of reconciliation
seems impossible. Moreover, because of our knowledge that, at
work, man alienates his labour to the organizational Other and
suffers psychologically by becoming estranged both from himself
(his potentialities) and from other people (because he responds to
them competitively and aggressively) it would not be inconsistent
to argue that *any* efforts to reconcile the difference between man's
mundane actuality and his spiritual possibilities in the work context would be undesirable because the inert power of the Other
would simply reassert itself and man once more would succumb to

its deadening embrace. Following this line of thought may tempt one to argue that a sudden, violent disruption of the Other's domination of the Self may be the only solution that allows man his freedom. However, I cannot find solace in hoping for a spontaneous socio-political revolution to alter the circumstances of work because my concern is for the ontological effects that change of this kind induces. Thus, I am interested in observing existing attitudes to work to see if latent within people a critical awareness of the estranging aspects of their jobs is to be found. For this reason as I noted earlier, the worker's adoption of an instrumental or functional attitude towards his work bears closer attention.

Possible transcendence of alienation and estrangement through instrumental job satisfaction

This attitude, through which employees appear interested only in work which 'enables them to achieve a higher level of economic return' (Goldthorpe *et al*. 1968: 33), can be seen as the antithesis of that advocated as necessary by those who, like Argyris and Maslow, are concerned with man's psychological and not his economic growth. In fact, Goldthorpe points out that it is understood by instrumentally-oriented employees that the work they do can never be as a Marxian or Maslovian self-productive or actualizing *activity* but must simply be treated as *labour* (Goldthorpe *et al*. 1968: 25). The individual has detached himself psychologically from the system's goals and commitments in the manner of the (Hegelian) estranged sceptic. As we saw in Chapter 3, one whose psychological relationship to the Other corresponds to that of the estranged sceptic is a person whose dissociation from the goals and ideals of the closed system can lead him to make the break from that system into a new psychological openness. This act requires very considerable ontological strength and a courage that can only arise through an awareness of one's potentialities. Such self-awareness is necessary to counter the sheer inert power of the givenness of the system, which encourages foreclosure of awareness either through the efforts of organization scientists to introduce their version of self-actualization, or less subtly through financial reward.

I suggest that, in the long term, the instrumental attitude to work *can* lead to a break into psychological openness but it largely depends on creative use of leisure time to stimulate psychological growth. Unfortunately, the evidence so far (e.g. Fisk 1964; Shimmin 1968; Argyris 1973) tends to show that those with dull routine jobs (who usually adopt an instrumental attitude to work will, through a 'carry-over effect', use their leisure time unimaginatively and prefer passive recreations like television watching (Parker 1971; Torbert 1972). Argyris (1973) adds that the carry-over effect appears to be more closely related to work content and context than the relevant social class variables; that is, it is a psychological problem rather than a sociological issue. While the dialectical interaction between job choice and social grouping probably places a large question mark on the validity of this assertion for the British work context, it is undoubtedly correct to point out that there exists a distinct psychological difference between instrumentally oriented workers and those who seek for actualized work. Goldthorpe's Cambridge research team asked workers from the former group what they aspired to in their personal lives over the next ten years: about 60 per cent had 'the simple aspiration to have more money to spend and more goods and possessions' (Goldthorpe *et al.* 1968: 136). In Fromm's (1978) terms they preferred 'to have' rather than 'to be', a preference Fromm (like Marx and Maslow) found quite unacceptable because it relegates psychological growth in favour of material acquisition. However, what is of interest to us is the other 40 per cent of Goldthorpe's instrumentally-oriented workers who did not give priority to the 'having' mode of existence. If these workers are seeking leisure activities that allow the 'being' of their lives to develop[11] one may imagine that the perceived contrast between their working lives and their leisure pursuits will reach a point where devoting approximately ten hours a day (including 'breaks' and travel time), five days a week to organized work becomes quite unacceptable. By raising this point one is obviously facing the risk of succumbing to speculation and wishful thinking, but we are not alone in this. Meakin (1976) has pointed out that:

'It is legimate to speak of a more or less concerted European literary tradition of radical speculation not only on the dangerous aspects of industrialism but also the possibility of some sort of salvation through a non-ascetic ethic of creative fulfilling work.'
(Meakin 1976: 17)

The writers and poets who sustain this radical speculation may have rather mundane jobs themselves, but, as Sartre (1963: 277ff) has remarked in his study of Genet, it allows them to see the contrast between the expression of their thoughts and ideas and the man-

---

[11] Because of the sociological nature of the research this issue is not made clear: they only say that some of the 40 per cent had 'aspirations which suggested the respondent's own abandonment of striving for "success" in any individualistic sense' (Goldthorpe *et al.* 1968: 136).

ifestations of the given system as expressed through the 'language of the bourgeois'. That is, through their own literary efforts they resist the socializing influence of that language and they keep alive language's true role: to transform meaning rather than to designate it. The assimilation of such a tradition into the minds of the working public may precipitate a rejection of work that requires the alienation of the Self to the organizational Other even though the overtly estranging characteristics of that alienation have become tolerable through financial incentives.

Possible transcendence of alienation and estrangement through the context of a self-actualized job

If what I have said above can be seen as an optimistic outline of the prospects for those instrumentally committed to their work but who have also acquired a growing awareness of the unacceptability of organized work, am I justified in retaining the same optimism for those who believe that they can actualize themselves at work?

A growing number of social scientists[12] think so. Their optimism is founded upon the realization that work in organizations can provide the individual with the necessary *opportunities* to develop what has been called his 'self-management' (Lefebvre 1969) or 'competence' (White 1959; Argyris 1965) *if* we understand that the work context is a *source* of ontological development or open-ended psychological growth and actualization and not a context that treats this kind of growth as a *requirement* for its ends. That is, one's existence and work-habits must not be arranged in a manner to suit the Other-based goals of the organization, but that these material goals of growth and high profitability are subsumed under the worker's ontological and social aspirations to provide him with the stimuli upon which he can act self-creatively and not instrumentally.

White (1959) has particularized my general concept of ontological growth by his use of the word competence, which describes the 'ego-growth' or learning qualities evident in:

'such things as grasping and exploring, crawling and walking,

---

[12] Including for instance, Anthony (1977), Argyris (1972), Cooper (1978), De Charms (1968), Emery (1974), Hampden-Turner (1971), Herbst (1972), Morgan (1980), and Trist (1959). These writers are not specifically concerned with organizations *per se* but with the plight of man in an organized world. Their field of study is social rather than organizational.

attention and perception, language and thinking, manipulating and changing the surroundings, all of which promote an effective – a competent – interaction with the environment.'

(White 159: 317–18)

Because there is no consummating climax in these actions he sees that satisfaction has to be found through a 'considerable series of transactions', in a trend of behaviour, rather than in a goal that is achieved. This considerable series of transactions develops ontological awareness because it gradually changes and enriches one's relationship with the environment allowing for new possibilities to emerge, or in Hebb's words, creates 'difference-in-sameness' (quoted in White 1959: 322). Thus, self-actualization in a non-Other based, or open system, represents a form of *learning* which permits a break from the giveness of the quotidian by creating new perceptions and interconnexions, whereas, we may note for comparison, actualization in a closed Other-based system is characterized by *adaptation* to that system. Competence, it should be made clear, is not at all connected with the ability to produce more goods with greater efficiency – if it were it would be significant only as the adaptive act of an individual within the context of the organized work system. Instead, it must be emphasized, it is the art of becoming more than one already is, regardless of the context, by transcending that context through one's effective actions upon it. If workers are seen to desire self-actualizing jobs this desire ought to be viewed as a manifestation of their general 'competence motivation'. White's concept of competence, because it places considerable weight on how man behaves towards other people, is more closely associated with Marx's notion of the social importance of self-productive activity than with Sartre's position, which by contrast, emphasizes isolationist free praxis. Argyris (1965) has developed White's concern for man's social awareness by proposing that certain factors, the 'plus characteristics' must be present before *interpersonal* competence can emerge. The important requirement at the basis of the plus characteristics according to Argyris is the ability of the individual to experiment or take risks with his self-esteem in order to enlarge his awareness of the relevant factors. By encouraging one to focus on the need to take risks, Argyris has correctly specified a factor necessary to the development of ontological strength and one that may eventually lead those who actualize within the work context to find that context unacceptable. Moreover, by suggesting that one must risk one's self-esteem in order to remain open to other possibilities, he has drawn attention to another facet of self-actualization – that of not taking oneself or one's actions completely seriously. I shall develop this point shortly.

Lefebvre's concept of 'self-management' takes us one step further than White's and Argyris's work in the process whereby the Self outgrows the realm of organized work. Self-management is closely associated both with what Marx understood to be the characteristics of self-productive activity and Sartre's praxis of the individual in his quest for freedom: through self-management the individual lifts himself out of the quotidian existence of 'apparent banality [to discover in the] depth beneath its triviality, something extraordinary in its very ordinariness' (Lefebvre, 1971: 37). That extraordinariness is found, as Heidegger (1978) has also shown, by realizing that in man's daily actions, before him lie all the resources necessary for his ontological development if he can only return to a referential, immediate level of interaction with it,[13] instead of perceiving it through the veil of a manipulative estranging metalanguage – a message or group of signals 'controlling the code of the same or another message' (Lefebvre 1971: 127). Morgan (1980) has recently developed these ideas through his powerful analysis of the 'root metaphors' (or ontological constructs) which pervade man's awareness of organizations. In our terms, the closed nature of the organized work system provides the sole language or context through which man's daily existence is perceived and acted out: if man's actions and perceptions operate through the system's metalanguage his behaviour affirms the system's potency over him, depriving him of a medium through which he may assault it or respond to the extraordinary thrown up by his praxis in it. Rose (1978), in an analysis of Lefebvre's ideas, puts the case for self-management succinctly: 'self-management *as praxis* refers to the process of uncovering the poetry[14] of everyday life and its cultural, organizational and societal transformation' (Rose 1978: 618). The praxis of self-management, I contend, can arise through what I have called the semi-autonomous interaction of the Self with the organization as Other to provide the individual with the material whereby, through his growing self-awareness, he transcends the organization's closedness and its metalinguistic influence. As Lefebvre

---

[13] And if, echoing White's recollection of Hebb's words, man can perceive the 'difference-in-sameness' of all things.

[14] The use of the word 'poetry' in this context suggests to me that perhaps Rose had Heidegger's (1975) comments in mind: 'Projective saying is poetry . . . poetry is the saying of the unconcealedness of what is. Actual language at any given moment is the happening of this saying, in which a people's world historically arises for it and the earth is preserved as that which remains closed. Projective saying is saying which, in preparing the sayable simultaneously brings the unsayable as such into a world. (Heidegger 1975: 74)

understands it, the praxis element of self-management is coupled with a *generalized* awareness of a 'utopia': this is not an Ideal in the closed sense but a yet-to-be-attained probability which may emerge through man's search for the possibilities inherent in a situation and which informs the direction of his praxis. I suggest that to supplement Lefebvre's requirements of a generalized awareness of 'utopia' as a praxis-director one needs to incorporate the awareness of self-actualization as a *particularized*, personal form of self-management, because this awareness creates its own 'utopia' through the enhancement of ontological growth in the form of the presence of meta-motivators and Being-cognition.

Conclusions

THE EMERGENCE OF A CRITICAL AWARENESS OF THE ARBITRARINESS OF MAN'S INVOLVEMENT WITH WORK ORGANIZATIONS

What this consideration of self-actualization and its other manifestations in the organized work context has sought to show is that although the presence of purposive rationalism and the unquestioning acceptance of the Protestant work ethic appears to extend into the research of many organization scientists, there are also a number of writers and practitioners whose research interests ensure the presence of a critical focus on man's behaviour in the context of work organizations. From these writers one may draw the hope that although the present system of work still rests on the alienation of man's Self to the organizational Other, there are within the organization's parameters sufficient scope for the critically aware individual to appreciate that while his efforts to attain self-actualization at work may lead to an over-dependence upon the organization's structures and goals (thus leading to the 'tent-like' Self), they can also lead to an emergence of a new-found inner strength or ontological courage to 'be' which can, in turn, serve as the spring-board for his participation in a form of work that does not have its origins in alienation to an Other. The individual whose psychological awareness has attained this stage thus approaches the poetry of everyday life authentically: the sincere pursuit of self-actualization within the context of organized work has been replaced by a new openness together with a willingness and an ability to *respond* to that openness. That is, the individual has attained the ability to see organizational goals for what they are: arbitrarily defined end-states which *give* the organization a purpose and a coherence that it does not have naturally.

It follows that the man who has emerged from a sincere attachment to the organized work context and who before earnestly sought after a self-actualizing job is able to see his actions in the light of their inherent arbitrariness. If he can see this, the strong moral qualities, which Anthony (1977) has pointed out govern attitudes to work, also disappear, thus freeing man of the necessity to take his work wholly seriously. Maslow (1976: 253) has argued that those whose cognitive awareness has transcended the striving to make up deficiencies state of 'D-cognition' and progressed to the striving towards being state of 'B-cognition' are much more likely to see the world, its events and themselves as amusing, comic, or even absurd.[15] This playful attitude to life can conceal true profoundity: Watts (1973) has shown in that in the Indian Vedanta (or Upanishads):

> 'the whole world is seen [in Hindu philosophy] as the *lila* and the *maya* of the Self, the first word meaning "play" and the second having the complex sense of illusion (from the Latin *ludere* to play), magic, creative power, art, and measuring – as when one dances or draws a design to a certain measure. From this point of view the universe in general and playing in particular are, in a special sense "meaningless": that is, they do not – like words and symbols – signify or point to something beyond themselves.'
>
> (Watts 1973: 116)

As I have already noted, Maslow, whom Watts knew when they worked together at the Esalen Institute in California, argued that to understand the world in this way required one to see everything in a 'sophisticated innocence' (Maslow 1976: 245), through which the individual can free himself of the strictures that surround him and perceive afresh with a playful eye. Although this requires further research, I suspect that in a special way the Irishman's 'stupidity' is the natural focus of jokes for Englishmen because the Irish retain a flavour of their Celtic forebears who (from what is known through their mythology and art-forms) did not perceive 'reality' in the rationalistic (Roman) manner preferred by the English but emphasized the profound *interplay* of occurrences and symbols in a way incomprehensible to the 'logical' mind. With this approach people

---

[15] They can, to paraphrase Argyris, take risks with their self-esteem – they need not recourse to pomposity to hide absurd aspects of themselves.

show great enthusiasm and commitment for their activities[16] but they are not as Pappenheim (1959) says, so absorbed in the relentless pursuit of their interests that nothing they experience has a meaning in itself, unless it can be turned into a means for attaining their ends. Not taking oneself or one's actions entirely seriously indicates that one is responding playfully to being-in-the-world. This, as I have indicated throughout this work, is the characteristic at the root of self-productive or non-alienated activity. The importance that I attribute to approaching life playfully may be seen in that it allows man to enhance his spiritual or psychological awareness of the 'poetry of everyday life' by transcending the purposive rationality that maintains the subject–object split alluded to by Gadalla and Cooper (1978), so that understanding of the world and the people around him, together with the metaphoric processes whereby he relates to them, can grow in open-ended complexity.

THE NEED TO REASSESS THE NATURE OF RESEARCH INTO MAN'S
BEHAVIOUR IN ORGANIZATIONS

If the 'reality' of the organized work context is seen as an arbitrary structure whose form is but one of several that could have appeared out of the ground of possible forms and whose psychological hold over people is equally arbitrary, scientists who wish to research into the effect of organized work on people's lives must bring with them a playfulness and an openness through which they can relate to the potential within those lives. Although I would like to think that the application of the principle of acting and thinking with playful absorption has infused the writing of this book, too often it appears that those who research into the effect of organized work upon man perceive their studies as a kind of serious industry:

'The scholar disappears. He is succeeded by the research man[17] who is engaged in research projects. These, rather than the cultivating of erudition, lend to his work its atmosphere of incisiveness. The research man no longer needs a library at home. Moreover, he is constantly on the move. He negotiates at meetings and collects information at congresses. He contracts for commissions with publishers. The latter now determine along with him which books must be written.'

(Heidegger 1977: 125)

---

[16] If they do not, their 'play' may be mere caprice. As Buber (1970, p. 109) said, 'capricious man does not believe and encounter . . . he only knows the feverish desire to use'.

[17] Goldmann (1969: 13) has called him one of the new host of 'illiterate scholars'.

As we have seen, the result of this attitude is shown most clearly in the treatment of the principle of self-actualization by (usually American)[18] organization scientists whose emphases on pragmatic rationalism has brought about a bulging 'literature' replete with statistics showing the effect of self-actualization programmes on work output levels and job commitment. Heidegger also adds that for the researcher, as technologist, the sustained activity of research degenerates to *'des blossen Betriebs'* (mere busyness). The researcher has reduced himself to a technologist devoid of any awareness of the absurdity of either his own activities or of the processes he studies. As I indicated in the Introduction, in this examination of the effects of man's interaction with the Other-based working environment, I have used the concepts of alienation and authenticity to inquire into man's working life in a manner which sought to keep open the different permutations of psychological attributes and environmental or Other-based processes. In this way I have tried to avoid what Bateson (1972) has seen as the result of an excessive preference for inductive thought which, he argues, characterizes the present state of the behavioural sciences, 'a mass of quasi-theoretical speculation unconnected with any core of fundamental knowledge' (Bateson 1972: 26).

I have endeavoured not to foreclose the difference aspects under consideration, save to resolve the confusion surrounding the concepts of alienation and estrangement and to emphasize the interweaving of their dual psychological and contextual qualities. Thus, my intent has been two-fold: on one hand, to clarify the understanding of alienation and estrangement both in an attempt to establish a core of knowledge about these concepts that can serve as a basepoint for fresh research in the work context, and, less importantly, so that when these concepts appear in the literature one may appreciate what the author, whether he be researcher or technologist, had in mind. On the other hand, I have tackled this study using a methodology, an approach which although 'unscientific' in the conventional sense of that word, can serve as a guide to those who have failed to appreciate that research must be playfully undertaken before one can comprehend the ever-open complexity of man's vital processes.

---

[18] In line with the comments from my study of Calvinism in Chapter 2, May (1976) has suggested that the admonition *'behave* yourself' and the American pre-occupation with studying man's rational overt *behaviour* are both born of the moralistic puritanism with which Americans repress the so-called irrational (May 1976: 74).

References

ABRAMSON, P.R. (1972) Political efficacy and political trust among black children: two explanations. *Journal of Politics*, 34: 1243–275.

ADAMS, H.P. (1940) *Karl Marx in His Early Writings*. London: Frank Cass and Co.

AIKEN, M. and HAGE I. (1966) Organizational alienation: a comparative analysis. *American Sociological Review* 31(4): 497–507.

ALDERFER, C.P. (1972) *Existence Relatedness and Growth: Human Needs in Organizational Settings*. New York: Free Press.

ALLPORT, G.W. (1955) *Becoming*. New Haven: Yale University Press.

ALTHUSSER, L. (1970) *For Marx*. Translated by B. Brewster. London: Allen Lane.

ALTHUSSER, L. (1976) *Essays in Self-Criticism*. Translated by G. Lock. London: New Left Books.

ALTHUSSER, L. and BALIBAR, E. (1970) *Reading Capital*. Translated by B. Brewster. London: New Left Books.

ANGYAL, A. (1965) *Neurosis and Treatment*. New York: Wiley.

ANTHONY, P.D. (1977) *The Ideology of Work*. London: Tavistock.

ARGYLE, M. (1972) *The Social Psychology of Work*. Harmondsworth: Penguin.

ARGYRIS, C. (1957) *Personality and Organization*. New York: Harper.

ARGYRIS, C. (1965) *Organization and Innovation*. Homewood, Ill.: Irwin.

ARGYRIS, C. (1972) *The Applicability of Organizational Sociology.* Cambridge: Cambridge University Press.

ARGYRIS, C. (1973) Personality and Organization Theory revisited. *Administrative Science Quarterly* **18**: 141–67.

ARTAUD, A. (1974) *Collected Works.* Translated by V. Corti and A. Hamilton. London: Calder and Boyars.

AUGUSTINE, ST, Bishop of Hippo, (1955) *Later Works.* Edited and translated by J. Burnaby. Library of Christian Classics, v. VIII. London: S.C.M. Press.

AYER, A.J. (1956) *The Problem of Knowledge.* Harmondsworth: Penguin.

BAINTON, R.H. (1950) *Here I Stand – A Life of Luther.* Tennessee: Abington Press.

BARTH, K. (1961) *Church Dogmatics.* Edited and translated by G.W. Bromily. Edinburgh: T. and T. Clark.

BARTHES, R. (1967) *Elements of Semiology.* Translated by A. Lavers and C. Smith. London: Cape.

BATESON, G. (1972) *Steps to an Ecology of Mind.* London: Chandler.

BEHLING, O., LABOVITZ, G., and KOSMO, R., (1968) The Herzberg Controversy – a critical reappraisal. *Academy of Management Journal* **11**(1): 99–108.

BERGER, P. (1966) *Invitation to Sociology.* Harmondsworth: Pelican.

BERLIN, I. (1969) *Four Essays on Liberty.* Oxford: Oxford University Press.

BERTALANFFY, L. VON. (1973) *General System Theory.* Harmondsworth: Penguin University Books

BLACKLER, F.H.M. and BROWN, C.A. (1975) The impending crisis in job redesign. *Journal of Occupational Psychology* **48**: 185–93.

—— (1978) *Job Redesign and Management Control: Studies in British Leyland and Volvo.* London: Saxon House.

BLAU, P.M. (1964) *Exchange and Power in Social Life.* New York: Wiley.

BLAUNER, R. (1964) *Alienation and Freedom.* Chicago: Chicago University Press.

BOOKCHIN, M. (1974) *Post-Scarcity Anarchism.* London: Wildwood House.

BONJEAN, C.M. and GRIMES, M.D. (1970) Bureaucracy and alienation: a dimensional approach. *Social Forces* **48–9**: 365–73.

BRAYFIELD, A.H. and CROCKETT, W.H. (1955) Employee attitudes and employee performance. *Psychological Bulletin* **52**: 396–424.

BROWN, N.O. (1959) *Life Against Death*. New York: Wesleyan University Press.

BUBER, M. (1970) *I and Thou*. Translated by W. Kaufmann. Edinburgh: T. and T. Clark.

BULLOUGH, B.L. (1967) Alienation in the ghetto. *American Journal of Sociology* 70: 469–78.

CALVIN, J. (1954) *Theological Treatises*. Translated by J.K.S. Reid. London: S.C.M. Press.

—— (1960) *Institutes of Christian Religion*. Edited by J.T. McNeill. Philadelphia: Westminster.

CHERNS, A.B. and DAVIS, L.E. (eds) (1975) *The Quality of Working Life*. New York: Free Press.

CHERRY, C. (1967) But there is nothing I have is essential to me. In R. Jakobsen (Festschrift) *To Honor R. Jakobsen*: 462–74. The Hague: Mouton.

CHIODI, P. (1976) *Sartre and Marxism*. Translated by K. Soper. Hassocks: The Harvester Press.

COFER, C.N. and APPLEY, M.H. (1964) *Motivation Theory and Research*. New York: Wiley.

COHEN, S. and TAYLOR, L. (1978) *Escape Attempts*. Harmondsworth: Pelican.

COOPER, R. (1974) *Job Motivation and Job Design*. London: Institute of Personnel Management.

—— (1976) The Open Field. *Human Relations* 29: 11: 999–1017.

CORNFORD, F. MACD. (1952) *Principium Sapientiae*. New York: Harper.

CRAIK, K.J.W. (1967) *The Nature Of Explanation*. Cambridge: Cambridge University Press.

CROZIER, M. (1964) *The Bureaucratic Phenomenon*. London: Tavistock.

CULLER, J. (1976) *Saussure*. Fontana Books. Glasgow: Collins.

DAHRENDORF, R. (1959) *Class and Class Conflict in Industrial Society*. Stanford: Stanford University Press.

DE CHARDIN, P.T. (1959) *The Phenomenon of Man*. Translated by B. Wall. London: Collins.

—— (1970) *Hymn of the Universe*. Translated by G. Vann. Fontana Books. Glasgow: Collins.

DE CHARMS, R. (1968) *Personal Causation*. New York: Academic Press.

DERRIDA, J. (1976) *Of Grammatology*. Translated by G. Chakravorty. New York: Johns Hopkins.

DESCARTES, R. (1968) *Philosophical Works*. Translated and edited by E.S. Haldane and G.R.T. Ross. New York: Dover.

DEWART, L. (1967) *The Future of Belief.* London: Burns and Oates.

DUBIN, R. (1976) Ed., *Handbook of Work Organizations and Society.* New York: Rand McNally.

DUMAZEDIER, J. (1967) *Toward a Society of Leisure.* New York: Collier-Macmillan.

DUNNETTE, M.D., CAMPBELL J.P., and HAKEL M.D. (1967) Factors contributing to job satisfaction and job dissatisfaction in six occupational groups. *Organizational Behavior and Human Performance.* 2. pp. 143–174.

DURKHEIM, E. (1952) *Suicide: a Study in Sociology.* Translated by J.A. Spaulding and G. Simpson. London: Routledge and Kegan Paul.

—— (1964) *The Division of Labour in Society.* Translated by G. Simpson. New York: Free Press.

ELDRIDGE, J.E.T. (1971) *Sociology and Industrial Life.* London: Michael Joseph.

EMERY, F.E. (1974) Bureaucracy and Beyond. *Organizationl Dynamics* (Winter).

ERASMUS, D. (1969) *De Libero Arbitrio* (On the Freedom of Will) Translated by E.G. Rupp and A.N. Marlow. Library of Christian Classics, v. XVII. London: S.C.M. Press.

FAIRBAIRN, W.R.D. (1952) *Psychoanalytic Studies of the Personality* London: Tavistock.

FEIN, M. (1973) The Myth of Job Enrichment. *Humanist.* September: 30–31.

FEUER, L. (1963) What is alienation? The career of a concept. In M. Stein and A. Vidich, Eds., *Sociology on Trial.* Englewood Cliffs, New Jersey: Prentice-Hall.

FEUERBACH, L. (1966) *Principles of the Philosophy of the Future.* Translated by M.H. Vogel, New York: Bobbs-Merrill Co.

FINDLAY, J.N. (1958) *Hegel: A Reexamination. London:* Allen and Unwin.

FINIFTER, A. (ed) (1972) *Alienation and The Social System.* London: Wiley and Sons.

FIRESTONE, S. (1971) *The Dialectic of Sex: The Case for Feminist Revolution.* London: Cape.

FISCHER, C.S. (1973) On urban alienations and anomie: powerlessness and social isolation. *American Sociological Review:* 311–26.

FISK, G. (ed.) (1964) *The Frontiers of Management Psychology.* New York: Harper and Row.

FOX, A. (1966) Industrial Sociology and Industrial Relations. *Re-*

search *Paper No. 3. Royal Commission on Trade Unions and Employers Associations.* London: H.M.S.O.

—— (1974) *Man Mismanagement.* London: Hutchinson.

FRANKFORT, H., FRANKFORT, H.A., WILSON, J.A., and JACOBSEN, T. (1949) *Before Philosophy.* Harmondsworth: Pelican.

FRANZ, M.L. VON (1975) *C.G. Jung: His Myth in our Time.* London: Hodders.

FREUD, S. (1973) *New Introductory Lectures on Psychoanalysis.* Translated by J. Strachey. Harmondsworth: Pelican.

—— (1974) *Introductory Lectures on Psychoanalysis.* Translated by J. Strachey. Harmondsworth: Penguin.

FROMM, E., (1960) *Fear of Freedom.* London: Routledge and Kegan Paul.

—— (1963) *The Sane Society.* London: Routledge and Kegan Paul.

—— (1978) *To Be or to Have.* London: Cape.

GADALLA, J.E. and COOPER, R. (1978) Towards an epistemology of management. *Social Science Information* **17**(3): 349–83.

GASKELL, P. (1836) *Artizans and Machinery.* London: Frank Cass and Co.

GIBSON, J.J. (1966) *The Senses Considered as Perceptual Systems.* London: Allen and Unwin.

GLASS, J.M. (1972) Schizophrenia and perception. *Inquiry* **15**: 114–45.

—— (1974) Plato, Marx and Freud: The vision of eros and transcendence. *Psychiatry* **37**(2): 147–57.

GLAZER, N. (1947) the alienation of modern man. *Commentary* **3**: 360–81.

GOFFMAN, E. (1957) Alienation from interaction. *Human Relations* **10**: 47–59.

—— (1969) *The Presentation of Self in Everyday life.* Harmondsworth: Penguin.

GOLDMANN, L. (1969) *The Human Sciences and Philosophy.* Translated by H.V. White and R. Anchor. London: Cape.

GOLDSTEIN, K. (1939) *The Organism.* New York: American Books.

—— (1947) *Human Nature.* Harvard University Press.

GOLDTHORPE, J.H. (1966) Attitudes and behaviour of car assembly workers: a deviant case and theoretical critique. *British Journal of Sociology* **17**: 227–44.

GOLDTHORPE, J.H., LOCKWOOD, D., BECHOFER, F., and PLATT, J. (1968) *The Affluent Worker: Industrial Attitudes and Behaviour.* Cambridge: Cambridge University Press.

GOULDNER, A.W. (1969) The Unemployed Self. In R. Fraser (ed.)

Work: 20 Personal Accounts. Vols. I and II. Harmondsworth: Penguin.

—— (1980) *The Two Marxisms: Contradiction and Anomalies in the Development of Theory.* London: Macmillan.

GRATTON, L.C. (1981) 'An empirical validation of Maslow's Need Hierarchy in the work and non-work setting.' Unpublished PhD thesis, Liverpool University.

GROSS, E. (1961) A functional approach to leisure analysis. *Social Problems* 9(1): 2–8.

—— (1970) Work, organization and stress. In S. Levine and N. Scotch (eds) *Social Stress.* Chicago: Aldine.

GUIBERT, J. DE (1954) *The Theology of the Spiritual Life.* London: Sheed and Ward.

GYLLENHAMMAR, P.C. (1977) *People at Work.* New York: Addison Wesley.

HABERMAS, J. (1971) *Knowledge and Human Interests.* Boston: Beacon Press.

—— (1974) *Theory and Practice.* New York: Heinemann.

HAJDA, J. (1961) Alienation and integration of student intellectuals. *American Sociological Review* 26: 758–77.

HAMPDEN-TURNER, C. (1971) *Radical Man: The Process of Psycho-Social Development.* London: Duckworth.

HARRISON, J.E. (1905) *The Religion of Ancient Greece.* London: Archibald Constable and Co.

HEGEL, G.W.F. (1931) *The Phenomenology of Mind.* Translated by J.B. Baillie. London: Macmillan.

—— (1964) *The Philosophy of Right.* Translated by T.M. Knox. Oxford: Clarendon.

—— (1969) *Das Phanomenologie des Geistes in Werke.* E. Moldenhauer and K. Michel (eds), Frankfurt a. M.: Suhrkamp.

—— (1971) *Philosophy of Mind.* Translated by W. Wallace, introduction by J.N. Findlay. Oxford: Clarendon Press.

HEIDEGGER, M. (1959) *An Introduction to Metaphysics.* Translated by R. Manheim. New Haven: Yale University Press.

—— (1962) *Kant and the Problem of Metaphysics.* Translated by J.S. Churchill. Bloomington: Indiana University Press.

—— (1975) *Poetry, Language, Thought.* Translated by A. Hofstadter. New York: Harper and Row.

—— (1977) *The Question Concerning Technology and Other Essays.* Translated by W. Lovitt. New York: Harper and Row.

—— (1978) *Being and Time.* Translated by J. Macquarrie and E. Robinson. Oxford: Blackwell.

HELD, R. and HEIN, A. (1963) Movement-produced stimulation in the development of visually guided behaviour. *Journal of Comparative and Physiological Psychology* **56**: 872–76.

HELLER, F.A. (1976) Towards a practical psychology of work. *Journal of Occupational Psychology* **49**(1): 45–54.

HERBST, P.G. (1972) Socio-Technical Theory and Design. London: Tavistock.

HERRICK, N.Q. and MACCOBY, M. (1975) Humanizing Work: A priority goal of the 1970s. In A.B. Cherns and L.E. Davis (eds) *The Quality of Working Life*, v. 1. New York: Free Press.

HERZBERG, F. (1966) *Work and the Nature of Man.* London: Staples Press.

—— (1968) One more time: How do you motivate employees? *Harvard Business Review* **46**(1): 53–62.

HERZBERG, F., MAUSNER, B., and SNYDERMAN, B.B. (1959) *The Motivation to Work.* New York: Wiley.

HILL, W.A., and EGAN, D.M. (eds) (1966) *Readings in Organizational Theory.* Boston: Allyn and Bacon.

HOBBES, T. (1885) *Leviathan* (8th Ed.) London: Routledge and Sons.

HORNEY, K. (1950) *Neurosis and Human Growth.* New York: Norton.

HUSSERL, E. (1931) *Ideas: General Introduction to Pure Phenomenology.* Translated by W.R.B. Gibson. London: Allen and Unwin.

—— (1960) *Cartesian Meditations.* Translated by D. Cairns. The Hague: Nijhoff.

HYMAN, R. (1972) *Strikes.* Fontana Books. London: Collins.

ISRAEL, J. (1971) *Alienation: From Marx to Modern Sociology.* Boston: Allyn and Bacon.

JAKOBSEN, R. (1967) Festschrift: *To Honour R. Jakobsen.* The Hague: Mouton.

JAQUES, E. (1951) *The Changing Culture of a Factory.* London: Tavistock.

JENSEN, R. (1969) *God after God.* New York: Bobbs-Merrill.

JOHNSON, F. (ed.) (1973) *Alienation, Concept, Term and Meanings.* New York: Seminar Press.

JONES, J.N. (1971) *The Wages of Fear.* New York: McGraw-Hill.

JUNG, C.G. (1963) *Memoirs, Dreams, Reflections.* Translated by R. and C. Winston. London: Collins.

KAHLER, E. (1957) *The Tower and the Abyss.* New York: Braziller.

KANT, I. (1933) *Critique of Pure Reason.* Translated by N.K. Smith. London: Macmillan.

KAPLAN, M.A. (1976) *Alienation and Identification.* New York: Free Press.

KAUFMANN, W. (1975) *Existentialism from Dostoevski to Sartre.* New York: New American Library.

—— (1978) *Hegel: A Reinterpretation.* Notre Dame University Press, New York: Basic Books.

KENISTON, K. (1965) *The Uncommitted: Alienated Youth in Modern Society.* New York: Harcourt, Brace and World.

KIERKEGAARD, S. (1954) *Fear and Trembling* with *The Sickness Unto Death.* Translated by W. Lowrie. Princeton N.J.: Princeton University Press.

KING, M.L. (1969) *Strength to Love.* Fontana Books. Glasgow: Collins.

KING, N.A. (1970) A clarification and evaluation of the two-factor theory of job satisfaction. *Psychological Bulletin* 74:18–31.

KIRK, G.S. and RAVEN, J.E. (1975) *The Presocratic Philosophers.* Cambridge: Cambridge University Press.

KOJÈVE, A. (1969) *Introduction to the Reading of Hegel.* Translated by J.H. Nichols. New York: Basic Books.

KUHN, T.S. (1970) *The Structure of Scientific Revolutions* (second edition). Chicago: Chicago University Press.

LABEDZ, L. (1962) *Essays on the History of Marxist Ideas.* London: Allen and Unwin.

LACAN, J. (1977) *Ecrits: A Selection.* Translated by A. Sheridan. London: Tavistock.

—— (1979) *The four fundamental concepts of psycho-analysis.* Translated by A. Sheridan. Harmondsworth: Penguin.

LAFARGUE, M.P. (1917) *The Right to Be Lazy and Other Stories.* Translated by C.H. Kerr. Chicago: Kerr.

LAING. R.D. (1961) *The Self and Others.* London: Tavistock.

—— (1969) *The Divided Self.* Harmondsworth: Penguin.

LAWLER, E.E. (1973) *Motivation in Work Organizations.* California: Brooks-Cole.

LAWLER, E.E. and SUTTLE, J.L. (1972) A causal correlation test of the Need Hierarchy concept. *Organizational Behaviour and Human Performance* 7: 265–87.

LEE, A.M.C. (1972) An obituary for alienation. *Social Problems* 20: 121–27.

LEE, H.D.P. (ed.)(1955) *Plato: The Republic.* Harmondsworth: Penguin.

LEFEBVRE, H. (1969) *The Explosion.* New York: Monthly Review Press.

—— (1971) *Everyday Life in the Modern World.* Translated by S. Rabinovitch. London: Allen Lane.

LEMPRIERE, J. (1865) *A Classical Dictionary.* Halifax: Milner and Sowerby.

LENIN, V.I. (1972) *Materialism and Empiro-Criticism.* Peking: Foreign Languages Press.

LEVINE, S. and SCOTCH, N. (eds) (1970) *Social Stress.* Chicago: Aldine.

LIKERT, R. (1961) *New Patterns of Management.* New York: McGraw-Hill.

—— (1967) *The Human Organizations.* New York: McGraw-Hill.

LING, T.O. (1970) *A History of Religion East and West.* London: Macmillan.

LOWRY, R. (1962) The function of alienation in leadership. *Sociology and Social Research* 46(4): 426–35.

LUKACS, G. (1975) *The Young Hegel.* Translated by R. Livingstone. London: Merlin Press.

LUTHER, M. (1958) *Works.* Ed. J. Pelikan. St. Louis: Concordia Publishing House.

—— (1969) *De Serro Arbitrio (On the Bondage of the Will).* Translated by P.S. Watson and B. Drewery. Library of Christian Classics, v. XVII. London: S.C.M. Press.

MACINTYRE, A. (1965) Marxist mask and romantic face. *Encounter* **XXIV**(4): 64–72.

MACKAY, D.M. (1969) *Information, Mechanism and Meaning.* Cambridge, Mass.: Massachusetts Institute of Technology.

MCCLELLAND, D.C. (1961) *The Achieving Society.* New York: Van Nostrand.

MCCLOSKY, H. and SCHAAR, J. (1965) Psychological dimensions of anomy. *American Sociological Review* 30(1): 14–40.

MCGREGOR, D. (1960) *The Human Side of Enterprise.* New York: McGraw-Hill.

MCDERMOTT, J. (1969) Technology: the opiate of the intellectuals. *New York Review of Books* **XIII**: 25–35.

MCLELLAN, D. (ed.) (1971) *Marx's Grundrisse.* London: Macmillan.

—— (1975) *Marx.* Fontana Books. Glasgow: Collins.

MALRAUX, A. (1968) *Antimemoirs.* Translated by T. Kilmartin. Harmondsworth: Penguin.

MANNHEIM, K. (1936) *Ideology and Utopia.* London: Routledge and Kegan Paul.

MARCH, J.G. and SIMON, H.A. (1958) *Organizations.* New York: Wiley.

MARCUSE, H. (1964) *One Dimensional Man.* Sphere Books. London: Abacus.

—— (1966) *Eros and Civilization.* 2nd Ed. Boston: Beacon Press.

MARX, K. (1940) See H.P. Adams, 1940.

—— (1959) *The Economic and Philosophical Manuscripts.* Translated by M. Milligan. Moscow: Foreign Languages Publishing House.

—— (1963) *Early Writings*. Translated and edited by T.B. Bottomore. London: Watts.

—— (1965) With F. Engels. *The German Ideology*. London: Lawrence and Wishart.

—— (1970) *The Economic and Philosophical Manuscripts of 1844*. Translated by M. Milligan. London: Lawrence and Wishart.

—— (1971) See D. McLellan, 1971.

—— (1973) *Grundrisse*. Translated by M. Nicolaus. London: Allen Lane.

—— (1974) *Capital*. London: Lawrence and Wishart.

—— (1975) *Early Writings* (including Critique of Hegel's Doctrine of the State; Economic and Philosophical Manuscripts; Excerpts from J.S. Mill's Elements of Political Economy; On the Jewish Question.) Translated by R. Livingstone and G. Benton. Ed. L. Colletti. Harmondsworth: Penguin.

MARX, K. and ENGELS, F. (1973) *Manifesto of the Communist Party*. Translated by S. Moore. Moscow: Progress Publishers.

—— (1975) *Collected Works*. London: Lawrence and Wishart.

Marx-Engels Gesamtausgabe (MEGA) (1977) Berlin: Dietz.

MASLOW, A.H. (1954) *Motivation and Personality*. New York: Harper and Bros.

—— (1968) *Towards a Psychology of Being*. (Second Edition) Princeton, N.J.: Van Nostrand.

—— (1969) Theory Z. *Journal of Transpersonal Psychology* 1(2): 31–47.

—— (1976) *The Farther Reaches of Human Nature*. Esalen. Harmondsworth: Penguin.

MASTERSON, P. (1973) *Atheism and Alienation*. Harmondsworth: Penguin.

MAUROIS, A. (1962) *The Quest for Proust*. Translated by G. Hopkins. Harmondsworth: Penguin.

MAY, R. (1953) *Man's Search for Himself*. New York: Norton.

—— (1976) *The Courage To Create*. London: Collins.

MEAD, M. (1942) The comparative study of culture and the purposive cultivation of democratic values. In *Science, Philosophy and Religion* (Second Symposium). New York: Harper and Row.

MEAKIN, D. (1976) *Man and Work*. London: Methuen.

MERLEAU-PONTY, M. (1963) *In praise of Philosophy*. Translated by J. Wild and J.M. Edie. Northwestern University Press.

—— (1964) *Sense and Non-Sense*. Translated by H.L. and P.A. Dreyfus. Northwestern University Press.

—— (1968) *The Phenomenology of Perception*. London: Routledge and Kegan Paul.

MÉSZÁROS, I. (1975) *Marx's Theory of Alienation (Fourth Edition)* London: Merlin Press.

MILLET, K. (1971) *Sexual Politics*. New York: Hart-Davis.

MILLS, R. (1973) *Young Outsiders*. London: Routledge and Kegan Paul.

MORGAN, G. (1980) 'An Analysis of Metaphor in Organization Theory.' Unpublished Doctoral Thesis, Lancaster University.

MULFORD, H.A. and SALISBURY, W.W. (1964) Self-conceptions in a general population. *Sociological Quarterly* **5**: 35–46.

MURCHLAND, B. (1971) *The Age of Alienation*. New York: Random House.

MURE, G.R.D. (1940) *An Introduction to Hegel*. Oxford: Clarendon Press.

—— (1965) *The Philosophy of Hegel*. Home University Library. Oxford: Oxford University Press.

MYERS, M.S. (1970) *Every Employee a Manager*. New York: McGraw-Hill.

NEAL, A.G. and RETTIG, S. (1967) On the Multidimensionality of Alienation. *American Sociological Review* **32**: 54–64.

NETTLER, G. (1957) A measure of alienation. *American Sociological Review* **22**: 670–77.

NIETZSCHE, F. (1966) *Beyond Good and Evil*. Translated by W. Kaufmann. New York: Vintage.

NOVE, A. (1972) *An Economic History of the USSR*. Harmondsworth: Penguin.

OGDEN, C.K. and RICHARDS, I.A. (1923) *The Meaning of Meaning*. London: Routledge and Kegan Paul.

OLLMAN, B. (1976) *Alienation: Marx's Conception of Man in Capitalist Society*. Cambridge: Cambridge University Press.

OUSPENSKY, P.D. (1970) *Tertium Organum*. Translated by N. Bessaraboff and C. Bragdon. London: Routledge and Kegan Paul.

OWEN, R. (1858) *The Life of Robert Owen, by Himself*. London: Bell and Sons Ltd.

PAPPENHEIM, F. (1959) *The Alienation of Modern Man*. New York: Modern Review Press.

PARKER, S.R. (1971) *The Future of Work and Leisure*. New York: Praeger.

PARKER, S.R. and SMITH, M.A. (1976) Work and Leisure. In R. Dubin (ed.) *Handbook of Work Organizations and Society*: 37–62. New York: Rand McNally.

PASCALE, R.T. and ATHOS, A.G. (1981) *The Art of Japanese Management*. New York: Warner.

PERROW, C. (1972) *Complex Organizations*. Illinois: Scott, Foursman and Co.

PLAMENATZ, J. (1975) *Karl Marx's Philosophy of Man*. Oxford: Clarendon.

POPPER, K.R. (1966) *The Open Society and Its Enemies* (Fifth Edition). London: Routledge and Kegan Paul.

REICH, W. (1975) *The Mass Psychology of Fascism*. Translated by V.R. Carfagne. Harmondsworth: Penguin Books.

ROBERTSON, H.M. (1933) *Aspects of the Rise of Economic Industrialism*. Cambridge: Cambridge University Press.

ROSE, E. (1978) Generalized Self-Management: The Position of Henri Lefebvre. *Human Relations* 31(7): 617–30.

ROSE, N. (1977) Fetishism and ideology. *Ideology and Consciousness*, 2: 27–54.

RYLE, G. (1973) *The Concept of Mind*. Harmondsworth: Penguin University Books.

SADDHATISSA, H. (1971) *The Buddha's Way*. London: Allen and Unwin.

SAMUELSSON, K. (1961) *Religion and Economic Action*. Translated by E.G. French. New York: Harper.

SARTRE, J-P. (1963) *St Genet*. New York: Plume Books.

—— (1966) *Being and Nothingness*. Translated by H.E. Barnes. Pocket Books. New York: Washington Square Press.

—— (1976) *Critique of Dialectical Reason*. Translated by P. Sheridan. London: New Left books.

SCHACHT, R.L. (1971) *Alienation*. London: George Allen and Unwin.

SCHILLER, J.C.F. (1965) *On the Aesthetic Education of Man*. E.M. Wilkinson and L.A. Willoughby. Oxford: Clarendon.

SCOTT, M.B. (1965) The Social Sources of Alienation. In I.L. Horowitz (ed.) *The New Sociology*: 239–52. New York: Oxford University Press.

SEEMAN, M. (1959) On the meaning of Alienation. *American Sociological Review* 24(6): 738–91.

—— (1971) The Urban Alienations: some dubious theses from Marx to Marcuse. *Journal of Personality and Social Psychology* 19(2): 135–43.

—— (1972) Alienation and knowledge-seeking. *Social Problems* 30: 3–17.

—— (1975) Alienation Studies. *Annual Review of Sociology*: 91–123. Palo Alto: Annual Reviews Inc.

SEIDEL, G.J. (1964) *Martin Heidegger and the Pre-Socratics*. Nebraska University Press.

SEMEONOFF, B. (1976) *Projective Techniques.* London: Wiley.

SEYBOLT, J.W., and GRUENFELD, L. (1976) The discriminant validity of work alienation and work satisfaction measures. *Journal of Occupational Psychology* 49(4): 193–202.

SHERMAN, B. and JENKINS, C. (1981) *Leisure Shock.* London: Eyre Methuen.

SHEWEN, W. (1826) *Meditations and Experiences.* Bradford: Blackburn.

SHIMMIN, S.B.N. (1966) Concepts of work. *Occupational Psychology* 40: 195–201.

SILVERMAN, D. (1972) *The Theory of Organizations.* London: Heinemann.

SIMPSON, G.G. (1961) *Principles of Animal Taxonomy.* Columbia University Press.

SMILES, S. (1908) *Self Help.* London: Murray.

SPALDING, K. and BURKE, K. (1967) *An Historical Dictionary of German Figurative Usage.* Oxford: Blackwell.

SROLE, L. (1956) Social Integration and Certain Corollaries: An Exploratory Study. *American Sociological Review* 21(6): 709–16.

STEIN, M. and VIDICH, A. (eds) (1963) *Sociology on Trial.* Englewood Cliffs, New Jersey: Prentice-Hall.

STINCHCOMBE, A.L. (1964) *Rebellion in a High School.* Chicago: Quadrangle Books.

STRAUSS, G. (1966) Some Notes on Power Equalization. In W.A. Hill and D.M. Egan, (eds) *Readings in Organizational Theory.* Boston: Allyn and Bacon.

STREUNING, E.L. and RICHARDSON, A.H. (1965) A Factor-analytic exploration of the alienation, anomie and authoritarianism domain. *American Sociological Review* 30(5): 768–76.

SUZUKI, D. (1957) *Mysticism: Christian and Buddhist.* New York: Harper and Bros.

—— (1969) *An Introduction to Zen Buddhism.* London: Rider.

TAUSKY, C. and PARKE, E.L. (1976) Job enrichment, need theory and reinforcement theory. In R. Dubin (ed.) Handbook of Work Organizations and Society. 531–65. New York: Rand McNally.

TAYLOR, F.W. (1947) *Scientific Management.* New York: Harper and Bros.

TILLICH, P. (1954) *Love, Power and Justice.* Oxford: Oxford University Press.

—— (1977) *The Courage to Be.* Fontana Books Glasgow: Collins.

TOFFLER, A. (1970) *Future Shock.* London: Bodley Head.

TOLSTOI, L.N. (1925) *What Then Must We Do?* Translated by A. Maude. World's Classics, 281. Oxford University Press.

TORBERT, W.R. (1972) *Being For The Most Part Puppets* ... Cambridge, Mass.: Schenkman.

TOURAINE, A. (1971) *The May Movement: Protest and Reform*. New York: Random House.

—— (1974) *The Post-Industrial Society*. Translated by L.F.X. Maynew. New York: Wildwood.

—— (1977) *The Self-Production of Society*. Chicago: Chicago University Press.

TRILLING, L. (1972) *Sincerity and Authenticity*. Oxford: Oxford University Press.

TRIST, E.L. and SOFER, C. (1959) *Exploration in Group Relations*. Leicester: Leicester University Press.

TUCKER, R.C. (1972) *Philosophy and Myth in Karl Marx* (2nd Ed.). Cambridge: Cambridge University Press.

VEBLEN, T. (1935) *The Theory of The Leisure Class*. New York: Viking Press.

VROOM, V.H. (1964) *Work and Motivation*. New York: Wiley.

WADDINGTON, C.H. (1977) *Tools for Thought*. London: Paladin.

WALK, R.D. and GIBSON, E.J. (1961) A comparative and analytical study of visual depth perception. *Psychological Monographs* 75(15).

WALL, T.D. and LISCHERON, J.A. (1977) *Worker Participation*. New York: McGraw-Hill.

WALLACE, R.S. (1959) *Calvin's Doctrine of the Christian Life*. Edinburgh: Oliver and Boyd.

WARFIELD, B.B. (1935) *The Plan of Salvation*. Philadelphia: Presbyterian and Reformed Publishing Co.

WATTS, A.W. (1973) *The Book on the Taboo Against Knowing Who You Are*. Sphere Books. London: Abacus.

WEBB, S. and WEBB, B. (1920) *The History of Trade Unionism*. (Second Edition). Published privately.

WEBER, M. (1958) *The Protestant Ethic and the Spirit of Capitalism* T.T. Parsons. New York: Scribner.

WEIL, S. (1972) *Gravity and Grace*. Translated by E. Craufurd. Glasgow: Collins.

WHITE, R.W. (1959) Motivation reconsidered: The concept of competence. *Psychological Review* 66: 297–333.

WHORF, B.L. (1956) *Language, Thought and Reality*. Ed. J.B. Carroll London: Chapman and Hall.

WILDEN, A. (1972) *System and Structure*. London: Tavistock.

ZANDER, A. (1971) *Motives and Goals in Groups*. London: Academic Press.

Name index

Abramson, P. R. 40, 189
Adam *see* subject index
Adams, H. P. 128, 189
Aikcn, M. 1, 189
Alderfer, C. P. 165, 189
Allport, G. W. 53, 165, 168–69, 189
Althusser, L. 51–2, 118, 121–26, 141, 145, 189
Angyal, A. 20, 189
Anthony, P. D. 30–1, 185, 189
Appley, M. H. 166, 191
Argyle, M. 162–63, 189
Argyris, C. 171, 179–84, 189–90
Aristotle 59, 79, 137
Artaud, A. 11–12, 190
Augustine, St 21, 25, 28–9, 190
Ayer, A. J. 39, 190

Baillie, J. B. 75, 97, 194
Bainton, R. H. 21, 190
Balibar, E. 121, 189
Bateson, G. 2, 4, 92, 156–57, 188, 190
Becker, E. 110
Behling, O. 167, 190
Bell, D. 113
Berger, P. 145–46, 190

Berkeley, G. 41, 96
Berlin, I. 49, 51, 63, 190
Bertalanffy, L. von 124, 190
Blackler, F. H. M. 171, 190
Blake, W. 26
Blau, P. M. 137, 179
Blauner, R. 15, 162, 190
Bonjean, C. M. 98, 190
Bookchin, M. 144, 190
Bottomore, T. B. 76, 128, 198
Brayfield, A. H. 174, 190
Brown, C. A. 171, 190
Brown, N. O. 145, 190
Buber, M. 10, 45, 91, 191
Bullough, B. L. 40, 191
Burke, K. 78, 201

Campbell, J. P. 167, 192
Cherns, A. B. 172, 191
Chiodi, P. 152, 191
Cofer, C. N. 166, 191
Cohen, S. 146, 191
Coletti, L. 119, 129, 198
Cooper, R. 17, 26, 31, 36, 164–65, 171, 182, 187, 191, 193
Craik, K. J. W. 163, 191
Crockett, W. H. 174, 190
Crozier, M. 179, 191

Culler, J. 11, 191

Dahrendorf, R. 14–15
Davis, L. E. 172, 191
De Chardin, P. T. 32, 169, 191
De Charms, R. 169, 182, 191
Derrida, J. 11, 191
Descartes, R. 43–4, 55–6, 192
Dubin, R. 111, 175, 179, 192
Dumazedier, J. 9, 192
Dunnette, M. D. 167, 192
Durkheim, E. 27, 50, 83, 102–04,
    112, 192

Eldridge, J. E. T. 120, 192
Empedocles 18
Engels, F. 113, 119–20, 141, 198
Erasmus, D. 29, 48, 56, 192

Fairbairn, W. R. D. 86–7, 111, 192
Fein, M. 174, 192
Feuer, L. 1, 192
Fichte, J. G. 96
Findlay, J. N. 75, 79, 96, 192
Finifter, A. 5, 103, 192
Firestone, S. 124, 192
Fischer, C. S. 40, 192
Fisk, G. 180, 192
Fox, A. 83, 137, 192
Frankfort, H. and H. A. 10, 193
Franz, M. L. von 4, 193
Freud, S. 4, 11, 16, 145, 165, 193
Fromm, E. 15, 70, 72–3, 112, 145,
    181, 193

Gadalla, J. E. 165–66, 186, 193
Gaskell, P. 8, 193
Gibson, E. J. 6, 202
Gibson, J. J. 46, 193
Glass, J. M. 144, 193
Glazer, N. 72, 193
God *see* subject index
Goethe, J. W. von 78
Goffman, E. 1, 99, 193
Goldmann, L. 2, 187, 193
Goldstein, K. 165, 193
Goldthorpe, J. H. 33, 95, 179–81
Gouldner, A. W. 1, 170–71, 193
Gratton, L. C. 166, 194
Grimes, M. D. 98, 190
Gross, E. 9, 175, 194
Gruenfeld, L. 1, 201

Guibert, J. de 146, 194
Gyllenhammar, P. C. 172, 194

Habermas, J. 46, 142, 194
Hage, I. 1, 189
Hajda, J. 15, 111–12, 194
Hakel, M. D. 167, 192
Hampden-Turner, C. 182, 194
Harrison, J. E. 19, 194
Hebb, D. O. 183, 184
Hegel, G. W. F. *see* Hegelianism in
    subject index
Heidegger, M. 2, 11, 35, 39, 58–60,
    67, 99, 101, 184, 187, 194
Hein, A. 6–7, 27, 194
Held, R. 6–7, 27, 194
Heller, F. A. 2, 195
Heraclitus 10, 58–9
Herzberg, F. 167, 195
Hesiod 62
Hobbes, T. 107, 195
Hölderlin, J. C. 78
Homer 18
Horney, K. 87, 195
Hui-neng 45
Husserl, E. 41–5, 65, 195

Israel, J. 70, 195

Jaques, E. 31, 195
Jenkins, C. 95
Jensen, R. 112, 195
Johnson, F. 70, 110–11, 195
Johnson, S. 96, 137
Jones, J. N. 178, 195
Jung, C. G. 4, 21, 195

Kahler, E. 90, 195
Kant, I. 52, 56–7, 96, 195
Kaplan, M. A. 1, 195
Kaufmann, W. 33, 75, 78, 195
Keniston, K. 89–90, 111
Kierkegaard, S. 33–4, 52, 54, 64, 196
King, M. L. 124, 196
King, N. A. 167, 196
Kirk, G. S. 59, 62, 196
Knox, T. M. 75, 194
Kojève, A. 75, 196
Kosmo, R. 167, 190
Kuhn, T. S. 162, 196

Labedz, L. 113, 196

Labovitz, G. 167, 190
Lacan, J. 11, 80, 196
Lafargue, M. P. 178, 196
Laing, R. D. 11, 92, 196
Lakatos, I. 111
Lawler, E. E. 166, 175, 196
Lee, A. M. C. 1, 196
Lefebvre, H. 9, 182–84, 196
Lempriere, J. 17, 196
Lenin, V. I. 12, 123, 196
Likert, R. 173, 197
Ling, T. O. 115, 197
Lischeron, J. A. 177, 202
Locke, J. 107
Lockwood, D. 179, 193
Lowry, R. 111, 197
Lukacs, G. 91, 197
Luther, M. 20–1, 24, 28–9, 31, 48, 197

MacCallum, D. 49, 197
McClelland, D. C. 173, 197
McClosky, H. 112, 197
McDermott, J. 1, 197
McGregor, D. 173, 175, 197
MacIntyre, A. 3, 197
MacKay, D. M. 108, 197
McLellan, D. 113, 121, 197
Malraux, A. 28, 197
Mannheim, K. 16, 197
March, J. G. 174, 197
Marcuse, H. 12, 90, 170, 197
Marx, K. see Marxism in subject index
Maslow, A. H. 2, 20, 164–70, 173, 180–81, 186, 198
Masterson, P. 35, 198
Maurois, A. 65, 198
May, R. 170, 188, 198
Mead, M. 156, 198
Meakin, D. 181, 198
Merleau-Ponty, M. 40, 43–4, 50, 53, 62, 65, 198
Merton, R. K. 70
Mészáros, I. 119, 121, 199
Milgram, S. 111
Mill, J. 131
Millet, K. 124, 199
Milligan, M. 128
Mills, R. 40, 70, 199
Morgan, G. 182, 184, 199
Mulford, H. A. 98, 199

Murchland, B. 101, 199
Mure, G. R. D. 75, 96, 199
Musgrave, T. 111
Myers, M. S. 173–74, 199

Neal, A. G. 100, 199
Nettler, G. 100, 199
Nicolaus, M. 128
Nietzsche, F. 49, 63–4, 68, 199
Nisbet, R. A. 70
Nove, A. 145, 199

Ogden, C. K. 11, 199
Ollman, B. 116–17, 120, 129, 133, 145, 199
Ouspensky, P. D. 112, 199
Owen, R. 175–76, 199

Pappenheim, F. 186, 199
Parke, E. L. 175, 201
Parker, S. R. 9, 180, 199
Pelagius 28–9
Perrow, C. 173, 179, 200
Plamenatz, J. 128–30, 200
Plato 51, 55–6, 58–9, 67
Plotinus 10
Popper, K. R. 79, 200
Pospelova, O. 119
Proudhon, P. J. 139
Proust, M. 65, 99

Raven, J. E. 59, 62, 196
Reich, W. 89, 200
Rettig, S. 100, 199
Richards, I. A. 11, 199
Richardson, A. H. 111–12, 201
Robertson, H. M. 30, 200
Rose, E. 121, 184, 200

Saddhatissa, H. 30, 200
Sainsbury, W. W. 98, 199
Samuelsson, K. 30, 200
Santayana, G. 100
Sartre, J. P. see Sartre's thought in subject index
Saussure, H. de 11
Schaar, J. 112, 197
Schacht, R. L. 71, 75, 107, 161–62, 200
Schiller, J. C. F. 35, 200
Scott, M. B. 1, 40, 200
Seeman, M. 1, 15, 70, 72–4, 88, 112, 200

Seidel, G. J. 58, 200
Semeonoff, B. 109, 201
Seybolt, J. W. 1, 201
Shewen, W. 23, 201
Shimmin, S. B. N. 180, 201
Silverman, D. 116, 201
Simon, H. A. 174, 197
Simpson, G. G. 41, 201
Smiles, S. 18, 201
Smith, M. A. 9, 199
Socrates 55
Spalding, K. 78, 201
Srole, L. 103, 201
Steuart, J., Sir 127
Stinchcombe, A. L. 100, 201
Strauss, G. 175, 201
Streuning, E. L. 111–12, 201
Suttle, J. L. 166, 196
Suzuki, D. 44, 167, 201

Tausky, C. 175, 201
Tawney, R. H. 30
Taylor, F. W. 87, 172, 201
Taylor, L. 146, 191
Tillich, P. 54, 94, 112, 201
Toffler, A. 145, 201

Tolstoi, L. N. 177, 201
Torbert, W. R. 181, 202
Touraine, A. 1, 40, 73, 202
Trilling, L. 15–17, 202
Tucker, R. C. 118–19, 202

Veblen, T. 144, 202
Vroom, V. H. 174, 202

Waddington, C. H. 2, 150, 202
Walk, R. D. 6, 202
Wall, T. D. 177, 202
Wallace, R. S. 30, 202
Warfield, B. B. 24, 202
Watts, A. W. 186, 202
Webb, S. and B. 177–78, 202
Weber, M. 30, 202
Weil, S. 5–6, 202
Wesley, J. 30
White, R. W. 182–84, 202
Whitehead, A. N. 60
Whorf, B. L. 34, 202
Wilden, A. 2, 108, 117, 147, 202

Zander, A. 155, 202
Zurcher, L. A. 111

Subject index

Absolute Knowledge 43, 53, 57, 79, 102, 107, 126; see also ideal
actions in open form of existence 114–18
active force, work as 5–9
actualization see self-actualization
Adam, Fall of 13, 18–23, 35, 61
affirmation, self- 93, 160–61
agent-subject, man as 51–2
Alienated Soul 97
alienation: in closed form of existence 74–84; and estrangement, in open form of existence 113–63; Marx's views on 112–43; new perspective on 70–4; and scepticism and Unhappy Consciousness 98–104; transcendence of 164–88
alloplastic behaviour 89, 110
Also 86
analytical: distancing 39–41, 45, 47, 68, 89; knowledge 82
anomie 102–04, 110
antagonism 151–55
anti-Hegelianism 126–27
Apollonian principles 16–17
appropriation 120
archetypal forms of awareness 39–52

arch-indifference 97; see also scepticism
assertion, self- 35
authentic awareness see awareness
autonomy 14, 22, 27–8, 32–7, 39, 47, 49, 68, 111–12
autoplastic behaviour 89
awareness and existence: forms of 36–69; see also closed form; open form

bad faith 65–6
becoming 58–61, 168–69; see also self-actualization
Being 169: as becoming 58–61, 106; -cognition 166, 185; potentiality-for- 99; to, from being 54–8, 60
being: -for-itself 54, 65, 80; -for-something 168; -in-itself 54, 80; -in-and-for-itself 80; -in-the-world 43, 54, 99, 186; and knowledge 59; power of 94; species- 114, 117, 135–43; to . Being 54–8, 60; see also psychosystem
body and mind 42–4
Bondsman-Lord relationship 91–5, 114, 135

break in Marx's thought 118–19,
  122, 125
breath, life 25
Buddhism 22, 30; *see also* religion

Calvinism and Calvin 191; as
  non-autonomous existence 18,
  21–31, 68, 105, 159–60; and
  predestination 25–9, 34, 48; and
  revelation 29, 77–8; and work
  28–33, 168, 187; *see also* God;
  religion
capital *see* money
capitalism: and alienation 15,
  129–43; and Lord-Bondsmen
  relationship 94; and
  organizations 118–63 *passim*; as
  semi-autonomous existence
  28–33
certainty, self- 99, 101
chaos 62, 106
Christianity and estrangement 98,
  101–02, 105, 111; *see also*
  Calvinism; Lutheran; religion
class: middle 95; movement 51–2;
  struggle 123–25
closed form of authentic awareness
  and existence (essensism) 47,
  52–62; alienation in 74–84;
  change from open form 148–55;
  estrangement in 70–112, 123,
  126; self's relationship to 84–98,
  109; and transcendence of
  estrangement 104–07, 174
closed work context 134; *see also*
  capitalism
common sense 86–7
communication 115–18
conceptual thought 77
concrete mind, free 95–8, 109, 111
Consciousness 47, 84–6; false 16,
  40, 73; intentional 42; negation of
  92; self 86–97, 100, 106, 109, 111,
  115–16; Unhappy 97–104,
  108–12, 147
creativity 169
crisis 92
critical awareness of organizational
  involvement 185–87
critique of system 177–79
cultural estrangement 72, 88, 112
cultural norms 40

deficiencies (D-aspects) 166, 186
dialectical awareness 81–4
differentiation 62
Dionysian principles 16–17
discretionary content of work 31
discrimination 115–18
distancing, analytical 39–41, 45, 47,
  68, 89
division of labour 103, 120
drives *see* needs
dualism 42–4

economic factors, potency of
  171–72
ecstasy (ekstasis) 146
eidetic (phenomenological)
  reduction 42–4
ends-directed view of reciprocity
  156–57
entäusserung (alienation) 75–6,
  113, 117, 119–29, 151
entfremdung (estrangement) 75–6,
  99, 113, 117, 127–29, 151
environment, interaction with
  5–37
epistemological awareness 39–47,
  59, 66–8, 89, 146–49; *see also*
  awareness
essensistic view *see* closed form
estrangement: as antagonism
  151–55; cessation of 104–08; in
  closed form of existence 70–112,
  123, 126; cultural 72, 88, 112;
  Marx's view of 27, 103, 105, 107,
  118–43 *passim*; in open form of
  awareness 113–63; in
  organizations 81, 83, 89, 104–07,
  164–88; transcendence of 104–07,
  164–88
existence *see* autonomous;
  awareness; closed form;
  non-autonomous; open form
existentialism 22, 27, 33–6 *see also*
  open form
experiment, kitten 6–8, 93, 115
exploitation 26–7, 141–43
expressive systems 17
externality 10, 86–90

factual being 54
Fall *see* Adam
false consciousness 16, 40, 73

fascist mentality 89
feed-back 46, 150–51
fetishism 121
free concrete mind 95–8, 109, 111
free will 29, 49
freedom, forms of 47–52, 63–4,
  95–6, 157

goal-getters 173
God: as father 32; Grace of 24,
  105–06, 111; as Ideal 98, 101–02,
  160; as locus of knowledge 77–8;
  and metaphysics 57; as Other
  13–14, 61; Will of 18, 21, 24, 26,
  29–31, 34, 49, 105; *see also*
  Adam; religion
good, highest 33–4
Grace 24, 105–06, 112
Greek philosophy and religion 10,
  51, 55–9, 62, 67, 79, 137
groundless floating 99

harmony, loss of 18–23
hearing 60
Hegelianism and Hegel 194; Anti-
  126–27; on alienation 52, 64, 69,
  71–6, 105, 107, 151, 153; on
  Bondsman 92–3, 97;
  epistemology of 59–61; on
  estrangement 42–3, 89–94, 99,
  152, 180; on Ideal 50, 53, 96; and
  Lacan 11; and Marx 106, 118–19,
  129–30; on Self and Other 16,
  57–8, 84–6, 91–2, 103, 105, 107,
  112, 115; on Spirit 57, 78–84, 87,
  90–1, 99, 110; on unity 77–8
Hinduism 10, 186; *see also* religion
homonomy and self-fulfilment
  19–21
honest soul 16
hope 102
hysterical conduct 163

Ideal 41, 53–61, 68, 95–6, 117, 123,
  126; God as 98, 101–02, 160; *see
  also* Absolute Knowledge
Ideas 58–9
identification 11
ideological bias 125
idiographic approach to history 124
ignorance, self- 22

immersion *see* epistemological
  awareness
inactivity 5–9
inauthenticity 16
individuality 21–3, 33–4, 38, 81
instinct *see* needs
institutions, social 149
instrumentalism 33, 180–81
interaction: between man and
  enviroment 5–37; with work
  organization 178–79
internal constraints 10, 64
irrational, suppression of 186–87
isolation 72, 88, 107, 112
It-world *see* Other
I-world *see* Self

job: satisfaction 180–81; type and
  self-actualization 171, 174–75

kitten experiment 6–8, 93, 115
knowledge: Absolute 43, 53, 57, 59,
  79, 102, 107, 126; analytical 82;
  and being 59; dialectical 81; locus
  of 77–8; self- 22

labour: alienation of 131–43;
  concept of 116; division of 103,
  120; *see also* capitalism; work
language 11–12, 58
langue 11
law of nature 12
leisure 95, 144
liberty *see* freedom
listening 60
logos (truth) 58–60
long-focus awareness *see*
  epistemological awareness
look, Other's 35, 148
Lord-Bondsman relationship 91–5,
  114, 135
loss: of authenticity *see* Adam
loss of harmony 18–23
love 21, 28, 86–7
Lutheran thought 20–1, 24, 28–9,
  31, 48

management, self- 183–84
Marxism and Marx 197–98; on
  alienation 27, 52, 64, 70–4, 77,
  87, 112–43 *passim*; on
  authenticity 160; break in

Marxism and Marx—*Cont'd*
  thought 118–19, 122, 125; on
  creativity 169; on estrangement
  27, 103, 105, 107, 118–43 *passim*;
  and Hegel 106, 118–19, 129–30;
  on inauthenticity 16; on
  reciprocity 79, 157–59; on
  revolution 143–44; on Spirit 91,
  116; on work 9
masochism 20–1
materialism *see* capitalism
meaning 88, 98
meaninglessness 72
mediator, money as 114, 131–35
meditation 45, 78
metaphors, symbolic 60, 77
metaphysical awareness 43, 50,
  57–8
middle-class values 95
mind and body, distinction between
  42–4
models 124
money: accumulation of 30–3; as
  manifestation of social existence
  135–43; as mediator 114, 131–35;
  as reward 94; *see also* capitalism
moral judgement 57
motivation theory 167, 169
mutual alienation 136
mythology 10, 14, 21–2 *see also*
  religion

necessity 48–51, 160–61
needs 165–70
negation of consciousness 92
negative feedback 150–51
negative freedom 47–52, 63
no-mind, doctrine of 45
non-autonomous existence 36–9,
  47, 49, 111–12; Calvinism as 18,
  21–32, 68, 105, 159–60
non-self *see* Other
normlessness 72, 88, 112
North American Indians 34
Nothingness 62

object: awareness of 84–90; -choice
  11, 36; *see also* Other
obligation, social 48–51
occultism 10
Oedipus myth 11
ontological awareness 39–40,

46–52, 59, 66–8, 71, 162: and
  psychosystem 52–61; of
  revolution 146–49; *see also*
  awareness
ontological life 36–7
ontological necessity 48–52
open form of authentic awareness
  and existence (existentialism):
  alienation and estrangement in
  106, 108, 113–63; change from
  closed form 148–55; described 39,
  47, 52–66, 68, 71; and reciprocity
  79–84, 91, 166; *see also*
  existentialism
organizations, work: as closed
  systems 74; and estrangement 81,
  83, 89, 94; theory of 15, 125–27;
  transcendence in 104–07,
  164–88; *see also* capitalism
Other: death of 63; denial of 160;
  -directed system 8, 129–35;
  estrangement from 90–1, 95–7,
  109; God as 13–14, 61; as object
  36; organizational 170–71; *see
  also* Self

parole 11
participative management 173
passivity 5–9
paternalism 25
perception 84–98, 109, 117
permanence, lack of 65
pessimism 156–59, 168
phenomenology 42–4
play 35, 186–87
pluralism 50, 83
poetry of life 184
political revolution 105, 143–55
positive freedom 47–52
potentiality-for-Being 99
power: of being 94; -seeker, man as
  63–4
powerlessness 72, 88, 112
practico-inert 106, 149–51
prajna 44
predestination (preordination)
  25–9, 34, 48
priesthood 88–9
primogeniture 130
private property 129–43, 147, 158
productivity 5, 9, 135–36, 174–75;
  see also capitalism

Protestantism *see* Calvinism;
Lutheran; religion
psychoanalysis 11, 80, 87
psychology 9; of authenticity and
sincerity 13, 15–18; internal
traumata 61–6; of organizations,
interaction with 178–79; new 43;
and self-actualization 165–72,
175–76
psychosystem, awareness of 40,
52–61; *see also*
being-in-the-world

real self 87
realization, self- 54
Reason and awareness 81–3, 104,
106
reciprocity 39–47, 63, 79–84, 91,
156–61, 166
Recollection 55
reduction to sensation 41–4
religion 169; *see also* Buddhism;
Calvinism; Christianity; God;
Hinduism; mythology;
Protestantism; Taoism
renunciation, self- 23
revelation 29–30, 88, 105
revolution, political 105, 143–55
reward 94, 101; work as 135–36
ritualized union 19
role-playing 32–4, 98–9, 167

saddha 30
samadhi 10
Sartre's thought: on alienation
151–53, 160, 169; on bad faith
65–6; on Being 54, 62; on ekstasis
146; and Hegel 92; on love 28;
pessimism of 156–59, 168; on
practoco-inert 106, 149–51; on
Self and Other 17, 34–6, 64–5,
117, 148, 153–61, 183; on writers
181
satisfaction, personal *see*
self-actualization
Satori (enlightenment) 45
scarcity 158
scepticism: and cessation of
estrangement 104–07; and
Unhappy Consciousness 97–104,
110–11, 147
schismogenesis, symmetrical 92,

156; complementary 157
scientific management 87, 172–74
secularization 30
Self and Other: and alienation and
estrangement 113–63; and
estrangement, aetiology of
70–112; and forms of authentic
awareness 38–69; forms of
interaction between 5–37; and
self-actualization in
organizations 164–83; *see also*
closed form; open form
self-actualization 20–1, 31–2, 135,
164–88
self-affirmation 93, 160–61
self-alienation 57, 87, 107, 112
self-assertion 35
self-autonomy *see* autonomy
self-awareness 21–3, 39–40, 64; *see
also* awareness
self-certainty 99, 101
self-consciousness 86–97, 100, 106,
109, 111, 115–16
self-estrangement 72, 88, 111; *see
also* estrangement
self-fulfilment 19–21
self-help theology 18; *see also*
religion
self-ignorance 22
self-isolation 107
self-knowledge 22
self-love 21
self-management 184–85
self-productivity 5, 9, 135–36
self-realization 54
self-relating 34
self-renunciation 23
self-sufficiency 20
self-transformation 34
semi-autonomous existence 14, 20,
28–33, 39, 49, 68, 111–12
semiology 11
separation 71, 82
sexuality 11
short-focus awareness *see*
epistemological awareness
sincerity 15–18, 39–40, 42, 54, 66
snake symbol 21–2, 61
social existence, loss of 135–43
social isolation 72, 88, 112
social obligation 48–51
social relations 9, 114–17

social scientists' views of alienation
72, 88, 111–13, 116, 161; of
organizations 164–88
sociality and reciprocity 157–59
sociological bias 125–26
soul 16, 97
species-being 114, 117, 135–43
speech 11, 58
Spielraum 35
Spirit 57, 78–84, 87, 90–1, 99, 112.
116, 126
subjectivity 50, 57, 62, 108
suicide 50, 102
superman, 50, 68
surrender 71, 161
survival, work for 8–9
symbolism 21–2, 60–1, 77
synthetic judgements 56

Taoism 168; *see also* religion
technological factors 171–72
theology *see* religion
this, here and now 84–5
thought 77, 106
timelessness 10–13
transcendence of alienation and
estrangement: in closed form of
existence 104–07; in
organizations 164–88

translation problems 75–6, 127–29
traumata, psychological 61–6
truth, apart from being 58–9

unalienated work 35
Understanding 82–3, 86–90, 97, 99,
105
un-estrangement 156–61
Unhappy Consciousness 97–104,
108–12, 147
Unions 177–78
unity 77–80

value isolation 72

'What is' question 40–7, 67
'What ought to be' 40, 46–52, 67
will, free 29, 49; *see also* God, will
of
work: as active force 5–9;
alienation from 5, 9, 23, 70–1;
changing attitudes to 94–5;
sociological approach to 164–88;
unalienated 35, 135–36; *see also*
capitalism; labour; organizations
worthlessness 88, 96, 112

Zen enlightenment 43–6, 67, 78,
107